MECHATRONICS FOR BEGINNERS

21 PROJECTS FOR PIC MICROCONTROLLERS

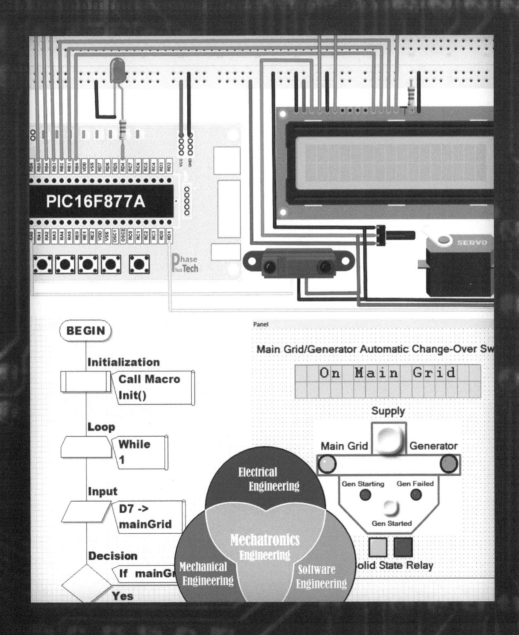

FLOWCODE GRAPHICAL PROGRAMMING PROJECTS' DEMONSTRATION BOOK

AuthorHouse™
1663 Liberty Drive
Bloomington, IN 47403
www.authorhouse.com
Phone: 1-800-839-8640

Published by AuthorHouse 10/22/2012

ISBN: 978-1-4772-3378-8 (sc)
*   978-1-4772-3161-6 (e)*

authorHOUSE®

Abubakar S. Imam

Mechatronics for Beginners

Flowcode Graphical Programming Projects' Demonstration Book

21 Projects for PIC Microcontrollers

Contents

II.   Hands-on-Projects

List of Tables

The Author

Abubakar Surajo Imam, MNSE is a Captain in the Nigerian Army Electrical and Mechanical Engineering (NAEME) Corps. He has earned Bachelors' degree in Mechanical Engineering from Bayero University Kano, Nigeria and Masters' degree in mechatronics Engineering from Newcastle University United Kingdom (UK). Presently, Imam is a third year PhD student in the School of Mechanical and Systems Engineering Newcastle University under the sponsorship of Petroleum Technology Development Fund (PTDF). His research interest is on the autonomous use of aerial robots for surveillance of oil and gas pipelines. He was commissioned into the Nigerian Army in December 2002 as a Second Lieutenant. Captain Imam has served in various capacities, been the Information and Communication Technology (ICT) officer at both NAEME headquarters in Lagos Island and Technical Group at Yaba Lagos. He spent a year at the Defence Industries Corporation of Nigeria (DICON) Kaduna where he was instrumental to developing a research group in unmanned aerial vehicles (UAVs) at the corporation research and development centre under the command-ship of Major General SU Labaran. Captain Imam has attended numerous military courses and passed his Captain to Major practical promotion exams in October 2010. He has authored six international conference papers, attended over 40 workshops and trainings internationally on capacity building and he is participating in teaching and demonstration in the School of Mechanical and Systems Engineering, Newcastle University. He is married to Maryam and blessed with a son - Khalid.

About the Technical Reviewers

Dr Robert Bicker:

Robert Bicker, MIMechE, CEng, PhD, MSc, BSc is a senior lecturer in the School of Mechanical and System Engineering Newcastle University, United Kingdom and Head of Robotics Research Group in the University. He graduated from the same University with First Class Honours in Mechanical Engineering in 1977, had completed his PhD, entitled *'Force Control in Telemanipulation'* in 1989 and has been a member of staff at University since 1981. To date, he has supervised over twenty PhD students and he is presently supervising six others in different areas of robotics applications.

Prior to joining the University he was employed by Northern Engineering Industries [NEI] Nuclear Systems, Gateshead immediately after his bachelors and within four years of taking up the appointment he was promoted to Group Leader. Robert Bicker is a Registered Interviewer for the IMechE, and regularly sits on interview panels. He is actively involved with the professional development of young Graduate Engineers, and is registered as a Mentor for the Institution's Monitored Professional Development Scheme (MPDS).

Before his undergraduate study, the young Robert Bicker had completed an Apprenticeship at NEI Reyrolle (now part of Rolls-Royce) followed by two years as a Draughtsman. He then went on to spend two years as a Laboratory Technician at Hebburn Technical College, before leaving to take his first degree.

Robert Bicker is still leading an active lifestyle that includes playing 5-aside football and golf on a weekly basis, and up until recently squash. He has a passion for finding out how things work, and not surprisingly he is particularly fond of taking things apart - *"you name it he will probably have fixed it! Anything from watches and clocks, domestic appliances, cars, hi-fi's, robots (of course) and machine tools etc"*.

Engr. M. B. Shehu:

Engr. Mustapha Balarabe Shehu is the 28th President of the Nigerian Society of Engineers (NSE). A Fellow of the Society and a winner of many distinguished awards for service to the Society. He was Vice-President several times and Deputy President and member of Council. The President has put in over 25 years in the practice of engineering both in government agencies and as a private consultant. He was inaugurated at a colourful investiture ceremony on the 11th of February 2012 at the International Conference Centre, Abuja.

Major General Suleman Labaran:

Major General Labaran was born on 6th January 1960 at Umaisha, in Toto LGA, Nasarawa State is the Director General (DG) Defence Industries Corporation of Nigeria (DICON). He holds a B. Eng. in Electrical Engineering. He was commissioned into the Nigerian Army on 6th of April 1981 and has attended several professional and military training courses both within and outside the country during the course of his career. He took over the corporation mantle of leadership on 23rd June 2009. The DG's philosophy in life is that "hard work pays no matter how long it takes". He enjoys playing lawn tennis and golf.

Engr Muttaqha Rabe Darma:

Engr. Muttaqha Rabe Darma, mnse, mnim was appointed Executive Secretary in November, 2008. He has Bachelors' degree in Mechanical Engineering and two Masters' degrees in Engineering (production) and Business Administration (Management) . He served variously as Hon. Commissioner of works, Housing and transport; Rural, Social development, Youth and Sports; and Rural, Social Development, Women Affairs, Youth and Sports in the Katsina State Government between August 2003 and May 2007. He also taught Mechanical Engineering in the Polytechnic and the University. His professional affiliations include the Nigerian Society of Engineers, Nigerian Institute of Management and Renewable and alternative Energy Network.

Acknowledgments

Many people have assisted in one way or the other in the preparation of this book. Due to space constrain, their contributions cannot all be mentioned here. Nonetheless, I wish to recognize the contributions, both directly and indirectly of my supervisor Dr Robert Bicker who immensely influenced my mechatronics knowledge and skills when I first enrolled as one of his MSc students in September 2008. I am forever grateful to my wife and son, Maryam Munir and Khalid, for their love and understanding, and for providing me continuous support when preparing the book's manuscript which translated into many long nights and too short weekends.

I am grateful to the Nigeria Army especially the Chief of Army Staff (COAS), Lieutenant General OA Ihejirika GSS psc(+) fwc fniqs, who in November 2010 approved my release to undertake the on-going PhD study in the United Kingdom. Without his approval, I would not have been in the position to write this book.

Special acknowledgments to my reviewers Major General SU Labaran, Engr M. B. Shehu, Engr (Dr) Mutaqqa Rabe Darma and Professor O. A. Fakinlede for patiently checking and spotting the mistakes. Without them this book would never have been a reality. Many thanks to the current members of my research group namely Ahmad Alsaab, Simon Ignace, Paramin Neranon and Alaa Jaber for their support, suggestions and constructive criticism.

I appreciate the contributions and suggestions of Dr Jameel Yusha'u, Waziri Galadima, Engr. Stephen Akande, Muhammad Alhaji Muhammad, Valentine C. Eze, Auwal Aliyu, Abdullahi Bello, Hassan Shuaibu, Murtala Kwara and Sadis Bara'u and Mr Titus Ogata. I also want to express my sincere gratitude to the entire management and staff members of Petroleum Technology Development Fund (PTDF) for their help and support during the writing and publishing process of this book. I am particularly grateful to Mr Ahmed G. Aminu, Mr Tanimu Ahmed and Mr Kalu Otisi for their professional advice and guidance in getting the book reaching-out to wider audience.

Preface

As the title suggests, this book is a project demonstration book for building smart systems. The primary purpose of the book, is to serve as a demonstration material for teaching mechatronics in vocational and technical colleges. It can also serve as a reference material for a course taken by first-year mechatronics engineering students in the universities and polytechnics. The book is a self-content resource for persons interested in acquiring the requisite skills for building mechatronics systems. It presents a step-by-step procedure of implementing mechatronics systems. Mechatronics systems function autonomously, in most cases, requiring no human operator's input. They are interlaced with embedded software, sensors and actuators and have a high degree of integration of mechanical, electrical and information-processing components.

The concept and procedure for building mechatronics systems are made easy in this book using a combination of software called Flowcode and custom hardware platform developed by PhasePlus Technologies Ltd. Flowcode is a graphical programming software developed by Matrix Multimedia ©. Flowcode software allows those with little or non-programming experience to create complex automated systems without writing traditional codes line by line.

The first three chapters in the book lay foundation for the projects in the subsequent chapters. Chapter one is a general overview on the subject's evolution and its position in the industry and education. Chapter two discusses the basic electrical/electronic terminologies, components and components identification techniques. While chapter three presents the common hardware and software required for implementing the projects in Part II, which begins with simpler projects and gradually advances to more complex ones. However, for those with a firm grounding in electrical/electronic can skip Chapter two. I recommend Part II of the book to be followed chapter by chapter as the preceding chapters laid foundation to the succeeding ones.

Furthermore, the majority of the projects can be made into commercial products with little modifications. Therefore, I enjoin readers to open their minds to these possibilities. Do not be limited to what the projects do but rather how to apply the concepts in the projects to solving physical problems. The projects codes, supporting files and demonstration version of Flowcode software can be downloaded for free from the book's website (www.mechatronicsforbeginners.com). The book has a companion kit which contains all the components used in the projects and can be ordered through the book website or any of the designated distributors.

AS Imam

October 2012

Part I

Basic Background

Chapter 1

Evolution of Mechatronics

Often, mechanical, electronic and software engineers in many companies are in different locations of the company. Better still, in some cases, they may be in the same building or the same office but the chances are they live in different worlds, speaking different languages and therefore cannot effectively communicate with each other when it comes to product design or problem solving. Simply because they come from different backgrounds knowing very little about other related disciplines. For instance, when the Mechanical engineers design a system they pass it over to the Electrical/Electronic engineers to design and fit the control systems and they, in turn, roll it over to the Software engineers to write the control program. This serial and disjointed engineering practice result in producing an unoptimized product or solution. To overcome these difficulties, mechatronics evolves as a trans disciplinary approach to solving engineering problem based on open communication systems and concurrent practices, to design better engineering products.

1.1. What is Mechatronics

Mechatronics has been defined in several ways. For instance, Harashima, Tomizuka, and Fukada [4], defined mechatronics as the synergistic integration of mechanical engineering, with electronics and intelligent computer control in the design and manufacturing of industrial products and processes. While Auslander and Kempf [6] defined mechatronics as the application of complex decision making to the operation of physical systems. Shetty and Kolk [10] defined mechatronics as a methodology used for the optimal design of electromechanical products. However, more recently, W. Bolton [11] viewed mechatronics system as not just a combination of electrical and mechanical systems or just control system, rather it is a complete integration of all of them.

All the definitions given above about mechatronics are accurate and informative, yet none has fully defined in totality what mechatronics represents. Robert, Bishop and Ramasubramanian [8] concluded that, despite continuing efforts to define mechatronics, to classify mechatronics products, and to develop a standard mechatronics curriculum, a consensus opinion on an all-encompassing description of "what is mechatronics" eludes us. Even without an unarguably definitive description of mechatronics, engineers understand from the definitions given above and from their own personal experiences the essence of the philosophy of mechatronics.

1.2. Key Element of Mechatronics System

A typical mechatronics system picks up signals, processes them, and, as an output, generates forces and motions. A fully mechanical system can be modified to an autonomous system by integrating sensors, microcontrollers/microprocessor and other electronic components to it. Therefore, mechatronics system is made up of the following subsystems and components:

1. The physical system.
2. Sensors
   a) Linear and rotational sensors.
   b) Acceleration sensor.
   c) Ranging and proximity sensors.
   d) Force, torque and pressure sensors.
   e) Temperature and humidity sensors.
   f) etc.
3. Actuators.
   a) Motors including stepper motors, servo motors, brushed and brushless DC motors.
   b) Electra-mechanical actuator.
   c) Piezoelectric actuators.
   d) Pneumatic and hydraulic actuators.
   e) etc.
4. Signal conditioning circuits.
   a) Filters.
   b) Amplifies
5. Computers and logic systems.
   a) Microcontrollers.
   b) Microprocessors.
   c) Integrated circuits.
6. Software applications.
   a) Operating systems (OS).
   b) Graphical user-interfaces (GUI).
   c) etc.

1.3. Historical Perspectives

The genesis of mechatronics began in Japan in1969 when Testura Mori, a senior engineer for Yaskawa Electric Corporation coined the term. Back then, mechatronics was viewed strictly as electro-mechanical systems or control and automation engineering. During 1970s, mechatronics focused on servo technology in which simple implementation aided technologies related to sophisticated control methods such as automatic doors and auto-focus cameras. In the 1980s, mechatronics systems implementation were computer technology based, whereby microprocessors were embedded into mechanical systems to improve performance, such as in automobiles and house hold appliances.

In the 1980s, mechatronics came to mean engineering centred on communication technology connecting products into large networks. The advances in digital electronics that have enabled the possibility to invent, create, and improve systems that rely on mechanical components to perform their intended action. A synergistic integration of different technologies started taking place, a notable example being in optoelectronic (i.e., an integration of optics and electronics). During this stage, the co-design concept of hardware/software has already been developed and was in use. Mechatronics technology development has been driven initially by the; explosive trend in automation within the automobile industry and the increased electronics content in the vehicle and control of system features via software, such as electronic engine controls and anti-lock-braking systems; Industrial machinery and numerically controlled systems, product integration and manufacturing in consumer electronics, and by the semiconductor industry. During the second half of the 1980s mechatronics quality product life cycles started to be compressed dramatically in which new technology must be developed, manufactured, and introduced to the marketplace, in cost effective approach and quickly ahead of the competition, as early market entry for the product provided a critical competitive edge.

1.4. Mechatronics in the Industries and Education

The adoption of mechatronics design philosophy, and concurrent practices by the industries require engineers with a new range of skills, attitudes and abilities. Such engineers are able to work across the boundaries of constituent disciplines to identify and use the right solution to the problem at hand. Engineers with good management skills that enable them to work in and lead design teams. This eventually guided academic institutions towards creating dedicated mechatronics degree programmes. They were aiming to develop interdisciplinary and integrated approach to problem solving where the most effective engineering solution can be reached without bias from any given traditional engineering discipline. Systems engineers were the first who had to deal with such technical and complex issues raised by interactions between software, mechanical hardware and electronics. The relative complexity of design had increased enormously with many thousands of engineers working on the same mega project. The question that remains is how to develop a curriculum and teach such different philosophy within traditional engineering departments.

With the beginning of the 1990s, mechatronics attained an education and research identity as it emerged as an important engineering discipline. The most notable features of the third stage are: the increased use of smart functions in mechatronics products and systems; miniaturization of the product, enhance human computer-interaction; shortening the development cycle time by adopting the use of virtual prototyping and computer simulation. Closely related topics of development during the 1990s were: rapid prototyping; human-computer interaction; optoelectronics, electronic manufacturing and packaging; micro electromechanical systems, advanced manufacturing technology for polymer composite structures, knowledge-based systems, material handling technologies, etc. Furthermore, a new breed of intelligent components and systems started to come out that combined an optimum blend of all available technologies featured by, innovation, shorter development cycles, better quality, high reliability, better performance, compactness, and low cost. In addition, the consideration of human factors during the design process led to ease of product use, safety and increased benefits to the end user. Individual devices such as sensors and actuators had built-in intelligence requiring local computer-based signal processing and control functions. Engineers began to embed microprocessors in mechanical systems to improve their performance. Embedded systems and real-time software engineering are accomplished through various types of embedded microcontrollers, which are indispensable components of modern mechatronics systems.

1.5. Mechatronics and ICT

The early part of 1990s, highlighted the beginning of a new era that merged mechatronics as a technology with modern information and communication technologies (ICTs). Information technology through intelligent software development started to become a more important constituent of mechatronics system functionality. Information and communications technologies were added to yield intelligent products that are portable and could be connected within large networks. This development made functions such as the remote operation of robots, home appliances, manufacturing, biomedical devices and health facilities possible. In addition, recent fundamental and applied developments in mini-, micro- and nano-scale electromechanics (especially micro scale electromechanical systems (MEMS) and micro-opto-electromechanical systems (MOEMS)), control, informatics, and power electronics have motivated and accelerated such growth and have found a wide range of applications. Micro-electromechanical systems, such as the tiny silicon accelerometers that trigger automotive air bags, are examples of the latter use. Furthermore, by the mid 1990s, mechatronics had gained a tremendous international attention and its importance was widely and globally recognized.

1.6. Mechatronics in the 21st Century

Since 2000, processor speed and advancements of building memory capacity heralded the boom in in-car navigation systems and other audio-visual consumer electronic products, as well as passive and active safety systems. The start of the 21st century marked the identity of mechatronics as an engineering and science discipline. The interdisciplinary mechatronics field has experienced phenomenal growth since its beginning over three decades ago due to rapid advances in enabling technologies: actuators, sensors, power electronics, motion devices, solid state devices, integrated circuits, microprocessors and microcontrollers, digital signal processors, high performance computer aided design, system intelligence, and computation intelligence software and techniques. Today, the term mechatronics encompasses a large array of technologies and it represents most of the research issues of modern design. The mechatronics design methodology is not only concerned with producing high quality products, but maintaining these products as well. This area referred to as life cycle design consideration. The life cycle design factors include delivery, reliability, maintainability, serviceability, upgradeability, and disposability. Life cycle factors should be considered during all stages of mechatronics product design and manufacturing, resulting in products that are designed from conception to retirement

Due to the intensive demands for high performance electromechanical systems, designers apply a mechatronics concept because the performance of such systems has been examined, assessed, and optimized. Modern engineering encompasses diverse interdisciplinary areas, and accordingly it is critical to identify new directions in research and engineering filed that address, pursue, and implement interdisciplinary development. mechatronics integrates the classical fields of mechanical engineering [13], electrical engineering, computer engineering, information technology and many more disciplines as indicated in Fig.1.1. This helps in establishing the basic principles for a contemporary engineering design methodology thereby providing interdisciplinary leadership and support current gradual changes.

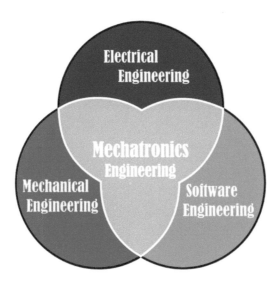

Figure 1.1. *Mechatronics as a confluence of other disciplines.*

Mechatronics represents a new philosophy to engineering design that is likely to be of increasing importance to the success of a wide range of industries as well as academic institutions. It became and remains a significant design trend that has impacted the nature of both the product development process and technological change, both in effect as well as pace [2]. Mechatronics has a significant and increasing impact upon engineering and engineering education as a defining approach to the design, development, and new way of thinking. Hence, it is important for both industry and academic institutions to work together in order to tune the required infrastructures to support and enhance the identity of mechatronics as engineering science discipline and to help engineers gaining the required skills.

1.7. Mechatronics Education and Training

In order to achieve the needed operational quality and efficiency in products, production and systems, current and future engineering workplace requires skills of graduates that go beyond those taught in traditionally designed university and technological colleges programmes. Creative response to the need to provide education and training for a new breed of engineers and technologists who are proficient in the combined application of systems design as well as mechanical, electronic and computer-based control to managing sophisticated manufacturing processes and technology-intensive operations; developing high value-added products of mechatronics nature, and providing quality interdisciplinary engineering services. Mechatronics discipline is attracting students to be part of the new era of industrialization to support advanced product development, and to enable the interdisciplinary engineer to look forward to a high quality of job satisfaction with enhanced employment prospects. This new concept requires strong scientific background and experimental techniques as well as a broad knowledge in engineering. This trend enhances the need for mechatronics engineers.

Education in mechatronics is a relatively new discipline in engineering education, as is mechatronics itself. At the first developmental stages, the content of courses and programmes in mechatronics formed spontaneously and were primarily based on the developer-professional experience. As a rule, mechatronics courses were initiated independently by tutors in mechanical or electrical and computer engineering departments. In the case of the former, this was generally through the inclusion of courses on microprocessors and control within a primarily mechanical engineering programme while in the latter, the primary emphasis tended to be on the electrical and electronic components of mechatronics systems.

During the 1990s, mechatronics became a common elective course and frequently, also a required course in many undergraduate mechanical engineering systems worldwide. Nevertheless, during that time, in the overwhelming majority of cases, engineers resorted to mechatronics as a part of their work, meaning that it was essentially self-taught. As a rule, this occurred, and still is occurring, due to collaborations between mechanical, electrical and computer engineers. This often results in an ineffective learning scheme, since the tutors involved had different backgrounds, and indeed often used different engineering terminologies.

1.7.1. Mechatronics Course Structure

Gradually, the discipline of mechatronics evolved as modifications to engineering courses in existing engineering programmes to the creation of new programmes in mechatronics, culminating in the creation of organizations devoted exclusively to the field of mechatronics. This process was to a large extent propelled by active scientific studies in the field of mechatronics systems. Analysis reveals that integration of various teaching courses into mechatronics took place in the research activities of many higher education institutions globally. The growth of interest in mechatronics has identified a need for the provision of engineers whose education and training enable them to operate in an interdisciplinary manner. Mechatronics engineering represents a fundamental shift away from the engineering specialist to an engineer with expectation to solve open ended problems while fusing mechanical, electronic and computer technologies. The need for mechatronics education has grown due to the increase in the number and importance of such systems and devices. The structure of a mechatronics programme should:

▷ Provide synthesis experiences and motivation, and integrate theoretical and practical skills.

▷ Provide in-depth knowledge in the fundamentals of design and analysis, along with implementing the engineering aspects related to utilization, operation, maintenance and management of mechatronics systems, processes and devices.

▷ Be designed to incorporate foundational subjects in physics, mathematics and statistics, computation and IT, static and dynamic, fluid power, electrical and electronics, measurements, and materials.

▷ Have core subjects in modeling and simulation, control systems and analysis, embedded systems and microcontrollers, sensors and perception, real-time and intelligent systems, engineering design and smart products, robotics, and computational intelligence.

In addition, it should include supporting subjects in management, product development and marketing, and engineering practices. The supporting subjects be designed to provide graduates with the unique skills required to tackle problems that span the full electro-mechanical spectrum integrated with information and communication technologies. A strong feature of the course should have emphasis on practical and project work that allow students to consolidate their learning and develop planning and communication skills that are considered an integral part of the engineering profession.

The theoretical and practical components of the curriculum should be integrated so that the topics for the lectures emerge from the direction leading to the solutions of real life challenges and subsequent development of systems capable of addressing the identified challenges. The projects should be designed to lead students to develop a greater interest in engineering and the teaching should reflects more closely real needs. This enables the student to build upon the knowledge and skills that they have developed during previous stages while subjecting them to new challenges through diversity. There was a significant evidence of the educational and motivational benefits of incorporating projects into earlier years of degree programmes. This increases students curiosity, physical understanding and insight. It is important to strengthen and sustain the quality and integrity of a targeted mechatronics programme by having a peer review and professional self-regulation. At the same time, an internal review process presents an invaluable opportunity to analyze how to conduct affairs and where to improve.

1.7.2. Mechatronics - Vocational Education

Having realized this disparity between industrial requirements and knowledge imparted to the graduates at various levels, ISESCO and Festo Didactic Germany ventured to elaborate a series of curricula to meet the futuristic dire need for skilled human workforce in mechatronics in one hand, and to contribute to creation of excellent job opportunities in industries on the other. A curriculum entitled Vocational Education/Technician Studies/Bachelor Studies is one in a series of curricula for mechatronics, designed to draw the guidelines for principal structure of a mechatronics system, assumption for regular and future education, a full account of prerequisite and advanced necessary modules, laboratory and equipment needs and last but not least the entrance qualification and final examination in the course of study. The curriculum is designed based on profound practical experience in vocational education and industrial placement through involvement in various international projects. This series of curricula if followed will promote the integration of mechatronics in the educational and vocational systems.

However, to effectively train competent mechatronics technicians who are capable of maintaining mechatronics equipment the following subjects should form the training foundation:

▷ Mathematics
▷ Physics
▷ Mechanical Engineering/Mechanics
▷ Electrical Engineering/Electronics
▷ Computer Systems
▷ Microcontroller/Microprocessor Systems
▷ Material Technology
▷ Sensors and Actuators
▷ Mechatronics Systems
▷ Automation and Control
▷ Graphical Programming and Analysis Tools (e.g. Labiew, Flowcode, Matlab, etc.)
▷ Laboratory experiments, hand-on practicals and project

1.7.3. Mechatronics in Higher Education Institutions

A considerable number of high education institutions in various countries offer mechatronics degrees. However, their approach to the challenge of educating mechatronics engineer varies depending on culture, system, and availability of existing courses and resources. Several of mechatronics programme seem to be based on simply adding electronics, PLCs and logic circuits to existing mechanical engineering curriculum, thus lacking a coherent integrative theme. This is obviously not ideal. On the other hand, some institutions are designing mechatronics degree programmes from scratch with integrating design projects running through the programme. mechatronics engineering courses at undergraduate and postgraduate levels as well as vocational training courses, have been rapidly increasing in higher education institutions in Europe, particularly in the U.K., U.S., Australia, and Japan [1]. While very few African countries embraced the development. For instance:

1. **Japan:** Japanese universities educational system tends to foster engineers with a transdisciplinary approach. Japanese educationalists see the mechatronics engineer as a broader based mechanical engineer who has a good hands on knowledge and ability in microprocessor hardware and software, electronics, actuators, and control.

2. **Australia:** The Australian Agency for International Development, AusAID supported the initiative of developing new mechatronics courses at six different Australian Universities. The courses were pitched at the undergraduate level. The aim was to establish a common understanding of the objectives and nature of a mechatronics course with a view to focus the development on satisfying the regional industrial demands. The programme objective was to equip students with the necessary knowledge and skills and prepare them to holistically and creatively manage, in a professional manner, the multidisciplinary tasks which include design, development and service of modern-day machines and devices.

3. **United States of America:** Up until the early 90s, most universities teaching mechatronics in USA mainly offer a course (module or unit) in microprocessor or microcontroller applications usually at the senior year level. The continuous relevance of mechatronics in the industries, necessitated the Massachusetts Institute of Technology (MIT) to convene a commission that studied the productivity and performance of the USA industries [1]. The Commission recommended that the MIT School of Engineering should offer as an alternative path to the existing four-year curriculum a broader undergraduate programme of instruction which would paved way for the training of mechatronics engineer. The Commission's recommendations reflect on the need for a new nucleus of engineers who have broader backgrounds but with specialist knowledge of a discipline and abilities to operate in a multidisciplinary project team. This proposition agrees with the concept of the mechatronics engineer. As of today, there over 60 higher institution offering various vocational, undergraduate and graduate level courses in USA.

4. **United Kingdom (UK):** In recent years mechatronics has increasingly gained more prominence in the UK higher education scene. This is clearly visible from the rapidly increasing number of undergraduate degree programmes and M.Sc. programmes offered by a number of higher education institutions. Lancaster University established the first undergraduate degree course in mechatronics as a specialist option of their electronic and mechanical engineering courses. The University of Hull and Leeds University have followed soon after. Several other universities and colleges have since embraced the subject to the extent of offering mechatronics courses at B.Sc., B.Eng., and M.Eng. levels. These include King, College London, Sussex University, Staffordshire University, Manchester Metropolitan University, Middlesex University, De Montfort University, University of Abertay Dundee, Glamorgan University and Newcastle University.

5. **Africa:** In Africa, very few countries to date have introduced mechatronics as course in their education curriculum. The following gives some insight into the level of mechatronics education compliance in Africa.

   a) **South Africa:** In 2006 South Africa launched a five-year partnership to train mechatronics engineers at three South African Universities of Technology in order to grow the country's indigenous technology and skills base. In another development, the country has introduced mechatronics in the new National Curriculum for Vocation (NCV) at NQF levels 2, 3 and 4, and is experiencing growing demand at Further Education and Training (FET) Colleges throughout South Africa by both students and employers [3]. Colleges in South Africa are now responding to the demand for practical, relevant skills by investing in hands-on industrial training equipment. leading.

   b) **Egypt:** Mechatronics has been in the Egypt's education system for over a decade. The programme is offered by several university and colleges at vocational, undergraduate and graduate levels. Most popular institutions offering mechatronics programme in Egypt are MISR University for Science and Technology, German University in Cairo (GUC), Egypt-Japan University of Science and Technology among others.

c) **Nigeria:** The body responsible for regulation of university education in Nigeria, the National University Commission (NUC) earmarked 14 pilot Nigerian institutions for introduction of mechatronics engineering degree programme in 2010. To date, the programme has fully been taken up in the majority of the institutions. Some of these institutions are Bayero University Kano (BUK), University of Lagos (UniLag), Abubakar Tafawa Balewa University (ATBU) Bauchi among others. However, other private universities, such as Afe Babalola University Ekiti and Bells University of Technology Ogun have introduced mechatronics at the undergraduate level. Also, the principal organ of Federal Ministry of Education which is a specifically created to handle all aspects of Technical and Vocational Education outside University Education in Nigeria, National Board for Technical Education (NBTE), some few years back drafted curricula for teaching mechatronics at national diploma (ND), technical and vocational education levels and is in effect now. Another private and non-profit vocational school in Lagos, Nigeria, Institute for Industrial Technology (IIT) also offers six months mechatronics training for engineering graduates of universities and polytechnics.

Chapter 2

Mechatronics Essentials

This chapter presents a general discussion on electronic components identification methods and terminologies used to describe these components. The chapter concludes with some highlights on the fundamental and practical considerations required to build mechatronics systems.

2.1. Electric Circuits and Components

An electric circuit is formed when a conductive path is created to allow free electrons to continuously move. This continuous movement of free electrons through the conductors of a circuit is called a current.

2.1.1. Current

Current (I) is the rate of charge flow past a given point in an electric circuit, measured in Coulombs/second which is named Amperes. In most DC electric circuits, it can be assumed that the resistance to current flow is a constant so that the current in the circuit is related to voltage and resistance by Ohm's law as in Equation 2.1. The standard abbreviations for the units are 1 A = 1C/s.

2.1.2. Voltage

Voltage (V) attempts to make electrons to flow in a circuit. It is is a specific measure of potential energy that is always relative between two points. The voltage difference between any two points in a circuit is known as the potential difference (pd) or voltage drop and it is the difference between these two points that makes the current flow. Unlike current which flows around a circuit in the form of electrical charge, potential difference does not move it is applied. The unit of potential difference is the volt and is defined as the potential difference across a resistance of one ohm carrying a current of one ampere.

2.1.3. Resistance

Free electrons tend to move through conductors with some degree of friction, or opposition to motion. This opposition to motion is more properly called resistance. The amount of current in a circuit depends on the amount of voltage available to motivate the electrons, and also the amount of resistance in the circuit to oppose electron flow. Just like voltage, resistance is a relative quantity between two points. For this reason, the quantities of voltage and resistance are often stated as being "between" or "across" two points in a circuit. Resistance is measured in a unit called Ohms, represented with a Greek letter notation Ω.

2.1.4. Practical Analogy to Understanding Current, Voltage and Resistance

A good analogy to help understand the relationship between current, voltage and resistance is a water pipe system. Lets consider a fixed diameter water pipe with a constant flow pressure through the inlet to the outlet, and having a plunger midway along its length. If the plunger is totally down, Fig. 2.1, no water will flow due to the high flow resistance.

Figure 2.1. *Practical analogy to understanding current, voltage and resistance (1).*

However, pulling the plunger up reduces the flow resistance and results in partial water flow to the outlet, Fig. 2.2.

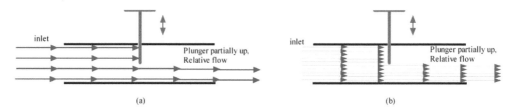

Figure 2.2. *Practical analogy to understanding current, voltage and resistance (2).*

Further raising up the plunger or increasing the inlet pressure will result in more water flow to the outlet (Fig. 2.3).

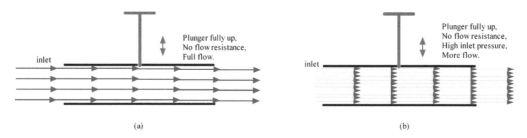

Figure 2.3. *Practical analogy to understanding current, voltage and resistance (3).*

In this analogy, water inlet pressure represents voltage, plunger position represents resistance and water flow rate represents current. Increasing the inlet pressure is like increasing the voltage and will result in more current flow. Pulling up the plunger is like decreasing the flow resistance which will also allow more current to flow.

2.1.5. Current, Voltage and Resistance Relationship - Ohms Law

The first, and perhaps most important, relationship between current, voltage, and resistance is called the Ohm's Law, discovered by George Simon Ohm. Mathematically, the relationship is written as;

$$I = \frac{V}{R} \tag{2.1}$$

where: I = current (I) in apms (A), V= voltage in volts (V) and R = resistance in ohms (Ω)

This can easily be remembered by using what is called the Ohm's Law Triangle (Fig. 2.4).

Figure 2.4. *Ohm's Law triangle*

The triangle is used as follows:

1. To calculate voltage, V: place a finger over V, this leaves I R, so the equation is:

$$V = I \times R \tag{2.2}$$

2. To calculate current, I: place a finger over I, this leaves V over R, so the equation is:

$$I = \frac{V}{R} \tag{2.3}$$

3. To calculate resistance, R: place a finger over R, this leaves V over I, so the equation is:

$$R = \frac{V}{I} \tag{2.4}$$

2.2. A Typical Electric Circuit

A simple electric circuit consists of voltage loops and current nodes in a closed connection of power source and switches together with various kinds of electrical components. Some basic electrical components typically found on electric circuits are resistors, capacitors, inductors, diodes, transistors and integrated circuits (ICs).

2.2.1. Resistor

Resistors *(R)* are the most fundamental and commonly used of all the electric components. There are many different types of resistors (Fig. 2.5) available, from very small surface mount chip resistors up to large wire-wound power resistors.

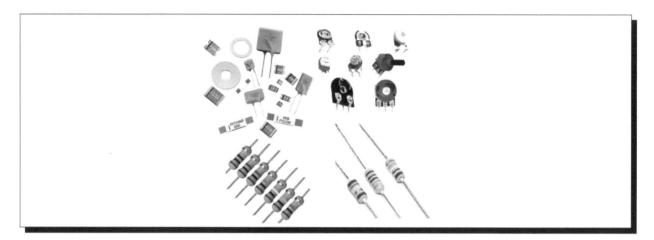

Figure 2.5. *Assorted resistors*

In an electric circuit, the resistance of the wires in the circuit can be ignored, because it is very low. Motors, light bulbs, and heating coils are all examples of resistors. Resistances are extremely useful in electrical circuits, they can be used to reduce the current flow or the voltage produced across them. The electrical symbols used to represent a resistor are depicted in Fig. 2.6.

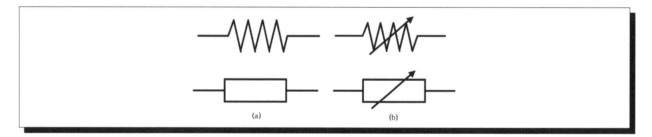

Figure 2.6. *Resistor electrical symbols (a) Normal resistor (b) Variable resistor*

2.2.2. Capacitor

A capacitor is a component made from two (or two sets of) conductive plates with an insulator between them. The insulator prevents the plates from touching. When a DC current is applied across a capacitor, positive charge builds on one plate (or set of plates) and negative charge builds on the other. The charge will remain until the capacitor is discharged. When an AC current is applied across the capacitor, it will charge one set of plates positive and the other negative during the part of the cycle when the voltage is positive; when the voltage goes negative in the second half of the cycle, the capacitor will release what it previously charged, and then charge the opposite way. This then repeats for each cycle. Since it has the opposite charge stored in it each time the voltage changes, it tends to oppose the change in voltage. If a mixed DC and AC signal is applied across a capacitor, the capacitor will tend to block the DC and let the AC flow through. The strength of a capacitor is called capacitance and is measured in farads (F). Figure 2.7 depicts the symbols used to represent a capacitor.

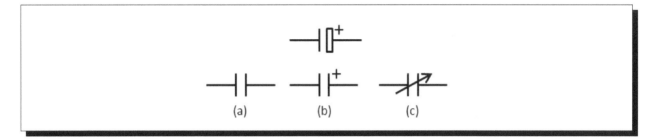

Figure 2.7. *Capacitor symbols (a) Unpolarized capacitor (b) Polarized capacitor (c) Variable capacitor*

As with resistors, there are many different types of capacitor, ranging from ceramic capacitors, electrolytic capacitors and silver mica capacitors as well as other various forms of plastic (e.g. polyester) capacitors. Each capacitor type has its own advantages and disadvantages and therefore, their usage differ. Some are better for high frequency applications, whereas others can be used for low frequency applications. Indeed it is necessary to have the right capacitor for the right application, otherwise the circuit will not work properly.

Capacitor Circuit

The circuit shown in Fig. 2.8 consists of a capacitor, a switch and a battery. When the switch is closed, current flows from the battery to the capacitor. The capacitor side attaches to the negative terminal of the battery gets electrons from the battery. The other side of the capacitor attaches to the positive terminal of the battery loses electrons to the battery. This charges the capacitor to the battery voltage. For a small capacitor, the capacity is small. However, large capacitors hold larger charges.

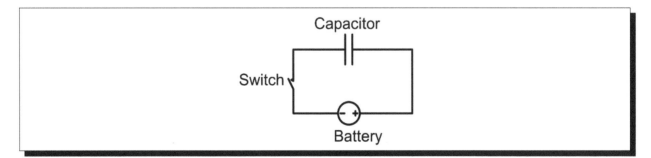

Figure 2.8. *Capacitor circuit*

In Fig. 2.9, a bulb is added to the circuit. If the the switch is closed, current will flow from the battery to charge the capacitor and hence turning on the bulb. However, the bulb will get dimmer as the capacitor is charging and eventually goes off when the capacitor is fully charged. If the battery is replaced with a piece of wire after the capacitor is fully charged, current will now flow from one side of the capacitor to the other turning off the bulb

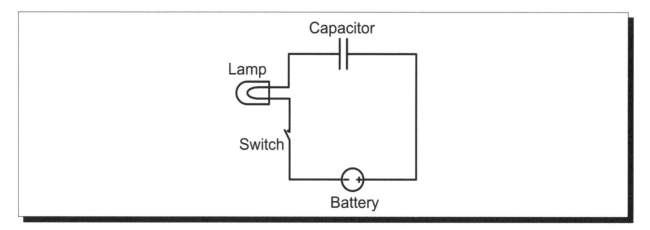

Figure 2.9. *Capacitor circuit with a bulb*

Capacitor Types

Electrolytic and tantalum capacitors are basically the two commonly large capacitors in use. Most large capacitors are clearly marked with the value of the capacitor, its polarity and working voltage. Small value capacitors are unpolarised and therefore can be connected into a circuit either way around. They are available in a wide range of values, with the various polyester types and ceramic capacitors being popular choices.

1. **Electrolytic:**
   The electrolytic type capacitor depicted in Fig. 2.10 is probably the most common large capacity capacitor. This type of capacitor offers a very high level of capacitance per unit volume. They are polar and therefore have to be incorporated into the circuit with the correct polarity. While they offer a high level of capacitance, the maximum frequencies at which they can operate is limited to around 100 kHz.

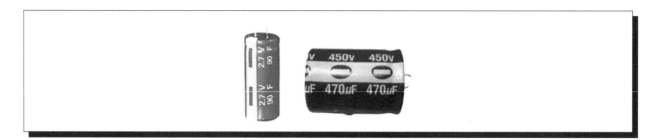

Figure 2.10. *Electrolytic capacitors*

Most electrolytic capacitors are clearly marked with the value of the capacitor in microfarads (μF), the polarity of the leads, and the working voltage. For this reason electrolytic capacitors are often the easiest capacitors to identify and use. It is very important to remember that most electrolytic capacitors are polarized i.e. the must be connected the correct way round in the circuit - to identify polarity these capacitors will generally have a (usually white) stripe down one side with a negative sign to indicate that lead is to go only to the negative side of the circuit and the positive lead will usually be longer than the negative. If it is connected the wrong way round it may explode.

2. **Tantalum:**
   The tantalum capacitor is another type of capacitor that is available in large capacities. It is a form of electrolytic capacitor that uses a tantalum based compound as the dielectric. It has exceedingly high levels of capacitance per unit volume. Like the standard aluminum electrolytic capacitor it is polar, and very sensitive to incorrect polarity voltages or voltages exceeding the maximum rated working voltage. They are much smaller than electrolytic capacitors and also usually have lower working voltages. Tantalum capacitors must be connected the right way round in the circuit. Modern tantalum bead capacitors have the value printed on the casing along with the voltage and polarity marking as shown in Fig. 2.11. Older ones use a colour code in the form of stripes or spots.

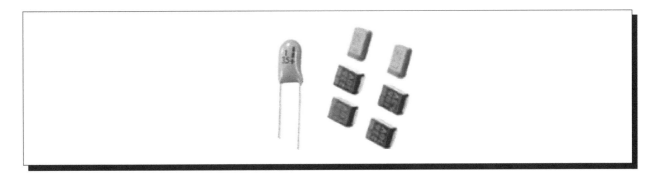

Figure 2.11. *Tantalum capacitors*

3. **Ceramic capacitor:**
   Ceramic capacitors, shown in Fig. 2.11 are one of the most commonly used capacitors on electronics components this days. As the name suggests, this capacitors use ceramic as the dielectric between the plates of the capacitor. They are classified into three classes based on stability, accuracy, temperature coefficient and volumetric efficiency. In addition to this ceramic capacitor types normally perform well at high frequencies and available in values ranging from a few picofarads (pF) up to around 0.1microfarads (μF).

Figure 2.12. *Ceramic capacitors*

4. **Plastic film capacitors:**
   Figure 2.13 depicts a combination of different kinds of plastic film capacitor. These capacitors are made out of different plastic materials, such as polyester, polystyrene and polycarbonate. Their capacitance values largely depend on the construction materials. Plastic film capacitors generally have small range of tolerances and high reliability and are used in many general-purpose applications. Example of these capacitor are;
   a) Polyester: suitable for use in filter circuits;
   b) Polycarbonate: Known for their reliability and stability over different environmental conditions.

Figure 2.13. *Plastic film capacitors*

5. **Silver mica capacitor:**
   Silver mica capacitors depicted in Fig. 2.14, use mica as the dielectric and have silver plates. They offer a high degree of performance for radio frequencies and in particular they offer a low temperature coefficient (typically around 50 ppm/^{0}C). Although expensive, ideal for applications such as filters and RF oscillators. However, as other ceramic and some plastic film capacitor types, they have been developed with very good levels of performance. These capacitors are now used much less than previously.

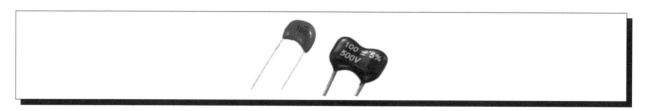

Figure 2.14. *Silver mica capacitors*

Uses of Capacitors

Capacitors are widely used in electronic circuits in a variety of applications such as:

- ▷ In electrical filters.
- ▷ Store charges such as in a camera flash circuit.
- ▷ Smoothing the output of power supply circuits.
- ▷ Coupling of two stages of a circuit (coupling of an audio stage with a loud speaker).
- ▷ Tone control of an audio system.

▷ Delay applications (as in 555 timer IC controlling the charging and discharging).

▷ Tuning radios to particular frequencies.

▷ Phase alteration.

2.2.3. Inductor

An inductor depicted in Fig. 2.15 is essentially a coil of wire. When current flows through an inductor, a magnetic field is created, and the inductor will store this magnetic energy until it is released. In some ways, an inductor is the opposite of a capacitor. While a capacitor stores voltage as electrical energy, an inductor stores current as magnetic energy. Thus, a capacitor opposes a change in the voltage of a circuit, while an inductor opposes a change in its current. Therefore, capacitors block DC current and let AC current pass, while inductors do the opposite. Inductance, the property of an inductor is measured in Henry (H).

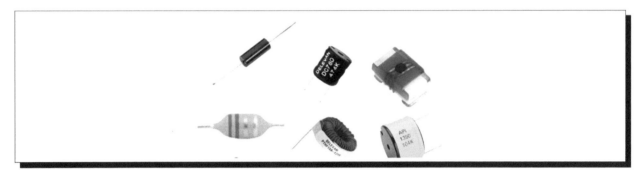

Figure 2.15. *Assorted inductors (a) Normal inductor (b) Iron core inductor (c) Variable inductor*

Inductors are available in different models and for a variety of applications. Most commonly found in commercial and industrial applications are coupled, multilayer, ceramic core, and moulded inductors. Inductors can have a core of air in the middle of their coils, or a ferrous (iron) core. Figure 2.16 depicts the electrical symbols used to represent inductors.

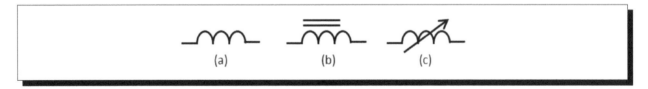

Figure 2.16. *Inductor symbols (a) Normal inductor (b) Iron core inductor (c) Variable inductor*

Factor Influencing the Strength of Inductors

1. *Number of coils, more coils mean more inductance.*
2. *The material that the coils are wrapped around (the core).*
3. *The cross-sectional area of the coil - More area means more inductance.*
4. *The length of the coil - A short coil means narrower (or overlapping) coils, which means more inductance.*

Inductor Circuit

The circuit shown in Fig. 2.17 consists of an inductor, a bulb, a battery and a switch. If the inductor were to be remove, the circuit is reduced to a flash light. Whereby if the switch is closed, the bulb lights up. However, with the inductor, if the switch is closed, the bulb lights up brightly and then dims gradually. When the switch is opened, the bulb lights up brightly and quickly lights off.

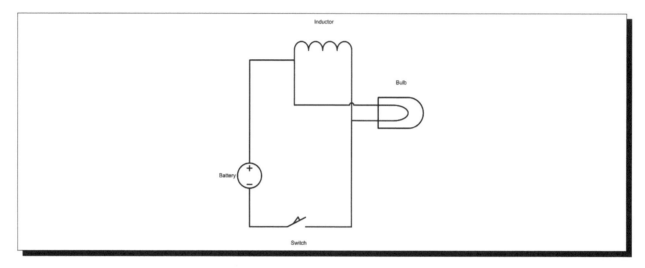

Figure 2.17. *Inductor circuit*

This behaviour is a consequence of the inductor property. As soon as current flows into an inductor, it begins building up a magnetic field. So on closing the switch, current will flow into the inductor and the inductor begins building up a magnetic field. The inductor hinders current flow while the magnetic field is building. As soon as the field is built, current then flows normally. If the switch is opened, the magnetic field in the inductor keeps the current flowing for its active period. The current in turn keeps the bulb glowing. Hence, inductor stores energy in its magnetic field.

2.2.4. A Switch

An electrical switch is any device used to interrupt the flow of electrons in a circuit. Switches are essentially binary devices: they are either completely on ("closed") or completely off ("open"). There are many different types of switches such as: toggle, rotary, push-button, rocker, pull-chain, slide, magnetic, mercury, timer, voice-activated, touch-sensitive, joystick, temperature, proximity among others. Figure 2.18 depicts symbolic representation of switches.

The simplest switch is one where two electrical conductors are brought in contact with each other by the motion of an actuating mechanism. Some switches are more complex than others, containing electronic circuits capable of turning on or off depending on some physical stimulus (such as light or magnetic field). In any case, the final output of any switch is at least a pair of wire-connecting terminals that are either connected together by the switch's internal contact mechanism ("closed"), or not connected together ("open").

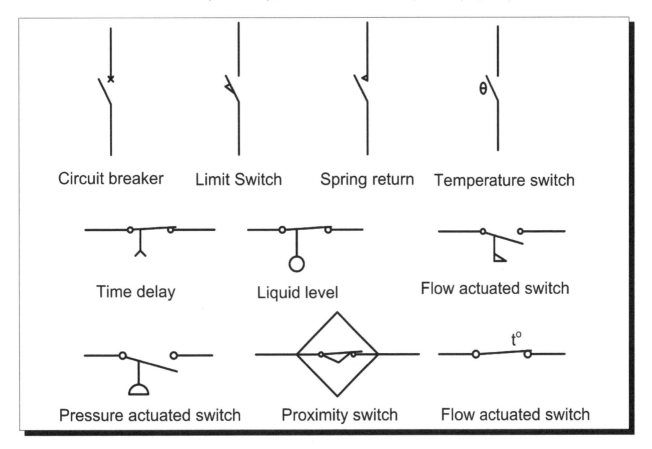

Figure 2.18. *Switch symbols and types.*

2.2.5. A Fuse

A fuse, symbolically depicted in Fig. 2.19 is a device designed to protect other components from accidental damage due to excessive current flowing through them. Fuse rating is based on the amount of current it can handle before it blows. Upon, fuses are rated for the voltage they can tolerate before blowing. As long as the current in the circuit is kept below this value, the fuse passes the current with little opposition. If the current rises above the rating of the fuse due to a malfunction of some sort or an accidental short-circuit, the fuse will blow and disconnect the circuit, causing a physical gap in the circuit and saving other devices from the high current. They can then be replaced when the problem condition has been corrected.

Figure 2.19. *A fuse symbol.*

2.2.6. DC Power Supply

A power supply is a device which supplies power to another device at a certain voltage and current levels. For instance, a 12VDC @ 400mA power supply (Fig. 2.20) can provide as much as 400mA of current and the voltage will be at least 12VDC up to that maximum current level. Selecting a power supply for a given application is governed by the power requirement of the overall system and the power supply rating.

Figure 2.20. DC power supply.

Basic Elements in a DC Power Supply

There are numerous types of elements in a power supply adapter. These are some of the basic elements found. Although, they may not all be present in every power adapter.

▷ **Input transformer:**
The input transformer is used to transform the incoming line voltage down to the required level for the power supply. Typically the input transformer provides a step down function. It also isolates the output circuit from the line supply.

▷ **Rectifier:**
The power supply rectifier converts the incoming signal from an AC format into raw DC. Either half wave or more commonly full wave rectifiers may be used as they make use of both halves of the incoming AC signal.

▷ **Smoothing:**
The raw DC from the rectifier is far from constant falling to zero when the AC waveform crossed the zero axis, and then rising to its peak. The addition of a reservoir capacitor here fills in the troughs in the waveform, enabling the next stage of the power supply to operate. Large value capacitors are normally used within this stage.

▷ **Regulator:**
At this stage, a power supply takes the smoothed voltage and uses a regulator circuit to provide a constant output virtually regardless of the output current and any minor fluctuations in the input level.

Types of Power Supply

The two commonly forms of power supply used in electronics equipment are regulated and unregulated DC power sources. Although, a battery is another source of power to electronic equipment.

1. **Unregulated:**
   This is the most common DC power supply adapter found in electronic stores. It consists of a rectifier section and a capacitor or capacitor and inductor for smoothing. The DC output voltage is this power supply depends on an internal voltage transformer and relates to the amount of current used by the load. If a large current is drawn the voltage would fall as a result of the resistive losses, and also the smoothing would not be as effective.

2. **Regulated DC power supply:**
   In this, the DC output voltage always stays within the rated value regardless of the amount of current consumed by the load, as long as the rated output current of the power adapter is not exceeded. Typically, it incorporates a voltage reference, and the output voltage is compared to this and altered accordingly by control circuitry within the regulated power supply.

2.3. Components Colour Codes/Marking Identification

In the last decade, electronics components have been miniaturized. When constructing electronic projects, it is necessary to determine the exact value of components to use. Some standards have been established over the years for identifying the rating of electronic components. These standards are normally based on colour coding or marking on the components body. Although the components values may be printed on their bodies or indicated by a colour code. The colour codes currently in use are; Joint Army-Navy (JAN) code, Radio Manufacturer's Association (RMA) code and Electronic Industries Alliance (EIA) code. For each of these codes, colour dots or bands are used to indicate components value.

2.3.1. Resistor Colour Code

When a resistor is large enough to accommodate markings, such as large power resistors, the resistance value, tolerance, and wattage rating are generally printed on the body of the resistor as numbers or letters. However, when the resistor is small, these specifications are shown using colour painted bands to indicate both their resistive value and their tolerance. The colour painted bands produce a system of identification known as *Resistors Colour Code*.

Figure. 2.21 depicts a table for resistor values identification based on colour code. The colour bands, normally four or five bands are always read one band at a time starting from the left to the right, with the larger width tolerance band oriented to the right side indicating its tolerance. Matching the colour of the first band with its associated number in the digit column of the colour chart, the first digit is identified. This represents the first digit of the resistor's value. Again, by matching the colour of the second band with its associated number in the digit column of the colour chart the second digit of the resistor's value is obtained and so on.

Four Colour Bands Resistors

Commonly used resistors are usually four colour bands. The first two bands show the first two digits, the third band provides the multiplier by which the first two digits must be multiplied (i.e number of zeros); together this gives the value of the resistor (the resistance) in Ohms. The fourth band indicates the tolerance of the resistor; that is how close the actual resistance may be to the value indicated. A 1K (1000Ω) resistor with a 20% tolerance could have a value anywhere between 800 and 1200Ω. The *tolerance band* is sometimes spaced further apart from the other three bands, which helps when deciding which way round to read off the value, which is sometimes difficult to establish immediately.

Example 2.1. Calculate the values of resistors shown in Fig. 2.22.

SOLUTION (Fig. 2.22(a):
From the colour code Table, Fig. 2.1.10, the four band colours of the resistor are:
1st band: Red = 2
2nd band: Blue = 6
3rd band: Orange(Multiplier): = $\times 1,000$
4th band: Gold(Tolerance): = $\pm 5\%$
Therefore, the resistor value is: $26 \times 1,000 = 26,000$ **Ohms (Usually expressed as 26K)** $\pm 5\%$

SOLUTION (Fig. 2.22(b):
From the colour code Table, Fig. 2.21, the four band colours of the resistor are:
1st band: Brown = 1
2nd band: Black = 0
3rd band: Silver (Multiplier) = $\times 0.01$
4th band: Silver Tolerance): = $\pm 10\%$
Therefore, the resistor value is: $10 \times 0.01 = 0.1$ **Ohms (Usually expressed as 0.1R)** $\pm 10\%$

SOLUTION (Fig. 2.22(c):
From the colour code Table, Fig. 2.21, the four band colours of the resistor are:
1st band: Red = 2
2nd band: Brown = 1
3rd band: Silver (Multiplier) = $\times 10$
4th band: Gold(Tolerance): = $\pm 5\%$
Therefore, the resistor value is: $21 \times 10 = 210$ **Ohms (Usually expressed as 210R)** $\pm 5\%$

SOLUTION (Fig. 2.22(d):
From the colour code Table, Fig. 2.21, the four band colours of the resistor are:
1st band: Orange = 3
2nd band: Orange = 3
3rd band: Yellow (Multiplier) = $\times 10,000$
4th band: Silver(Tolerance): = $\pm 10\%$
Therefore, the resistor value is: $33 \times 10,000 = 33,000$ Ohms (Usually expressed as 330K)
$\pm 10\%$

SOLUTION (Fig. 2.22(e):
From the colour code Table, Fig. 2.21, the four band colours of the resistor are:
1st band: Brown = 1
2nd band: Black = 0
3rd band: Orange (Multiplier) = $\times 1,000$
4th band: Gold(Tolerance): = $\pm 5\%$
Therefore, the resistor value is: $10 \times 1,000 = 10,000$ Ohms (Usually expressed as 1K)
$\pm 5\%$

SOLUTION (Fig. 2.22(f):
From the colour code Table, Fig. 2.21, the four band colours of the resistor are:
1st band: Yellow = 4
2nd band: Violet = 7
3rd band: Green (Multiplier) = $\times 100,000$
4th band: Gold(Tolerance): = $\pm 10\%$
Therefore, the resistor value is: $47 \times 100,000 = 4,700,000$ Ohms (Usually expressed as
4.7M) $\pm 10\%$

Five Colour Bands Resistors

Other commonly used resistors are the five colour bands. The first three bands indicate the first three digits, the fourth band provides the multiplier by which the first three digits must be multiplied (i.e. number of zeros) the result gives the value of the resistor. The fifth band indicates the tolerance. Again it is often difficult to tell which way round to read off the value, but the tolerance band is usually spaced a little further apart from the first four bands as shown in the lower part of Fig. 2.21.

Example 2.2. Find the value of the following five colour band resistors in Fig.2.23.

SOLUTION (Fig. 2.23(a):
From the colour code Table, Fig. 2.21, the four band colours of the resistor are:
1st band: Red = 2
2nd band: Red = 2
3rd band: Black = 0
4th band: Yellow (Multiplier) = ×10,000
5th band: Gold(Tolerance): = ±5%
Therefore, the resistor value is: $567 \times 100 = 56,700$ **Ohms (Usually expressed as 56.7K)** ±5%

SOLUTION (Fig. 2.23(b):
From the colour code Table, Fig. 2.21, the four band colours of the resistor are:
1st band: Brown = 1
2nd band: Black = 0
3rd band: Black = 0
4th band: Black (Multiplier) = ×1
5th band: Brown(Tolerance): = ±1%
Therefore, the resistor value is: $100 \times 1 = 100$ **Ohms (Usually expressed as 100R)** ±1%

SOLUTION (Fig. 2.23(c):
From the colour code Table, Fig. 2.21, the four band colours of the resistor are:
1st band: Yellow = 4
2nd band: Violet = 7
3rd band: Black = 0
4th band: Brown (Multiplier) = ×10
5th band: Brown(Tolerance): = ±1%
Therefore, the resistor value is: $470 \times 10 = 4,700$ **Ohms (Usually expressed as 4.7K)** ±1%

SOLUTION (Fig. 2.23(d):
From the colour code Table, Fig. 2.21, the four band colours of the resistor are:
1st band: Orange = 3
2nd band: Orange = 3
3rd band: Black = 0
4th band: Orange (Multiplier) = ×1,000
5th band: Gold(Tolerance): = ±5%
Therefore, the resistor value is: $330 \times 1,000 = 330,000$ **Ohms (Usually expressed as 330K)** ±5%

SOLUTION (Fig. 2.23(e):
From the colour code Table, Fig. 2.21, the four band colours of the resistor are:
1st band: Red = 2
2nd band: Red = 2
3rd band: Black = 0
4th band: Yellow (Multiplier) = ×10, 000
5th band: Red(Tolerance): = ±2%
Therefore, the resistor value is: $220 \times 10,000 = 2,200,000$ **Ohms (Usually expressed as 2.2M)** ±1%

SOLUTION (Fig. 2.23(f):
From the colour code Table, Fig. 2.21, the four band colours of the resistor are:
1st band: Yellow = 4
2nd band: Blue = 6
3rd band: Red = 2
4th band: Silver (Multiplier) = ×0.01
5th band: Silver (Tolerance): = ±10%
Therefore, the resistor value is: $462 \times 0.01 = 4.62$ **Ohms (Usually expressed as 4.62R)** ±10%

Surface Mount Resistors

This type of resistor helps to achieve very low power dissipation along with very high component density. Most modern circuits use tiny SMD (surface mount devices) components. Surface mount resistors are made by depositing a film of resistive material such as tin oxide on a tiny ceramic chip. The edges of the resistor are then accurately ground to give precise resistance across the device. Tolerances may be as low as 0.02%. A contact is provided at each ends of the resistor, which is soldered directly onto the conductive print on the circuit board, usually by automatic assembly methods. These resistors are mostly used where space is an important factor.

Three Digits Surface Mount Resistors

The first two digits are the significant digits, the third is the number of zeros (i.e. Power of 10). For instance,

- ▷ **151 stands for a 150 Ohm device: 15 plus 1 zero (10^1) = 150 Ohms**
- ▷ **242 stands for a 2.4K Ohm device: 24 plus 2 zeros (10^2) = 2,400 Ohms**
- ▷ **363 stands for a 36K Ohm device: 36 plus 3 zeros (10^3) = 36,000 Ohms**
- ▷ **444 stands for a 440K Ohm device. 44 plus 4 zeros (10^4) = 444,000 Ohms**
- ▷ **515 stands for a 5.1M Ohm device. 51 plus 5 zeros (10^5) = 5,100,000 Ohms**

Less Than 10 Ohms Surface Mount Resistors

Surface mount resistors having values lower than 10Ω have the letter $'R'$ in between the digits. Where the R indicates a decimal point position. For example,

> ▷ **0R55 = 0.55 ohms**
> ▷ **1R2 = 1.2 ohms**
> ▷ **5R08 = 5.08 ohms**

Four Digits Surface Mount Resistors

For a four digits surface mount resistor, the first three digits represent the significant digits. While the fourth digit indicates the number of zeros (i.e. the Power of 10). For example,

> ▷ **1500 represents a 150 Ohm device: 150 plus no zeros (10^0) = 150 Ohms**
> ▷ **3003 represents a 300K Ohm device. 300 plus 3 zeros (10^3) = 300,000 Ohms**
> ▷ **5904 represents a 5.97M Ohm device. 590 plus 4 zeros (10^4) = 5,900,000 Ohms**

However, a device marked 000 or 0 has essentially no resistance and would be used as a *link* on the circuit.

2.3.2. Ceramic Capacitors Colour Code

Generally, the actual values of a capacitance, voltage or tolerance for ceramic capacitor are marked onto the body of the capacitor in the form of alphanumeric characters. However, when the value of the capacitance is of a decimal value problems arise with the marking of a "Decimal Point" as it could easily not be noticed resulting in a misreading of the actual value. Instead, letters such as p (pico) or n (nano) are used to identify the decimal point position and the weight of the number. For example,

Two digits markings: A capacitor labelled:

> ▷ **47 = 47pF**
> ▷ **n47 = 0.47nF**
> ▷ **4n7 = 4.7nF**
> ▷ **47n = 47nF**

Also, sometimes capacitors are marked with the capital letter K to signify a value of one thousand pico-Farads (pF), this is called a coded three digit marking. For example,

A capacitor with the markings of:

> ▷ **100K = 100 x 1000pF or 100nF**
> ▷ **10K = 1000 x 1000pF or 10nF**
> ▷ **1K = 1nF**

To reduce the confusion regarding letters, numbers and decimal points, an International colour coding scheme was developed as a simple way of identifying capacitor values and tolerances. It consists of colour bands known commonly as the Capacitor Colour Code system as shown in Fig. 2.24

Example 2.3. Calculate the value of the polyester capacitor shown in Fig. 2.25.

SOLUTION (Fig. 2.25(a):
From the colour code Table, Fig. 2.24, the four band colours of the capacitor are:
1st band: Blue (Temperature coefficient) = -470
2nd band: Violet = 7
3rd band: Red = 2
4th band: Brown (Multiplier) = ×10
5th band: Green(Tolerance): = ±5%
Therefore, the capacitor value is: $72 \times 10 = 7,200$ pH ±5%

SOLUTION (Fig. 2.25(b):
From the colour code Table, Fig. 2.24, the four band colours of the capacitor are:
1st band: Orange (Temperature coefficient) = -30
2nd band: Blue = 6
3rd band: Orange = 3
4th band: Green (Multiplier) = ×100,000
5th band: Green(Tolerance): = ±1%
Therefore, the capacitor value is: $63 \times 100,000 = 6,300,000$ pF or 6.3 μF ±1%

2.3.3. Mica Capacitors Colour Code

A mica capacitor is marked with either three dots or six dots. Both the three and the six dot codes are similar, but the six-dot code contains more information about the electrical ratings of the capacitor, such as working voltage and temperature coefficient. The capacitor schematic shown in Fig 2.26 represents either a mica capacitor or a moulded paper capacitor.

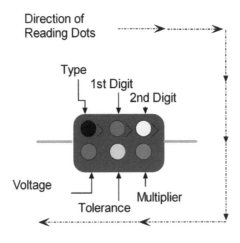

Figure 2.26. *Mica/paper capacitor schematic.*

The type and value of this kind of a capacitor is determined by holding the capacitor such that the three arrows point the to right. The first dot at the base of the arrow sequence (the leftmost dot) represents the capacitor *type*. This dot is either black, white, silver, or the same colour as the capacitor body. Mica capacitor is represented by a black or white dot and paper capacitor by a silver dot or dot having the same colour as the body of the capacitor. The two dots to the immediate right of the **type** dot indicate the first and second digits of the capacitance value. The dot at the bottom right represents the multiplier to be used. The multiplier represents **picofarads**. The dot at the bottom centre indicates the tolerance value of the capacitor. The dot beneath the *type* dot denotes the voltage of the capacitor. Figure 2.27 depicts the mica/paper capacitors colour code Table.

Color	1st Digit	2nd Digit	Multiplier	Tolerance (+/-) Percent	Voltage Rating
Black	0	0	1	1%	100
Brown	1	1	10	2%	200
Red	2	2	100	3%	300
Orange	3	3	1,000	4%	400
Yellow	4	4	10,000	5%	500
Green	5	5	100,000	6%	600
Blue	6	6	1,000,000	7%	700
Violet	7	7	10,000,000	8%	800
Grey	8	8	100,000,000	9%	900
White	9	9	1,000,000,000		1000
Gold			.1	10%	2000
Silver			.01	20%	

Figure 2.27. *Mica capacitor colour code*

Example 2.4. Determine the types, values and voltage ratings of the capacitors shown in Fig. 2.28.

SOLUTION (Fig. 2.28(a):
From the colour code Table, Fig. 2.27, the four band colours of the capacitor are:
1st dot: Black = Mica capacitor
2nd dot: Green = 5
3rd dot: Yellow = 4
4th dot: Orange (Multiplier) = ×10,000
5th dot: Blue (Tolerance): = ±10%
6th dot: Red = 300V
Therefore, the capacitor value is: 54 × 1,000 = 54,000 pF or 54nF ±10%
CONCLUSION:
Capacitor type: Mica
Capacitor value = 54nF ±10%
Voltage rating: 300V

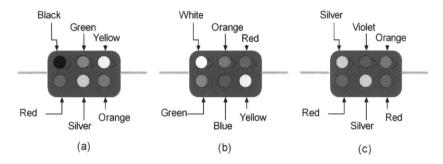

Figure 2.28. *Example 2.4 figures.*

SOLUTION (Fig. 2.28(b):
From the colour code Table, Fig. 2.27, the four band colours of the capacitor are:
1st dot: White = Mica capacitor
2nd dot: Orange = 3
3rd dot: Red = 2
4th dot: Yellow (Multiplier) = ×1,000
5th dot: Blue (Tolerance): = ±7%
6th dot: Green = 600V
Therefore, the capacitor value is: $32 \times 10,000 = 320,000$ **pF or 320nF ±7%**
CONCLUSION:
Capacitor type: Mica
Capacitor value = **32nF ±7%**
Voltage rating: **600V**

SOLUTION (Fig. 2.28(c):
From the colour code Table, Fig. 2.1.15, the four band colours of the resistor are:
1st dot: Silver = Paper capacitor
2nd dot: Violet = 7
3rd dot: Orange = 3
4th dot: Red (Multiplier) = ×100
5th dot: Silver (Tolerance): = ±10%
6th dot: Red = 300V
Therefore, the capacitor value is: $73 \times 100 = 7,300$ **pF or 7.3nF ±10%**
CONCLUSION:
Capacitor type: Mica
Capacitor value = **7.3nF ±10%**
Voltage rating: **300V**

2.3.4. Inductors Colour Code

The two major standards for inductors colour code identification are the Military and Electronic Industries Association (EIA) standards. Military standard defines five band colour code while EIA defines four band colour code for inductors.

1. **Military Five Band Inductor Colour Code:**

   The Military standard for cylindrical inductors specifies five colour bands like in the EIA four band code, with the first band (band 1), a double width sliver band used to signify Military Standard as depicted in Fig. 2.29.

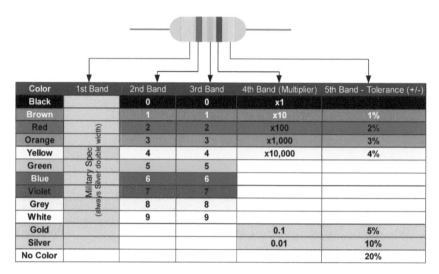

Color	1st Band	2nd Band	3rd Band	4th Band (Multiplier)	5th Band - Tolerance (+/-)
Black		0	0	x1	
Brown		1	1	x10	1%
Red	Military Spec	2	2	x100	2%
Orange	(always Silver double width)	3	3	x1,000	3%
Yellow		4	4	x10,000	4%
Green		5	5		
Blue		6	6		
Violet		7	7		
Grey		8	8		
White		9	9		
Gold				0.1	5%
Silver				0.01	10%
No Color					20%

Figure 2.29. *Five band Military standard inductor colour code.*

2. **EIA Four Band Inductor Colour Code:**

   The EIA is an ANSI-accredited standards development organization managed by the Electronic Components Association (ECA) Standards and Technology department. EIA provides a forum for industry to develop standards and publications for the electronic components industry. Although, the organization ceased operations in February 2011. However, the organization standard is still in use. Figure 2.30 depicts the EIA four band colour code for inductors.

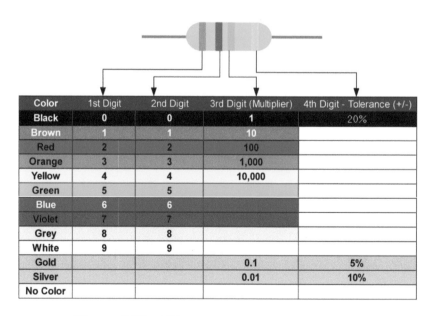

Color	1st Digit	2nd Digit	3rd Digit (Multiplier)	4th Digit - Tolerance (+/-)
Black	0	0	1	20%
Brown	1	1	10	
Red	2	2	100	
Orange	3	3	1,000	
Yellow	4	4	10,000	
Green	5	5		
Blue	6	6		
Violet	7	7		
Grey	8	8		
White	9	9		
Gold			0.1	5%
Silver			0.01	10%
No Color				

Figure 2.30. *EIA four colour band inductor code.*

Example 2.5. Find the value of the four colour band inductor shown in Fig. 2.31.

SOLUTION (Fig. 2.31(a):
From the colour code Table, Fig. 2.30, the five band colours of the inductor are:
1st band: Silver double band = Military identifier
2nd band: Orange = 3
3rd band: Green = 5
4th band: Red (Multiplier) = ×100
5th band: Brown(Tolerance): = ±20%
Therefore, the inductor value is: $35 \times 100 = 3,500\ \mu H$ or 3.5mH ±20%

Figure 2.31. *Example 2.5 figures.*

SOLUTION (Fig. 2.31(a):
From the colour code Table, Fig. 2.30, the five band colours of the inductor are:
1st band: Silver double band = Military identifier
2nd band: Blue = 6
3rd band: Yellow = 4
4th band: Gold (Multiplier) = ×0.1
5th band: Gold(Tolerance): = ±5%
Therefore, the inductor value is: $64 \times 0.1 = 6.4\ \mu H$ ±5%

The same procedure is followed to determine the value of an inductor having the four band colour EIA standard.

Example 2.6. Find the value of the four colour band inductor shown in Fig. 2.32.

SOLUTION (Fig. 2.32(a):
From the colour code Table, Fig. 2.30, the five band colours of the inductor are:
1st band: Red = 2
2nd band: Orange = 3
3rd band: Silver(Multiplier) = ×0.01
4th band: Black(Tolerance): = ±20%
Therefore, the inductor value is: $23 \times 0.01 = 0.23\ \mu H$ ±20%

SOLUTION Fig. 2.32(b):
From the colour code Table, Fig. 2.30, the five band colours of the inductor are:
1st band: Red = 2
2nd band: Violet = 7
3rd band: Orange(Multiplier) = ×1,000
4th band: Gold(Tolerance): = ±5%
Therefore, the inductor value is: $27 \times 1,00 = 27,000 \ \mu H \ \pm 5\%$

Surface Mount Inductor Code

For inductors having very small physical sizes, colour dots are used instead of bands. In such inductors, dots are used to mark the inductors. A silver dot indicates a Military (Mil) specification and is larger than the other dots. In some cases, only a single colour dot is used. In such a situation, it is necessary to refer to individual manufacturers datasheets for accurate interpretation. For inductors having three marking, dots 1 and 2 indicate the inductance in nH and dot 3 indicates the number of zeroes to be added.

Example 2.7. Find the value of the three Dots inductor shown in Fig. 2.331.6:

SOLUTION Fig. 2.33:
From Fig 2.33, the three dots colours of the inductor are:
1st dot: Red = 2
2nd dot: Green = 5
3rd band: Yellow(Multiplier) = ×10,000
Therefore, the inductor value is: $25 \times 10,000 = 250,000 \ nH$

2.4. Semiconductors

Conductors are materials which allow the passage of electric current due the present of free electrons in their atomic structure. Generally, metals are good conductors of electricity. While Insulators are kind of materials which do not pass electric current as they have tightly bound electrons in their atomic structure, for example, rubber and plastic. However, semiconductors are class of materials whose conductivity lies in between that of conductors and insulators. They have their current carrying capacity dependent on temperature or amount of light falling upon them. Most commonly used semiconductors are silicon and germanium.

The properties of semiconductor crystal can be improved significantly by inserting small quantities of impurity into the crystal lattice of the semiconductor a process referred to as "*doping*". These impurities are basically other materials which have three or five free electron in their outer atomic structure. Adding an impurity into a semiconductor element results in either an ***n-type*** or a ***p-type*** semiconductor, depending on the impurity inserted. In an ***n-type*** semiconductor, the charge carriers are called ***"electrons"***. Whereas, in a ***p-type*** semiconductor, the charge carriers are called "holes" The process of the insertion is called "doping". Interaction between *n-type* and *p-type* semiconductor materials formed the basis for most semiconductor electronic devices.

2.4.1. Diodes

Like resistors being the most basic passive components in electronics, diodes are the most basic active components. Diodes are made by placing *n-type* and *p-type* regions on a piece of a semiconductor material creating what is called a *diffuse region*. The *p-type* side of the diode is referred to as the *anode*, while the *n-type* side is called the *cathode* as shown in Fig. 2.34.

Rectifier

A diode is termed as a rectifier when connected to a circuit in such that it only passes current in one direction. This is done by either connecting the diode in forward or reverse biased. If a voltage source is connected to the diode with the positive side of the voltage source connected to the anode and the negative side connected to the cathode, as shown in Fig. 2.35(a), the diode is said to be *forward biased*. However, if the voltage source is connected the other way round, i.e, positive to the cathode and negative to the anode as in Fig. 2.35(b), the diode is said to be *reverse biased*. When a diode is forward biased, the diffused region becomes narrower and wider if the diode is reverse biased.

Zener Diode

This is a distinct class of diode that has the ability of maintaining constant voltage over a wide range of currents. This quality of Zener diode makes it good candidate for building voltage regulators. In order to use a Zener diode in a circuit, it should be reversed biased with a voltage kept in excess of the zener voltage. Fig. 2.36 shows a simple voltage regulator circuit using a zener diode and a resistor.

Light Emitting Diodes (LEDs)

LEDs are diodes that emit photon when forward biased. The positive terminal (anode) of an LED is longer than the negative terminal (cathode). LED Light intensity is related to the magnitude of current passing through it. Typically, an LED has a voltage drop of between 1.5 to 2.5 and requires current of between 10 to 25mA for save operation. Therefore, it is necessary to connect a series currentlimiting resistor to the positive terminal to prevent excess current that may eventually destroy the device. Most microcontroller digital applications are 5V based. Fig. 2.37 depicts both pictorial and electrical symbols of an LED.

2.4.2. Transistor

Transistor is a three terminal active device made by placing three regions of doped semi-conductor materials adjacent to one another. The two possible placements of the doped silicon are *npn* or *pnp*. Transistor operates by controlling current between two terminals using voltage applied to the third terminal. Primarily, transistor has two basic functions *switching* in digital electronics or *amplification* in analogue electronics. Transistor comes in different packages examples of which are shown in Fig. 2.38.

The two basic transistors types are bipolar junction transistor (BJT) and field effect transistor (FET).

Bipolar Junction Transistor (BJT)

BJT basic construction consists of two *pn-junctions* connected back-to-back producing three connecting terminals namely: emitter (E), base (B) and collector (C) terminals. Figure 2.39 depicts the two basic BJT configuration. The *n-type* of the emitter in *npn* BJT is more doped with silicon than the collector and is the most common. BJT allows charge carriers to enter into a thin base region from the emitter and then attracted to the collector resulting in a large collector current controlled by a much smaller base current. Hence, BJT transistors are current regulating devices that control the amount of current flowing through them in proportion to the amount of biasing voltage applied to their base terminal acting like a current-controlled switch. The two transistor types principally operate in exactly the same way. They differ only in their biasing and the polarity of the power supply.

Field Effect Transistor (FET)

A field effect transistor (FET) is the type of transistor commonly used for weak signal amplification. FETs transistors exist in two major classifications, junction FET (JFET) and the metal-oxide-semiconductor FET (MOSFET). Figure 2.40 depicts the symbols schematic of the four most common FETs transistors. FETs can be used for amplification of both analogue and digital signal and also as an oscillator.

In FET, the output current is controlled by the input voltage. The electric field produced by a voltage on one electrode controls the availability of charge carriers in the narrow region called *channel*, through which the current can be made to flow. The control electrode in the FET is called the *gate* and current flows along a semiconductor path called the *channel* which has at its end an electrode called the *drain*. The physical diameter of the channel is fixed; however, its effective electrical diameter can be altered by applying a voltage to the *gate*. FET electrical conductivity depends on the electrical diameter of the *channel*. A small variation in *gate* current causes a larger change in the current form the source to the *drain*. Hence, this is how a FET amplifies signals.

2.4.3. Integrated Circuits (ICs)

In digital system, data storage and processing are performed using logic circuitry. These circuits consist of logic gates elements. A typical IC chip contains a large number of micro-electronics circuit elements manufactured on a small slice of silicon. Each circuit element consists of small semiconductor elements such as diodes and transistors. These semiconductor elements are not present as conventional discrete components with leads and wiring for interconnection, but rather in the monolithic form. An integrated circuit is entirely produced through a delicate manufacturing process. Therefore, it is not possible to remove or replace any of the IC constituent components.

IC Classifications

Basically, IC chip classification is based on the circuit density. The four common classifications of ICs are given Table 2.1. The IC chip circuit density used in digital systems is expressed in terms of the number of elementary logic circuits present on the chip.

Table 2.1. Integrated Circuit Chip Classification Based on Circuit Density

IC Chip Type	Number of Basic Logic Gates Present
Small-scale integration (SSI)	Less than 10
Medium-scale integration (MSI)	10-1000
Large-scale integration (LSI)	1000-10,000
Very-large-scale integration (VLSI)	10,000 to over one million

IC Types

There are two basic kinds of ICs; analogue (or linear) and digital (or logic). Linear ICs are commonly used as amplifiers, timers and oscillators while digital ICs are used in microprocessors, microcontrollers and memories.

IC Applications

ICs are the building blocks for all mechatronics systems. ICs are used in applications such as automobile systems, intelligent home appliances, entertainment products as well as in the Military hardware. Most common applications of ICs are in DC motor control with chopper circuits, control of AC motor using variable frequency drives, intelligent systems with embedded control, etc. The listing below sindicates the basic areas of digital and analogue ICs application.

1. Analogue IC are used in:
   ▷ Power amplifiers
   ▷ Small-signal amplifiers
   ▷ Operational amplifiers
   ▷ Microwave amplifiers
   ▷ Voltage comparators
   ▷ Multipliers
   ▷ Radio receivers
   ▷ Voltage regulators
2. Digital IC's are mostly used in computers. They are also called switching circuits because their input and output voltages are limited to two levels; **HIGH** or **LOW**. They include:
   ▷ Flip-flops
   ▷ Logic gates
   ▷ Timers and counters
   ▷ Multiplexers
   ▷ Memory chips
   ▷ Microprocessors

▷ Microcontrollers

▷ Temperature sensors

2.4.4. Microcontrollers

A microcontroller, sometimes called a single-board computer, is a device which integrates numerous components onto a single chip thereby making up a complete control system suitable for mechatronics systems design. Examples of microcontrollers are ATmega328 by Atmel Corporation, ARM Cortex M4 by Philips semiconductors and PIC16F877A by Microchip Inc. Figure 2.41 is a block diagram representing a typical microcontroller unit.

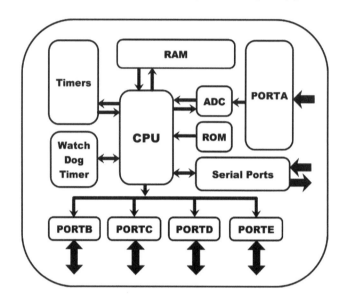

Figure 2.41. *Microcontroller block diagram.*

Unlike microprocessors, microcontroller has a number of built-in resources such as;

▷ **CPU (Central Processing Unit):**
Executes the software stored in the ROM and controls all other components.

▷ **RAM (Random Access Memory):**
Stores settings and values used by a running program.

▷ **ROM (Read-Only Memory):**
Used to store the program and any other permanent data. A ROM can be EPROM (Electrical Programmable Read-Only Memory) or EEPROM ((Electrical Erasable and Programmable Read-Only Memory). A software permanently stored on ROM is called *firmware*. Data stored in EEPROM is nonvolatile, meaning the program can access the data when the microcontroller is powered off.

▷ **Timers:**
— A microcontroller timer is simply a register which acts as simple clock in the microcontroller keeping the time that elapses since when the microcontroller was powered or when the program was started. Most timers are asynchronous, meaning they work independently of the CPU or program.

▷ **Analogue to Digital Converter (ADC):**
This is an input port which allows the microcontroller to take-in external analogue signal and converts it to a digital signal that can be processed, stored or sent to external peripherals.

▷ **Input/Output(I/O) port:**
These allow the transfer of binary data to and from the microcontroller using the external pins of the device.

▷ **Serial Communication Ports:**
Although, these are part of the I/O ports but, used basically for communication purposes, such as data exchange with others devices like memories, PCs, ICs, e.t.c. Data can be transmitted and/or received using these ports based on standard communication protocols. There are numerous standard for serial communication. Most famous among them are UART (universal asynchronous receiver-transmitter), I2C (inter-integrated circuit), SPI (serial peripheral interface), among others.

Microcontrollers are used in a wide range of fields mostly for building intelligent systems. Areas of microcontroller application include military hardware, robotic systems, industrial automation, home appliances, toys, etc.

2.5. Practical Considerations

Assembling a mechatronics project involves the use of a number of tools, such as bread board, multimeter, screwdrivers, cutters, pliers and an oscilloscope. Successful use of these tools requires the user to acquire certain basic skills and observe the safety regulations associated with electrical equipment. This section highlights on the use of the basic tools in building mechatronics system.

2.5.1. Using a Solderless Bread Board

A breadboard, shown in Fig. 2.42 is a temporary circuit making board for testing out ideas before building the main circuit. It does not require any soldering; hence it is always handy in any electronic project. Many electronics components could be assembled in a very short time using the breadboard. Circuit modification could be done easily for tuning and optimization purpose. The final circuit layout could be assembled in a printed circuit board (PCB).

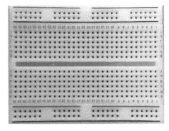

Figure 2.42. *A breadboard.*

Bread board has many strips of metal (copper usually), which run underneath the board. The metal strips are laid out as shown in Fig. 2.43. These strips connect the holes on the top of the board, making it easy to connect components together to build circuits. To use the bread board, the legs of components are placed in the holes (the sockets). The holes are made so that they will hold the component in place. Each hole is connected to one of the metal strips running underneath the board. Each wire forms a node. A node is a point in a circuit where two components are connected. Connections between different components are formed by putting their legs in a common node. On the breadboard, a node is the row of holes that are connected by the strip of metal underneath. The long top and bottom row of holes are usually used for power supply connections.

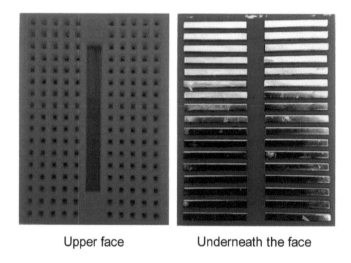

Upper face   Underneath the face

Figure 2.43. *The breadboard internals.*

2.5.2. Measurement with Multimeter

A multimeter is a device capable of measuring voltage, current, and resistance for both AC and DC sources. It is called a multimeter because it combines the functions of a voltmeter, ammeter, and ohmmeter. Some multimeters can measure diode and can be used in carrying out continuity test. Multimeters come in many flavours having varying features. However, for a beginner, a basic multimeter capable of measuring voltage levels up to about 20DCV is enough. A typical multimeter can measure the voltage level of a signal and the resistance of a component or load. The current can then be computed given the resistance and voltage. Figure 2.44 depicts a schematic of a standard multimeter. It has two insulated test-probes that plug into its base and used to contact the electrical device being tested.

Figure 2.44. *A multimeter.*

Measuring Voltage

Voltage appears in two forms; Alternating Current (AC) or Direct Current (DC). AC voltage is mainly from national grid supply or generating sets. A DC voltage is found in batteries or from conversion of AC voltage. Multimeter can measure both AC and DC voltages when set to correct level. To measure the voltage of a point, it is compared to a reference voltage of another point. Usually, ground (GND) is selected as a reference node with an assumed zero voltage. The voltage across a component is the difference of the voltages at its ends. It doesn't matter how the voltage polarity (plus and minus) is chosen, across a component or to the ground, it only changes the sign of the final result. To measure say, AA size battery voltage, the following steps should be followed;

1. Set the multimeter knob to correct voltage level to 2V in the DC range.

2. Plug the red probe to the multimeter port marked $V\Omega A$.

3. Plug black probe to the port marked COM on the multimeter.

4. Linked the other end of the red multimeter probe to the positive terminal of the battery.

5. Link the other end of the black multimeter probe to the negative terminal of the battery.

6. Read out the voltage displayed on the meter screen.

To measure *a 5VDC*, the same steps should be followed but only setting the multimeter selection knob to *20VDC* in the DC range. Reason for setting the multimeter to higher voltage range of *2V* while measuring *1.5VDC* and *20VDC* while measuring *5VDC* is that multimeters are generally not auto-ranging. It has to be set to the voltage close to the anticipated range it will measure. For example, to measures voltages from *2V-20V* the knob setting is 20V. So to measure a *12V* battery, *20V* setting is sufficient. Using a low voltage setting to measure high voltage source does not harm in any way, rather the meter may display a '1', meaning it is overloaded or out-of-range.

Measuring Current

Unlike voltage which is measured in parallel, current is measured in series. Measuring current entails physical interruption of the current flow. For instance, to measure current consumed by an LED connected to a circuit, the following steps should be followed:

1. Connect the multimeter probes as in voltage measurement.

2. Set the multimeter knob to 200mA setting.

3. Insert the multimeter inline in such away as connecting it as a piece wire along the positive of the power source and the circuit.

4. The meter having complete the circuit will measure the current as it flows through to the multimeter into the circuit.

5. The multimeter will display the instantaneous current in the circuit

Note: All multimeters take readings over time and then give the average values. Therefore, expect fluctuation of the displayed reading. Similarly, as in voltage measurement, interchanging the multimeter probes does not have grievous consequences other than indicating negative current.

Measuring Resistance

Resistors values can easily be determined using the colour code system or resistor calculator. However, in the absence of these calculators or when using the colour code table proved tedious, a multimeter can also be used to measure resistance. To measure 10K resistance, the following steps should be followed:

1. Set the multimeter to the 20K setting.

2. Connect the probes as in voltage measurement.

3. Hold the probes against the resistor legs.

4. The meter will display 9.90, meaning a 9.90K resistor.

Remember resistors have tolerance in percentage of their actual value. If the tolerance is say 5%, this means that the colour code may indicate 10K, but because of discrepancies in the manufacturing process a 10K resistor could be as low as 9.5K or as high as 10.5K.

2.5.3. Oscilloscope

Although, multimeter is capable of measuring voltage, resistance, and current. However, it is sometimes helpful to be able to observe the variation of a signal with time. A device called an oscilloscope enables measurement of time-varying signals and can detect repeated-patterns or oscillations in an electrical signal, and display the waveform of the signal. There are many brands of oscilloscopes. Most popular among them are; Tektronix TDS1000C-EDU

Education Oscilloscope series, Siglent 100mhz Digital Storage Oscilloscope SDS1102CN and Atten ADS1102CAL 100MHz Digital Oscilloscope Fig. 2.45 depicts a simple oscilloscope. Using an oscilloscope is beyond the scope of this book and therefore, will not be treated further.

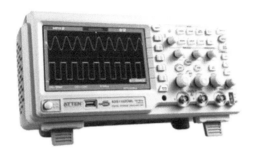

Figure 2.45. *An oscilloscope.*

2.5.4. Safety

Electricity can cause fatal burns or cause vital organs to malfunction. In general, a current of 5mA or less will cause a sensation of shock, but rarely any damage. Larger currents can cause hand muscles to contract. Currents on the order of 100mA are often fatal if passed through human body for even a few seconds. Although, the electronic circuits dealt with in this book are primarily of low-voltage electronics. Therefore, chances of injury due to electric shock are minute.

Nonetheless, because of the possibilities of personal injury, danger of fire, and possible damaged to equipment, the following basic safety procedures should be observed while implementing the projects in this book.

1. Unplug power from the circuit or equipment prior to working on it. Never assume the circuit is off, double check with a multimeter.

2. Remove and replace fuses only after the power to the circuit has been turned-off.

3. Make circuit wiring carefully, and be on the lookout for any signs of burning. Some components become hot when improperly connected. A hot wire or component can burn skin, hair, fabric, etc. Many burning electrical components have a sharp, choking odour, or may begin to smoke.

4. Make sure all equipment are properly grounded.

5. Use extreme caution when installing or removing batteries containing acid.

6. Use cleaning fluids and other chemicals only in well-ventilated places.

7. Dispose of cleaning rags and other flammable materials in tightly closed metal containers.

8. In case of electrical fire, switch off the circuit and report it immediately to the appropriate authority.

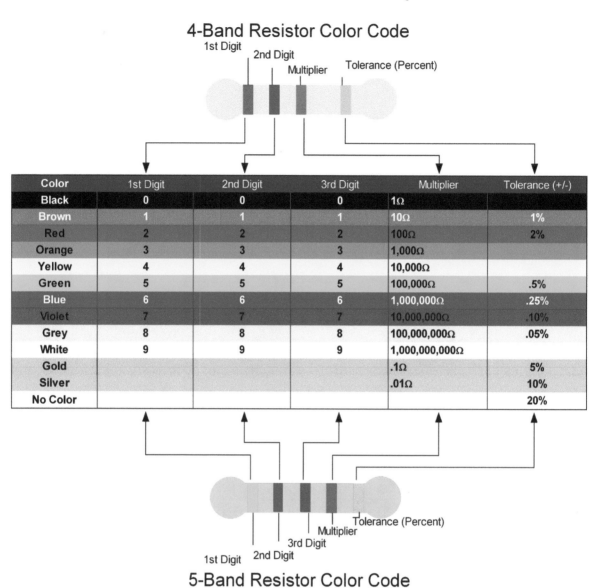

Figure 2.21. Resistor colour codes table.

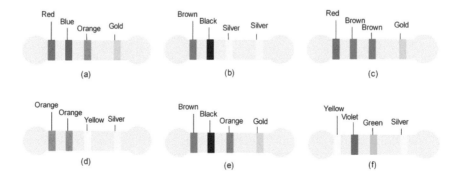

Figure 2.22. Example 2.1 figures.

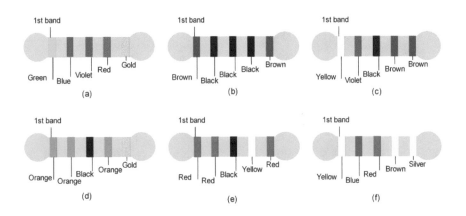

Figure 2.23. Example 2.2 figures.

Ceramic Capacitor Colour Code

A - Temperature Coefficient
B - 1st Digit
C - 2nd Digit
D - Multiplier
E - Tolerance (Percent)

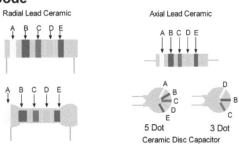

Color	1st Digit	2nd Digit	Multiplier	Tolerance (+/-) over 10pF	Tolerance (+/-) under 10pF	Temperature Coefficient
Black	0	0	1	20%	2.0pF	0
Brown	1	1	10	1%		-30
Red	2	2	100	2%		-80
Orange	3	3	1,000			-150
Yellow	4	4	10,000			-220
Green	5	5	100,000	5%	0.5pF	-330
Blue	6	6	1,000,000			-470
Violet	7	7	10,000,000			-750
Grey	8	8	.01		.25pF	+30
White	9	9	.1	10%	1.0pF	+120 to -750 (EIA) +500 to -330 (JAN)
Gold						Bypass or Coupling
Silver						+100 (Jan)

Figure 2.24. Ceramic capacitor colour code.

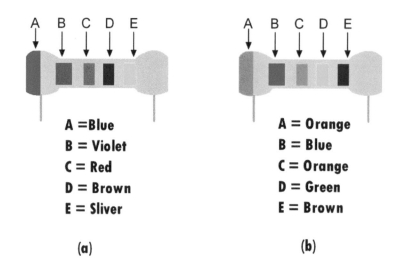

A =Blue
B = Violet
C = Red
D = Brown
E = Sliver

(a)

A = Orange
B = Blue
C = Orange
D = Green
E = Brown

(b)

Figure 2.25. *Example 2.3 figures.*

1st Band Military Id
2nd Band (Orange)
4th Band (Black)
3rd Band (Silver)
(a)

1st Band Military Id
2nd Band (Blue)
5th Band (Gold)
3rd Band (Yellow)
(b)

Figure 2.32. *Example 2.6 figures.*

3rd Dot (Black)

2nd Dot (Green)

1st Dot (Red)

Figure 2.33. *Example 2.7 figure.*

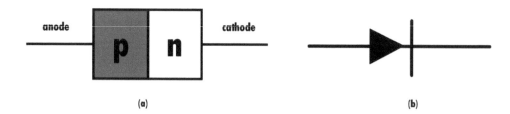

anode   cathode

p **n**

(a)   **(b)**

Figure 2.34. *A diode (a) Graphical representation (b) Schematic symbol.*

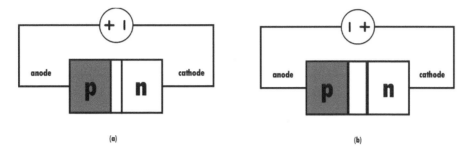

Figure 2.35. *Rectifier (a) Forward biased (b) Reverse biased.*

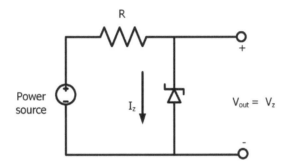

Figure 2.36. *Zener diode voltage regulator circuit.*

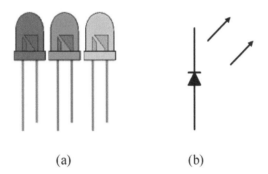

Figure 2.37. *Light emitting diode (a) LED pictorial representation (b) Electrical symbol.*

Figure 2.38. *Assorted transistors.*

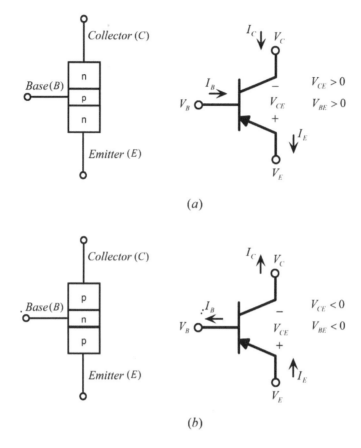

Figure 2.39. *Bipolar Junction Transistor (BJT) schematic symbols (a) npn (b) pnp.*

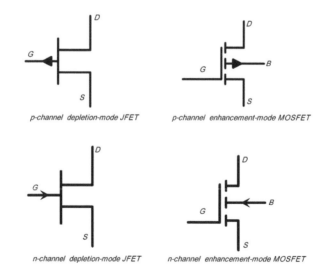

Figure 2.40. *Field-effect transistor schematic symbols.*

Chapter 3

Hardware and Software

This chapter highlights on the common hardware and software required to implement the projects in the subsequent chapters of the book. However, hardware or software specific to individual projects are discussed under those projects chapters.

3.1. Development Tools

The following tools are necessary for implementing the projects in the subsequent chapters.

1. A personal computer.
2. PhasePlus PIC16F877A Development Board.
3. A PIC programmer.
4. Development software.

3.2. A Personal Computer (PC)

A desktop or a laptop computer that at least meets the following minimum configurations.

▷ **Processor:**
  — A Pentium III upward or AMD Athlon based (PC).
▷ **Operating System:**
  — Microsoft Windows Windows XP or upwards.
▷ **Optical Drive:**
  — A CD or DVD drive.
▷ **Working Memory:**
  — 256MB RAM minimum.
▷ **Hard Disk Space:**
  — A minimum of 500MB.
▷ **Internet Access:**
  — An internet connection is recommended when using the License copy of Flowcode for product activation.

3.3. PIC Programmer

There are many PIC programmers in the market that are relatively cheap. A PICkit 2 or a PICkit 3 programmer is recommended for projects in this book. PICkit 3 is little more expensive but has advantage over PICkit 2 in that, it programs newer PIC microcontrollers. PIC microcontrollers can be programmed with either of the two programmers without having to remove the microcontroller from the prototyping board using the In-Circuit Serial Programming (ICSP) capabilities of the programmers. Figure 3.1 depicts a schematic for PICkit 3 programmer.

Figure 3.1. *PICkit 3 programmer.*

3.4. PhasePlus PIC16F877A Development Board

PhasePlus PIC16F877A development board is a demonstration and development platform for the 40-pins Microchip family of the microcontrollers developed by PhasePlus Technologies. The board schematically depicted in Fig. 3.2 provides a platform to explore the potentials of PIC16F877A device in building mechatronics systems. The board has the following physical features:

1. On-board chip - PIC16F877A microcontroller.

2. 8 x LEDs mapped to PORTD.

3. 4 x input switches mapped to PORTB pins B0-B3.

4. ICSP programming header.

5. 1 x RS232 communication interface.

6. MCLR reset switch.

7. 4 MHz external oscillator.

8. USB power port.

9. The power interface.

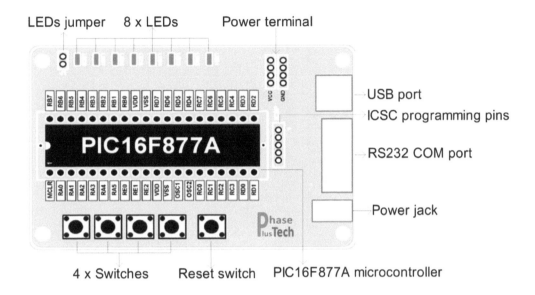

Figure 3.2. *PhasePlus PIC16F877A development board.*

3.4.1. Microchip PIC16F877A Microcontroller Features

Microchip PIC16F877A, shown in Fig. 3.3 is a 40-pin CMOS FLASH-based 8-bit microcontroller and one of the most commonly used microcontroller in the PIC microcontroller family. Mostly used in applications such as the automobile industry, industrial machinery, military hardware and home appliances. It features 200ns instruction execution cycles, 256 bytes of EEPROM data memory, self programming, ICD, 2 Comparators, 8 channels of 10-bit analogue-to-Digital (A/D) converter, 2 capture/compare/PWM functions, a synchronous serial port that can be configured as either 3-wire SPI or 2-wire I2C bus, a USART, and a Parallel Slave Port (PSP).

3.5. Programming PhasePlus PIC16F877A Development Board

PhasePlus PIC16F877A development board can be programmed with either a PICkit2 or PICkit3 programmer using an in-circuit serial programming (ICSP) interface based on Microchip's ICSP protocol. The Microchip's ICSP protocol is a fairly conventional synchronous communications protocol with the ability to control the state of the microcontroller using a high voltage (12 to 15 V) signal on the reset pin (MCLR) of the microcontroller. To program the board, the on-board ICSP header pins should be plugged to the programmer's ICSP pins as shown in Fig. 3.4 and following the chip programming wizard provided by the development software.

Figure 3.3. *PIC16F877A microcontroller.*

3.6. Development Software

The software used in implementing the projects in this book is called Flowcode. Flowcode is a graphical programming software developed by the Matrix Multimedia ©. It is one of the world's most advanced graphical programming languages for microcontrollers. The great advantage of the software is that it allows those with little or non-programming experience to create complex mechatronics systems. Flowcode contains standard flow chart icons and electronic components that allow virtual creation of electronic system on a PC screen. It facilitates the rapid design of mechatronics systems based on microcontrollers by simply dragging and dropping icons on to the Flowcode programming environment to create myriad mechatronics systems without writing traditional code line by line.

Flowcode has a host of high-level component subroutines, which allow the use of the flowchart programming method by users of all abilities to develop microcontroller programs rapidly. It also allows user to view C and ASM code for all the programs created and to customize them. It is available in more than twenty languages and currently supports the PIC microcontroller, dsPIC, PIC24, AVR and ARM series of microcontrollers. Flowcode v5 (Fig. 3.5) is the most current version for PIC microcontrollers as at the time of writing this book.

Flowcode is used in education as a means of introducing students to the concepts of programming and in the industry for rapid development and as a means of managing large projects.

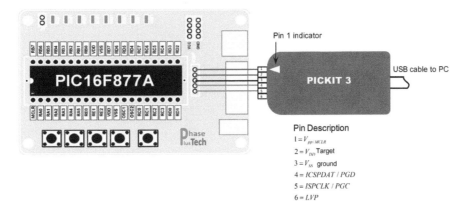

Figure 3.4. *Programming PhasePlus PIC16F877A development board.*

3.6.1. Flowcode v5 for PIC microcontroller

Flowcode v5 is a very high-level language optimized-programming software for PIC micro-controllers based on flowcharts. The projects in the subsequent chapters are implemented using the demonstration (demo) edition of Flowcode v5. Although, it has some limitations in terms of components but still it is sufficient.

3.6.2. Flowcode v5 Supported Devices

▷ **Supported microcontrollers:**
Microchip PIC10, PIC12, PIC16 and PIC18 microcontrollers.

▷ **Supported communication systems:**
Bluetooth, CAN, FAT, GPS, GSM, I2C, IrDA, LIN, MIDI, One wire, RC5, RF, RFID, RS232, RS485, SPI, TCP/IP, USB, Wireless LAN, Zigbee.

▷ **Supported components:**
ADC, LEDs, switch array, keypads, LCDs, Graphical colour LCDs, Graphical mono LCDs, Sensors, 7-segment displays, Internal EEPROM, communications systems, Touch-screen LCD, Webserver, Accelerometer, PWM, Servo, Stepper, Speech.

▷ **In-Circuit Serial Programming (ICSP):**
When used with PICkit 2 or PICkit 3 programmers.

▷ **In-Circuit Debug (ICD):**
When used with EB006 PIC Multiprogrammer or FlowKit.

3.6.3. Installing PIC microcontroller Flowcode v5 Demonstration Edition

The demonstration edition of Flowcode v5 for PIC microcontrollers can be downloaded from www.matrixmultimedia.com/ or from the book's website and burn to disk. To install from the disk follow the following steps:

1. Slot the disk in to PC's or laptop's optical drive.

Figure 3.5. *Flowcode for PIC v5.*

2. Click Start/Computer.

3. Double click on the disk drive icon to explore its contents.

4. Select Flowcode demonstration v5 for PIC microcontrollers folder and open it.

5. Double click on the *setup.exe* located inside the folder.

6. Follow the installation wizard to complete the installation.

After the installation, a window would appear to prompt for installation of a *PPP* application. A *PPP* is a program developed by Matrix Multimedia for Flowcode software that allows the *HEX* files to be download to the microcontroller. However, Flowcode is compatible with other third party programming software and hardware, and so it supports the microchip programming utilities developed for PICkit 2 and PICkit 3. Therefore since this book utilizes PICkit 3 programmer, then do not install the *PPP* application.

3.6.4. Launching and Configuring Flowcode

The following steps explained how to prepare the Flowcode software for implementing the projects in the subsequent chapters. This configuration is common to all but must be done on every project. For easy access to the Flowcode software, copy the **Flowcode V5 for PIC microcontrollers** icon from **Start/All Programs** and paste it on the desktop.

Step 1

▷ Double-click on the **Flowcode shortcut icon** located on the PC desktop.
▷ The action opens a window shown in **Fig. 3.3** prompting the user to **Create a new Flowcode flowchart** or to **Open and existing Flowcode flowchart**.
▷ Click **OK** to create a new Flowcode program.

Figure 3.6. *Launching a new Flowcode program.*

Step 2

▷ Select **Choose a Target.**
▷ Under **Choose a target for this flowchart** select **16**.
▷ Scroll and choose **16F877A** and the click **OK**.

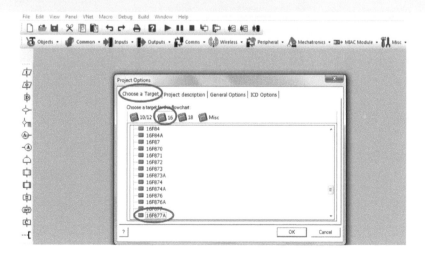

Figure 3.7. *Choosing a target device.*

Step 3

▷ An empty Flowcode environment.
▷ Flowcharts (program codes) are entered, compiled and loaded to the target device in this environment.

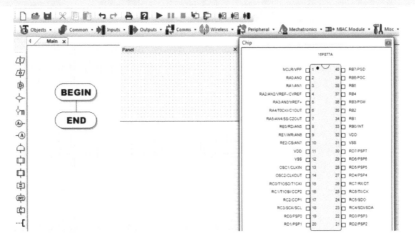

Figure 3.8. *A new Flowcode program environment.*

Step 4

▷ Click on **Build** tab and select **Project Options**.
▷ In the **Clock Speed (Hz)** menu select **4000000** for clock speed.
▷ Click **OK**.

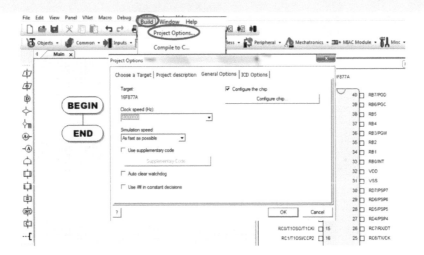

Figure 3.9. *Setting the microcontroller clock speed.*

Step 5

▷ Click on **Configure Chip** button and make this changes.
— select **HS** in the **Oscillator** menu.
— In the **Watchdog Timer** drop down menu select **Off**.
▷ Click **OK**.

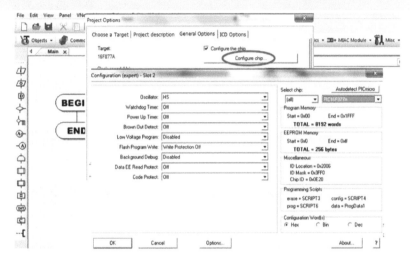

Figure 3.10. *Configuring the microcontroller.*

Step 6

▷ Click on **Build** again and select **Compiler Options**.
▷ Select **Programmer** tab and click on the **Browse** button.
▷ Point to **PK3CMD.exe** file located in the **Flowcode** installation directory (PICkit3 Programmer).
▷ Click **OK**.

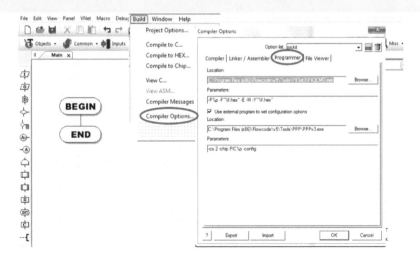

Figure 3.11. *Choosing the programmer option.*

3.6.5. Program Downloading to the Development Board

Connect the programmer USB cable to the development board and PC as shown in Fig. 3.12. Ensure pins matching between the programmer and the development board. The white triangle mark on the programmer indicates pin 1 (MCLR). Click on the **Build** tab and select **Compile to Chip** button to download the program to the microcontroller. If prompted to save the program, accept and continue. A small window will appear displaying execution status which eventually ends with a **Return Code = 0** for successful download.

Figure 3.12. *Downloading program to the development board.*

3.6.6. Flowcode Icons Description

Table 3.1. *Description of Flowcode icons*

Input	
	This checks a specified port and/or pin(s) of the microcontroller for their value and then places the resulting value into a specified variable.
Output	
	This sends a value or variable to a specified port and/or pin(s) of the microcontrller in binay format.
Delay	
	This imposes an absolute value or variable delay in millisecond/ seconds to slow down program execution and for program timing.
Decision	
	This allows a condition test to redirect the program flow according to the condition's outcome. The condition may be based on a calculation in which variables can be used along with following operators; Equal to (=), Not equal to (!=), Greater than (>), Less than (<) and Boolean operators (AND, OR, XOR, NOT), etc.
Switch	
	This is used to improve program clarity by reducing repetitive coding or as a substitute for long if statements that compare a variable to several certain values.
Connection points	
	These are used to link from one part of a program to another and always used in pairs.
Loop	
	This is used to repeat a task until specified condition is fulfilled, or to facilitate a program to repeatedly execute a block of code.
User-defined Macro	
	This facilitates a call to a macro function defined by user. Macros are sections of code, that can be used and reused in program
Component Macro	
	These are pre-defined macros supplied with the Flowcode components. For example LED macro is used to turn on/off an LED component. Only available for use with that particular component.

Calculation	
	This allows a variable to be defined or modified and can be used for checking inputs or to create outputs.

Interrupt	
	This facilitates the activation of an interrupt. An Interrupt is a signal that tells the microcontroller that something has happened that needs its attention. Interrupts are called to react to an event such as an external stimulus, or a timing event.

C Code	
	This allows programs written in C and Assembly code to be embedded into the Flowcode program.

Comment	
	This allows comments to be added to a program in order explain functions, variable settings etc., or other documentation task. Applying comments to a code is an excellent programming practice. It posters easy understanding of codes written by others.

Part II

Hands-on-Projects

Chapter 4

Project 1: LED Flashing

4.1. Objective

The purpose of this project is to demonstrate how to interface an LED to a microcontroller. This is a basic mechatronics application as LEDs are the most commonly used means of visual communication and indication in mechatronics systems. Most mechatronics systems have at least an LED to indicate system status, such as power or operation mode.

An LED is a semiconductor device that emits infrared or visible light when charged with an electric current. Visible LEDs are used in many electronic devices as indicator lamps, in automobiles as rear-window and brake lights, and on billboards and signs as alphanumeric displays or even full-colour posters. Infrared LEDs are used in applications such as auto-focus cameras and television remote controls. Owing to the LED's importance in mechatronics systems, this project is chosen to be the first in this book.

Hardware

- ▷ Red LED
- ▷ 220Ω resistor
- ▷ Connection wires
- ▷ PhasePlus PIC Development Board

4.2. LED Overview

LEDs are available in numerous colours, such as red, orange, amber, yellow, green, blue and white. Blue and white LEDs are much more expensive than the other colours. The colour of an LED is determined by the semiconductor material, not by the package colour (the plastic body). Other LED packages are tri-colour and bi-colour. The most popular type of tri-colour LED has a red and a green LED combined in one package with three terminals. They are called tri-colour because mixed red and green light appears to be yellow, and this is produced when both the red and green LEDs are on. A bi-colour LED has two LEDs wired in inverse parallel (one forwards, one backwards) combined in one package with two leads. Only one of the LEDs can be lit at one time, and they are less useful than the tri-colour LEDs.

The applied voltage in most LEDs is quite low, in the region of 2.0 volts; the current depends on the application and ranges from a few milliamperes to several hundred milliamperes. An LED must be connected obeying its polarity markings. The longer LED terminal is the positive (+) or anode, and the shorter terminal is the negative (-) or cathode. LEDs can be damaged by heat when soldering, but the risk is minimal. An LED should always be connected with a series resistor to limit forward current. Connecting an LED directly to a battery or power supply will destroy it almost instantly. If an LED is connected without the current limiting resistor, too much current will pass through and destroy it.

4.3. Circuit Schematic

The circuit schematic for this project is shown in Fig. 4.1. The longer LED terminal (anode) connects to pin B0 via a 220Ω current limiting resistor. While the shorter LED terminal (cathode) directly connects to ground (GND) via the bread board GND rail. Note: Any pin designated as an output on a microcontroller delivers +5V (VCC) when it receives a high logic. The GND terminal of the development board is connected to the bread board GND rail.

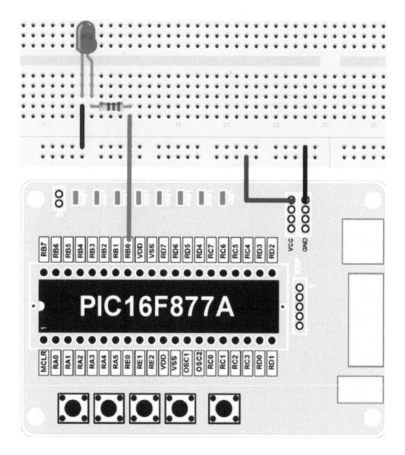

Figure 4.1. *Project 1 circuit schematic.*

4.4. Implementation Steps:

Project 1: Step 1

▷ Launch *Flowcode*.
▷ Select *Create a new Flowcode*, click *OK* and select *16F877A*.
▷ Click *OK*.

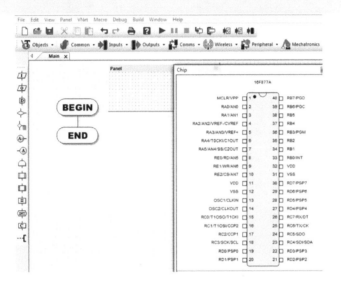

Figure 4.2. *An empty Flowcode project environment.*

Project 1: Step 2

▷ Click, drag and drop a *Loop* icon into the program to insert a loop.

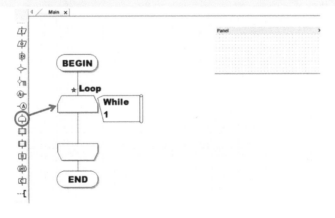

Figure 4.3. *Adding a continuous loop.*

Project 1: Step 3

▷ Click on the **Output** tab and select **LED** to insert an **LED** component.

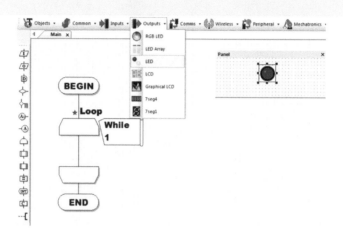

Figure 4.4. *Adding an LED component.*

Project 1: Step 4

▷ Right click on the **LED** and select **Connections**.
▷ In the **Connect to** fields select **PORTB** and **0** from **Port** and **Bit** menus.
▷ Click **Done**.

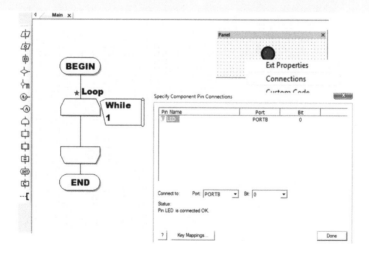

Figure 4.5. *Connecting the LED to output pin.*

Project 1: Step 5

▷ Insert a **Component Macro** icon and double click on it.
▷ Select **LED(0)** and **LEDOn** in the **Component** and **Macro** fields.
▷ Click **OK**.

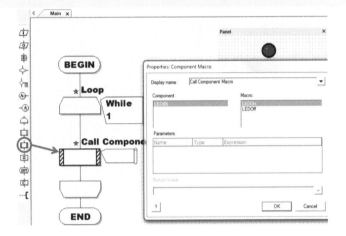

Figure 4.6. *Sending a high logic to the output pin.*

Project 1: Step 6

▷ Insert a **Delay** icon and double click on it.
▷ Set the delay time to **400 milliseconds**.
▷ Click **OK**.

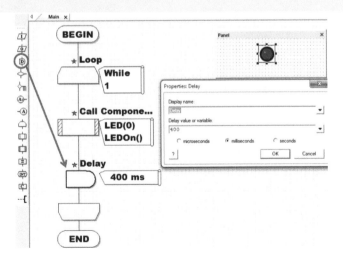

Figure 4.7. *Adding and configuring a delay.*

Project 1: Step 7

▷ Insert another **Component Macro** icon and double click on it.
▷ Select **LED(0)** and **LEDOff** in the **Component** and **Macro** fields.
▷ Click **OK**.

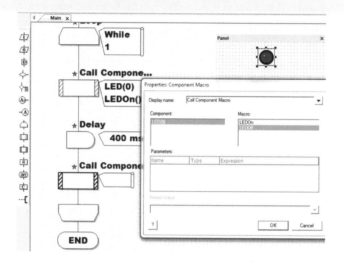

Figure 4.8. *Sending a high logic to the output pin.*

Project 1: Step 8

▷ Insert another **Delay** icon and double click on it.
▷ Set the delay time to **400 milliseconds**.
▷ Click **OK**.

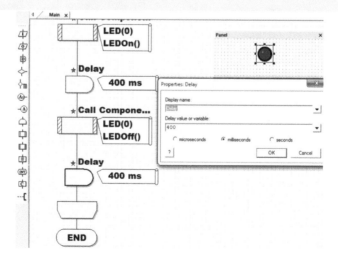

Figure 4.9. *Adding and configuring a delay.*

Project 1: Step 9

▷ Save the program and click **Run** for simulation.

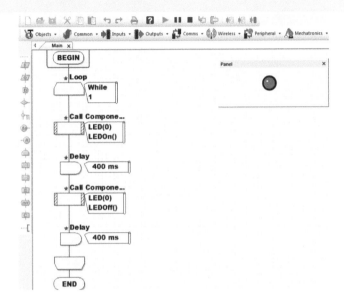

Figure 4.10. *Program completed ready for simulation and downloading.*

4.5. Program Description

This program implements an LED flasher. The program turns on the LED connected to the output pin of the microcontroller for 400 milliseconds and turns it off again for another 400 milliseconds. The LED can be made to flash very fast or very slow by tinkering with the delay time. The details of the program implementation steps are listed below;

▷ **Step 1:**
   — Launch **Flowcode** and start a new program.
▷ **Step 2:**
   — Add a **Loop** to make the program runs repeatedly.
▷ **Step 3:**
   — Add an **LED** component.
▷ **Step 4:**
   — Connect the LED to **PORTB** pin **B0** of the microcontroller.
▷ **Step 5:**
   — Send a high logic (+5V) to pin **B0** to turn on the LED connected to the pin.
▷ **Step 6:**
   — Keep the LED on for **400 milliseconds**.
▷ **Step 7:**
   — Send a low logic (0V) to pin **B0** to turn off the LED connected to the pin.
▷ **Step 8:**

    — Keep the LED off for *400 milliseconds*.

▷ **Step 9:**

    — Simulate the program by clicking on the *Run* button and download it to the micro-controller on the PhasePlus development board.

Chapter 5

Project 2: Running Light

5.1. Objective

The purpose of this project is to demonstrate further how to build another LED lightening project in the form of a running light display. Light displays are ubiquitous nowadays as they are found in the streets of major cities depicting various messages or advertisements. These displays come in different shapes and pattern each relaying a particular message.

Hardware

- ▷ 4 x Red LEDs
- ▷ 4 x 220Ω resistor
- ▷ Connection wires
- ▷ PhasePlus PIC Development Board

5.2. Circuit Schematic

The circuit schematic for this project is shown in Fig. 5.1. Anodes of the four LEDs connect to pins B0-B3 via current limiting resistors. While the LEDs cathodes connect to the development board GND.

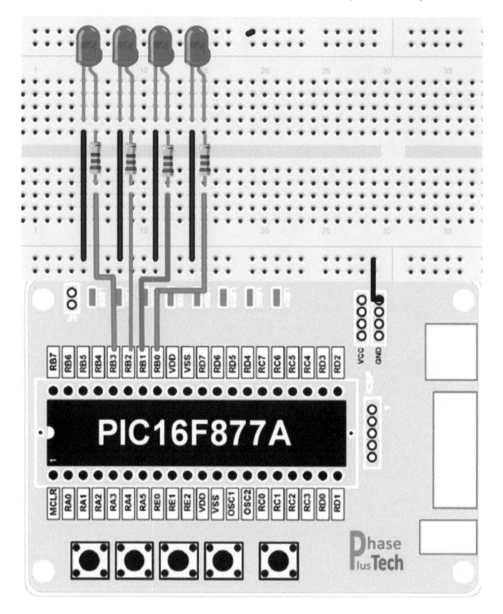

Figure 5.1. *Project 2 circuit schematic.*

5.3. Implementation Steps:

Project 2: Step 1

▷ Launch *Flowcode.*
▷ Select *Create a new Flowcode*, click *OK* and select *16F877A*.
▷ Click *OK*.

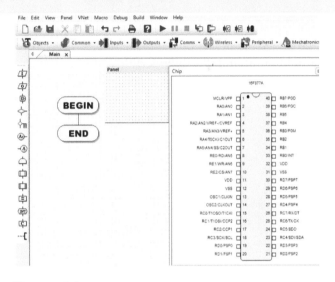

Figure 5.2. *An empty Flowcode project environment.*

Project 2: Step 2

▷ Insert a *Calculation* icon into the program.
▷ Double click on the *Calculation* icon to open up its *Properties* dialogue.

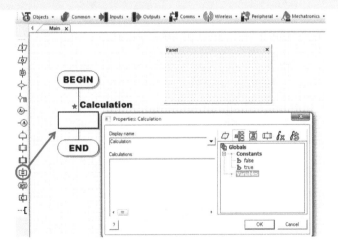

Figure 5.3. *Adding a calculation icon.*

Project 2: Step 3

▷ Double click on **Variables** to create a **Byte** type variable.
▷ In the **Name of new variable** field enter **counter**.
▷ Click **OK**.

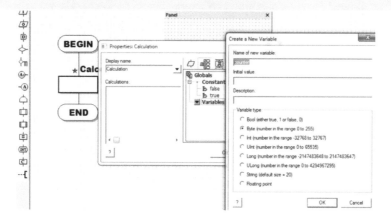

Figure 5.4. *Creating a variable.*

Project 2: Step 4

▷ In the **Calculations** field enter **counter = 0**.
▷ Double click on **Variables** again.
▷ In the **Name of new variable** enter **light[5]** and click **OK**.

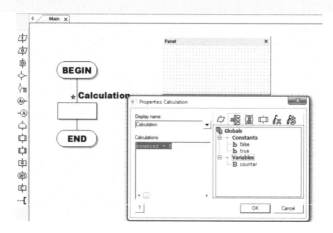

Figure 5.5. *Initializing a variable and creating an array variable.*

Project 2: Step 5

▷ In the **Calculation** field enter the following:
— **light[0] = 8**
— **light[1] = 4**
— **light[2] = 2**
— **light[3] = 1**
▷ Click **OK**

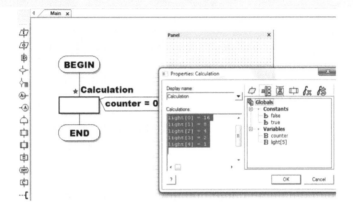

Figure 5.6. *Assigning values to the elements of the array variable.*

Project 2: Step 6

▷ Insert a **Loop** icon into the program
▷ Click on the **Output** tab and select **LED array**.
▷ Right click on the **LED array** and select **Ext Properties**.

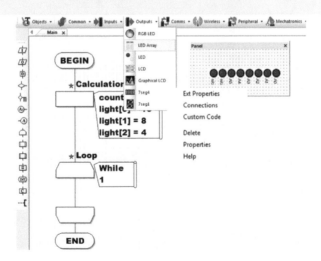

Figure 5.7. *Adding a loop and LED array.*

Project 2: Step 7

▷ In the **Number of LED** menu select *4*.
▷ Increase the LEDs size to 40 × 40 by dragging the **Size** horizantal slider.
▷ Click **OK**.

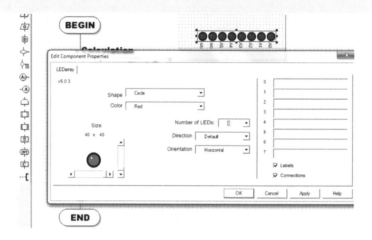

Figure 5.8. *Configuring the LED array.*

Project 2: Step 8

▷ Right click on the **LED array** again and select **Connections**.
▷ From the **Port** drop down menu select **PORTB**.
▷ Click **Done**.

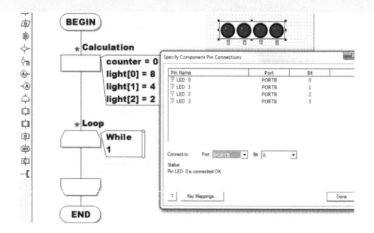

Figure 5.9. *Connecting LED array to the output pins.*

Project 2: Step 9

▷ Insert an *Output* icon and double click on it.
▷ Under the *Port* menu select *PORTB*.
▷ Type *light[counter]* in the *Variable or value* field and click *OK*

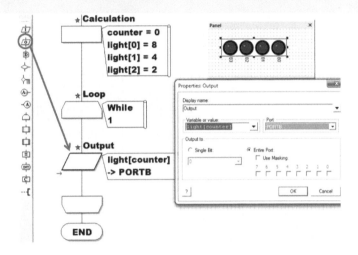

Figure 5.10. *Sending logic levels to the output pins.*

Project 2: Step 10

▷ Insert a *Delay* icon and double click on it.
▷ Set the delay time to *100 milliseconds*.
▷ Click *OK*.

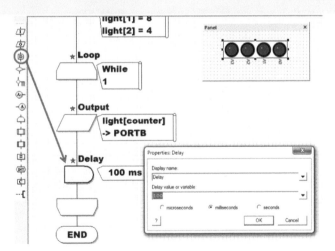

Figure 5.11. *Adding an configuring a delay.*

Project 2: Step 11

▷ Insert a *Calculation* icon and double on it
▷ In the *Calculation*s field enter: *counter = counter + 1*
▷ Click *OK*

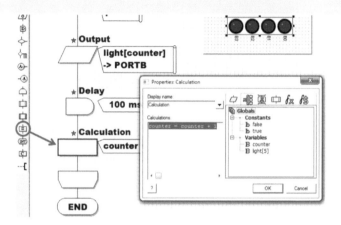

Figure 5.12. *Incrementing a variable.*

Project 2: Step 12

▷ Insert a *Decision* icon double click on it.
▷ In the *If* field enter *counter = 4*.
▷ Click *OK*.

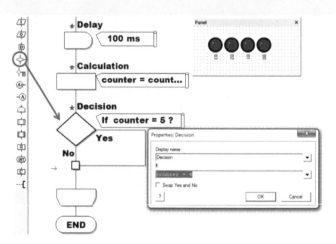

Figure 5.13. *Adding and configuring a decision for condition checking.*

Project 2: Step 13

▷ Insert a ***Calculation*** icon and double click on it.
▷ In the ***Calculation***s field enter: ***counter = 0***.
▷ Click ***OK***.

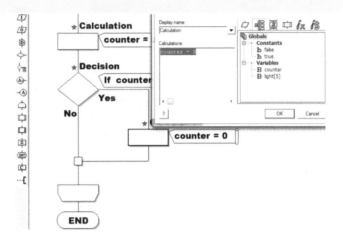

Figure 5.14. *Re-initializing a variable.*

Project 2: Step 14

▷ Save the program and click ***Run*** for simulation.

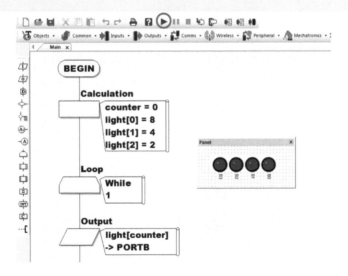

Figure 5.15. *Project completed ready for simulation and downloading.*

5.4. Program Description

This program implements a running light display pattern. The four LEDs attached to the microcontroller output pins are turned on and off serially and repeatedly at a 100 milliseconds interval. The result appears as if a light is running from the leftmost LED to the right most LED. The running speed can be made faster or slower by increasing or decreasing the delay interval. The details of the program implementation steps are listed below:

▷ **Step 1:**
— Launch *Flowcode* and start a new program.

▷ **Step 2:**
— Add a *Calculation* icon.
— Note: This is an environment which allows a variable to be defined or carrying out mathematical evaluations.

▷ **Step 3:**
— Declare a variable of *Byte* type and name it *counter*.

▷ **Step 4:**
— Initialized the variable *counter* to *zero*.
— Declare a *four-elements* array variable and name it *light[4]*.

▷ **Step 5:**
— Assign values to the array elements as indicated below:
  — *light[0]* = *8*.
  — *light[1]* = *4*.
  — *light[2]* = *2*.
  — *light[3]* = *1*.
— Sending the numeral *8* turns on the left most LED and numeral *1* turns on the rightmost LED, etc.

▷ **Step 6:**
— Add a *Loop* to make the program runs repeatedly.
— Also add an *LED array*.
— Configure the *LED array*.

▷ **Step 7:**
— In the configuration panel reduce the number of the LEDs in the array from *eight* to *four*.

▷ **Step 8:**
— Connect the four LEDs in the array to *PORTB* of the microcontroller.

▷ **Step 9:**
— Use the variable *counter* to index the elements of the array variable *light[]*.
— Send the array variable *light[]* to PORTB.

▷ **Step 10:**
— Slow down the speed of the serial turning *on* and *off* of the four LEDs by regulating the rate of incrementing the variable *counter* to *100 milliseconds*.

▷ **Step 11:**
— Increment the variable counter to move successively through the four LEDs.

▷ **Step 12:**

— Since there are only four LEDs in the display, therefore, the variable **counter** should run from **zero** to **four**.

— Check to ensure the index variable does not exceed *4*.

▷ **Step 13:**

— However, in the event the index variable exceeds *4*, reinitialized it to zero.

— Meaning, if the four LEDs are lit sequentially, start all over from the leftmost LED.

▷ **Step 14:**

— Simulate the program by clicking on the **Run** button and download it to the micro-controller on the PhasePlus development board.

Chapter 6

Project 3: Automatic Light Switch

6.1. Objective

The purpose of this project is to demonstrate how to build an automatic light switch. This project is meant to address the inconveniences associated with the routine of switching home security lights **on** at night and **off** in the morning. Often, people tend to forget to switch-off their lights in the morning, which translates to high electricity bills. The concept in this project can be used in areas such as home security lights, automatic car head lights, street lights, e.t.c.

Hardware

- ▷ 1 x LED
- ▷ 1 x Photocell
- ▷ 1 x 10KΩ
- ▷ 1 x KΩ
- ▷ 1 x PhasePlus PIC Development Board
- ▷ Connection wires

6.2. Photocell Overview

A photocell usually called Light Dependent Resistor (LDR) schematically shown in Fig. 6.1 is technically a resistor which changes its resistance based on light level. LDRs are used for numerous applications such as solar powered garden lights, camera flashers and night light switching. It converts light energy into electrical energy. In the absence of light, photocell has very high resistance in the order of millions of ohms. However, when light is present, its resistance diminishes to few ohms allowing the passage of more current. The resistance of LDR is of the order of Mega Ohms in the absence of light and reduces to a few ohms in the presence of light.

6.3. Circuit Diagram

Figure 6.1. *A photocell.*

The circuit schematic for this project is shown in Fig. 6.2. The LED anode connects to pin C4 via a current limiting resistor, and the cathode connects to the microcontroller GND via the bread GND rail. One of the LDR terminal connects to +5V (VCC) and the other to analogue pin AN0 and GND via a 10K resistor.

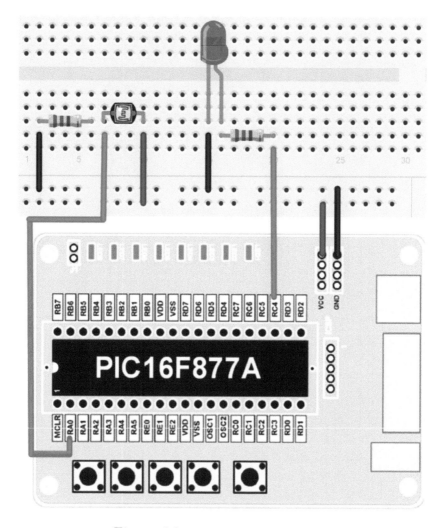

Figure 6.2. *Creating a new variable.*

6.4. Implementation Steps:

Project 3: Step 1

▷ Launch **Flowcode**.
▷ Select **Create a new Flowcode**, click **OK** and select **16F877A**.
▷ Click **OK**.

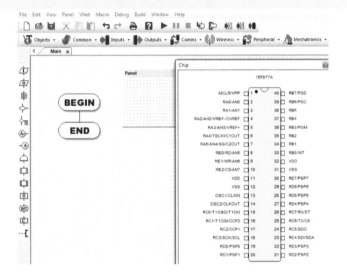

Figure 6.3. *An empty Flowcode project environment.*

Project 3: Step 2

▷ Insert a **Calculation** icon and double click it.
▷ Double click on **Variables** and create a new variable of **Uint** type.
▷ In the **Name of new variable** field type **lightLevel** and click **OK**.

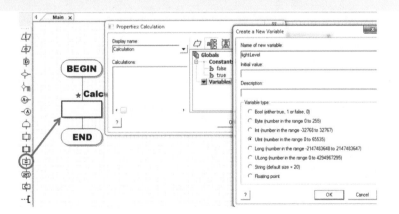

Figure 6.4. *Creating a new variable.*

Project 3: Step 3

▷ In the **Calculations** field enter **lighLevel = 0**.
▷ Click **OK**.

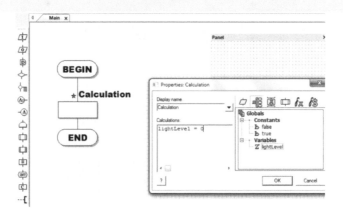

Figure 6.5. *Initializing a variable.*

Project 3: Step 4

▷ Insert a **Loop** icon.
▷ Click on the **Output** tab and select **ADC**.

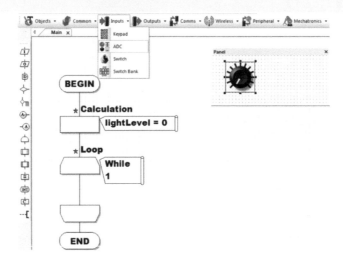

Figure 6.6. *Adding a loop and an ADC component.*

Project 3: Step 5

▷ Right on the **ADC** component and select **Connections**.
▷ Double check **AN0** (analogue pin 0) is selected in the **ADC** field.
▷ Click **Done**.

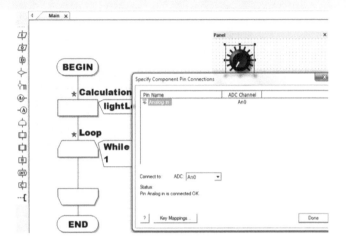

Figure 6.7. *Connecting an ADC component to the analogue pin.*

Project 3: Step 6

▷ Insert a **Component Macro** icon and double click on it.
▷ Select **ADC(0)** in the **Component** field and **ReadAsInt** in the **Macro** field.
▷ In the **Return value** field enter **lightLevel** and click **OK**.

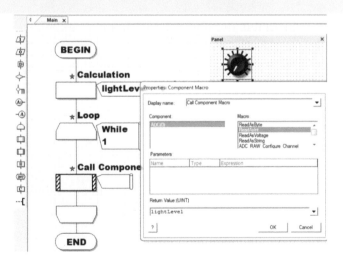

Figure 6.8. *Reading an analogue device and returning the read value to the Main program.*

Project 3: Step 7

▷ Insert a **Delay** icon and double click on it.
▷ Set the delay time to **50 milliseconds**.
▷ Click **OK**.

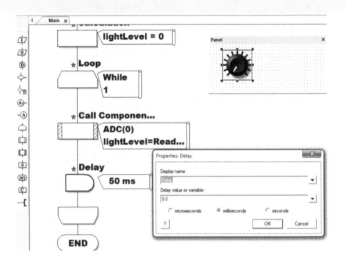

Figure 6.9. *Adding and configuring a delay.*

Project 3: Step 8

▷ Insert a **Decision** icon and double click on it.
▷ In the **If** field enter **lightLevel < 150**.
▷ Click **OK**.

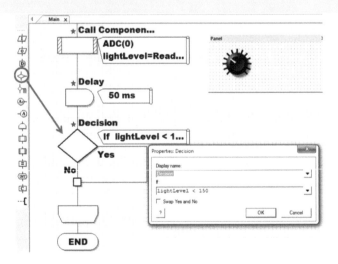

Figure 6.10. *Adding a decision to monitor a defined condition.*

Project 3: Step 9

▷ Click on on the **Output** tab and select **LED**.

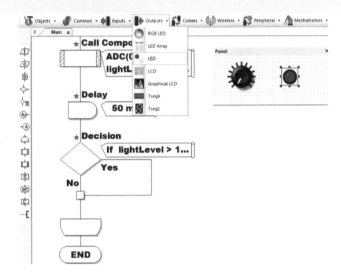

Figure 6.11. *Adding an LED component.*

Project 3: Step 10

▷ Right click on the **LED** component and select **Connections**.
▷ In the **Port** and **Bit** fields choose **PORTC** and *4*.
▷ Click **Done**.

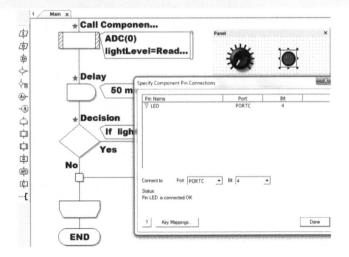

Figure 6.12. *Connecting the LED to the output pin.*

Project 3: Step 11

▷ Insert a **Component Macro** icon and double click on it.
▷ Select **LED(0)** and **LEDOn** in the **Component** and **Macro** fields.
▷ Click **OK**.

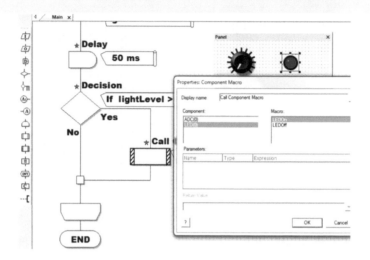

Figure 6.13. *Sending a high logic to the output pin.*

Project 3: Step 12

▷ Insert a **Component Macro** icon at **No** end of the loop
▷ Double click on it and select **LED(0)** in the **Component** field
▷ In the **Macro** field select **LEDOff** in the **Macro** field and Click **OK**

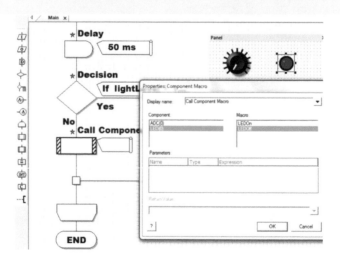

Figure 6.14. *Sending a low logic to the output pin.*

Project 3: Step 13

▷ Click on **Run** tab to run the program

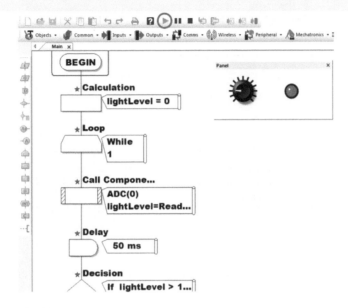

Figure 6.15. *Project completed ready for simulation and downloading.*

6.5. Program Description

This project implements an automatic light switch. The sensor was represented by an ADC device for Flowcode simulation. As described in Section 6.2, the resistance of an LDR is very high in the dark, but when illuminated the resistance drastically drops to fewer ohms. For instance, when a light level of 1000 lux (bright light) is directed towards an LDR, its resistance value drops to about 400Ω. On the other hand, when the light level is 10 lux (very low light level) the resistance rises to about 10MΩ.

The LED attached to the system turns on when the sensor receives a light level less than the defined threshold and turns off when the light level is greater than defined threshold. In the program, the low light level corresponds to the low ADC values and high light level corresponds to the high ADC values. An ADC value less 150 represents darkness and the LED turns on, while any ADC value above 150 represents day time, and hence the LED turns off. The details of the program implementation steps are listed below;

▷ **Step 1:**
▷ Launch **Flowcode** and start a new program.
▷ **Step 2:**
 — Declare an unsigned variable type and name it *lightLevel*.
▷ **Step 3:**
 — Initialized the declared variable to zero.

▷ **Step 4:**

— Add a **Loop** to make the program runs repeatedly.

— Add an **ADC** component to represent the **LDR** as Flowcode does not have an **LDR** in its components library.

▷ **Step 5:**

— Connect the **ADC** device to pin **AN0** (analogue pin 0) of the microcontroller.

▷ **Step 6:**

— Read the state of the **ADC** device attached to pin **An0**.

— Store the state of the **ADC** device in the variable **lightLevel**.

— Return the value of variable **lightLevel** to the **Main** program.

▷ **Step 7:**

— Update the state of the **ADC** device every **50 milliseconds**.

▷ **Step 8:**

— Does the value of the variable **lightLevel** exceed **150**?

▷ **Step 9:**

— Add an LED component.

▷ **Step 10:**

— Connect the LED component to pin **C4** of the microcontroller.

▷ **Step 11:**

— However, if the value of the variable **lightLevel** exceeds **150** turn on the LED (it is dark).

▷ **Step 12:**

— Otherwise, turn off the LED (it is still day time).

▷ **Step 13:**

— Simulate the program by clicking on the **Run** button and download it to the microcontroller on the PhasePlus development board.

[1]**NOTE:** The built-in ADC in PIC 16F877A microcontroller is capable of converting analogue signals to the digital value through the analogue pins of the microcontroller. This digital value is in the range of 0 - 1024, where 0 represents 0V and 1024 represents +5V on each pin.

Chapter 7

Project 4: LED SOS Distress Signal

7.1. Objective

The purpose of this project is to demonstrate how to build a distress signalling system based on the Morse code using LEDs. Morse code is one of the internationally accepted distress signalling code. The commonly used description for international Morse code distress signal is the SOS. SOS signal was created and adopted as the universal international distress signal at the 1906 Berlin Radio-telegraphic conference. In Morse code, SOS is represented by three dots, three dashes and then three dots being sent together as one string. It is commonly held that SOS stands for *Save Our Ship* or *Save Our Souls*, eventhough SOS actually stands for nothing, neither is it an acronym for anything.

Hardware

- 3 x Any colour LED
- 3 x 220Ω
- PhasePlus PIC Development Board
- Connection wires

7.2. Circuit Schematic

Figure 7.1 depicts the circuit schematic for this project. Anodes of the four LEDs connect to pins D2, D4 and D7 via current limiting resistors. While the LEDs cathodes connect to the microcontroller GND via the bread GND rail.

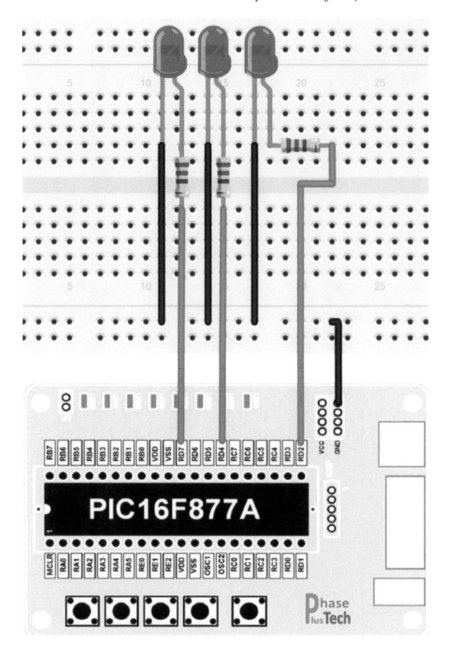

Figure 7.1. *Project 4 circuit schematic.*

7.3. Implementation Steps:

Project 4: Step 1

▷ Launch **Flowcode**.
▷ Select **Create a new Flowcode**, click **OK** and select **16F877A**.
▷ Click **OK**.

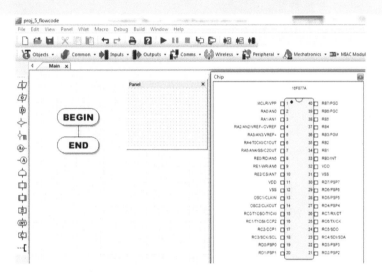

Figure 7.2. *An empty Flowcode project environment.*

Project 4: Step 2

▷ Insert a **Loop** icon.
▷ Click on the **Output** tab and select **LED array**.

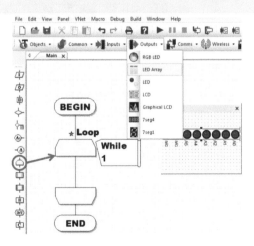

Figure 7.3. *Adding a loop and LED array.*

Project 4: Step 3

▷ Right click on the **LED Array** and select **Ext Properties**.
▷ Increase the **LEDs size** by drawing **Size** slide to the extreme right.
▷ From the **Number of LEDs** down menu select **3** and click **OK**.

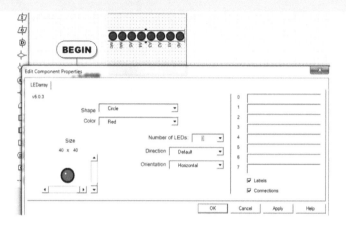

Figure 7.4. *Configuring the LED array.*

Project 4: Step 4

▷ Righ click on the **LED Array** again and select **Connections**.
▷ In the **Port** drop down menu select **PORTD**.
▷ Click **Done**.

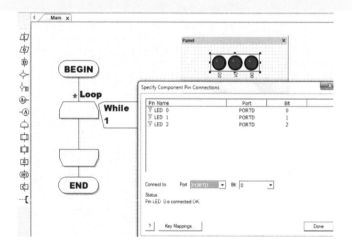

Figure 7.5. *Connecting the LED array to the output pins.*

Project 4: Step 5

▷ Click on the **Macro** tab and select **New** to create a new macro.
▷ In the **Name of new macro** field enter: **dih_ dih_ dih**.
▷ Click **OK** to edit the new macro.

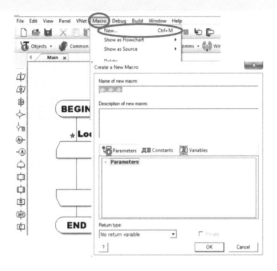

Figure 7.6. *Creating a user-defined macro.*

Project 4: Step 6

▷ Insert a **Loop** icon in the new macro.
▷ Double click on the **Loop icon** and check **Loop count** box.
▷ Enter **3** in **Loop count** field and click **OK**.

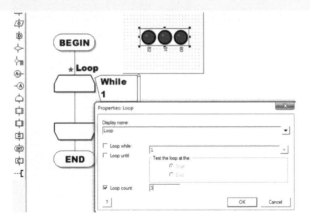

Figure 7.7. *Adding and configuring a loop.*

Project 4: Step 7

▷ Insert an **Output** icon and double click on it.
▷ In the **Variable or value** field enter **148** and select **PORTD**.
▷ Click **OK**.

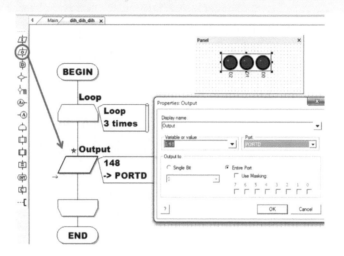

Figure 7.8. *Sending high logic to the output pins.*

Project 4: Step 8

▷ Insert a **Delay** icon and double click on it.
▷ Set the delay time to **150 milliseconds**.
▷ Click **OK**.

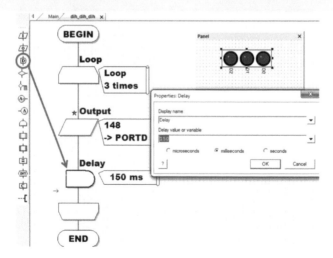

Figure 7.9. *Adding and configuring a delay.*

Project 4: Step 9

▷ Insert another **Output** icon and double click on it.
▷ In the **Variable or value** field enter **0** and select **PORTD**.
▷ Click **OK**.

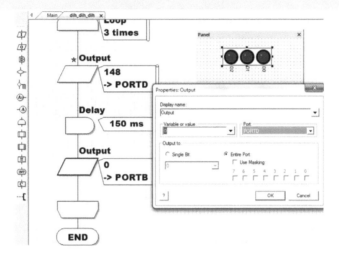

Figure 7.10. *Sending a low logic to the output pins.*

Project 4: Step 10

▷ Insert a **Delay** icon and double click on it.
▷ Set the delay time to **150 milliseconds**.
▷ Click **OK**.

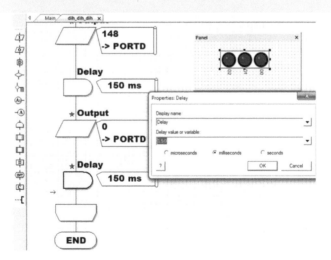

Figure 7.11. *Adding and configuring a delay.*

Project 4: Step 11

▷ Switch to the **Main** program by clicking on its tab.
▷ Insert a user-defined **Macro Call** icon and double click on it.
▷ In the **Macro** field select **dih_ dih_ dih** macro and click **OK**.

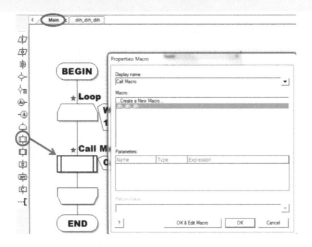

Figure 7.12. *A call to a user-defined macro..*

Project 4: Step 12

▷ Insert a **Delay** icon and double click on it.
▷ Set the delay time to **300 milliseconds**.
▷ Click **OK**.

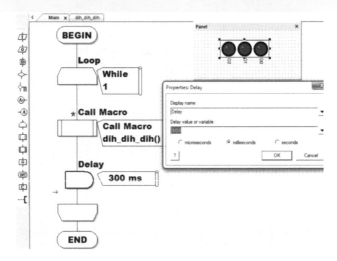

Figure 7.13. *Adding and configuring a delay.*

Project 4: Step 13

▷ Click on the **Macro** tab and select **New** to create a new macro.
▷ In the **Name of new macro** field enter: **dah_ dah_ dah**.
▷ Click **OK** to edit the new macro.

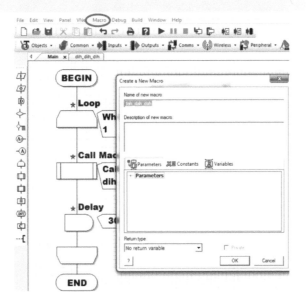

Figure 7.14. *Creating a new user-defined macro.*

Project 4: Step 14

▷ Click on the **dih_ dih_ dih** macro tab.
▷ Select and copy all the icons in the macro including the **While loop**.

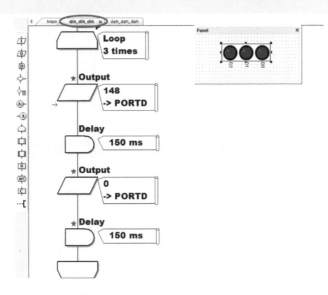

Figure 7.15. *Editing a macro.*

Project 4: Step 15

▷ Click on the **dah_dah_dah** macro tab.
▷ Click on the **BEGIN** side of the macro and paste the copied items.
▷ Edit the two delays to **250 milliseconds.**

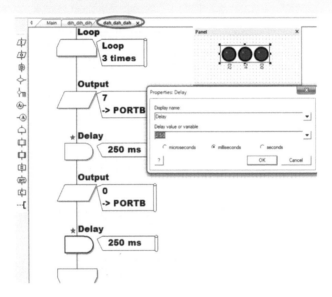

Figure 7.16. *Editing a macro.*

Project 4: Step 16

▷ Click on the **Main** program tab.
▷ Insert a **Macro Call** icon and double click on it.
▷ In the **Macro** field select **dah_dah_dah** macro and click **OK**.

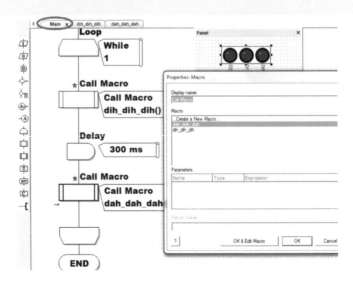

Figure 7.17. *A call to a user-defined macro.*

Project 4: Step 17

▷ Insert a **Delay** icon and double click on it.
▷ Set the delay time to **300 milliseconds**.
▷ Click **OK**.

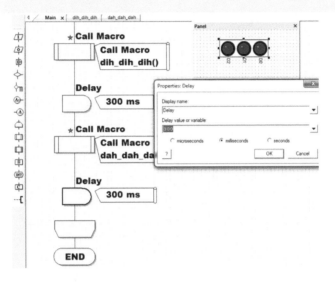

Figure 7.18. *Adding and configuring a delay.*

Project 4: Step 18

▷ Insert another **Macro Call** icon and double click on it.
▷ In the **Macro** field select **dih_dih_dih** macro.
▷ Click **OK**.

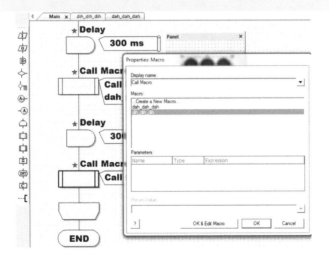

Figure 7.19. *Another call to user-defined macro.*

Project 4: Step 19

▷ Insert a **Delay** icon and double click on it.
▷ Set the delay time to **150 milliseconds**.
▷ Click **OK**.

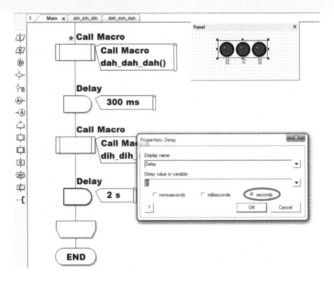

Figure 7.20. *Adding and configuring a delay.*

Project 4: Step 20

▷ Save the program and click **Run** for simulation.

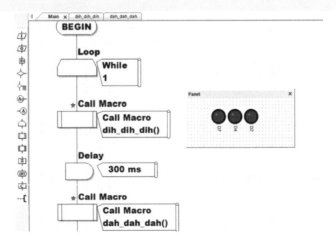

Figure 7.21. *Project completed ready for simulation and downloading.*

7.4. Program Description

This program implements a Morse code SOS distress signalling system. The system works as follows; Three LEDs are flashed three times together at 150 milliseconds interval, then turned off for 300 milliseconds. Followed by another 250 milliseconds flashing and turned off again for 300 milliseconds, and finally flashed at 150 milliseconds interval and turned off for 2 seconds. The sequence repeats over and over. The details of the program implementation steps are listed below;

▷ **Step 1:**
▷ Launch **Flowcode** and start a new program.
▷ **Step 2:**
  — Add a **Loop** to make the program runs repeatedly.
  — Add an **LED array** component.
▷ **Step 3:**
  — Reduce the LEDs number in the array from **8** to **3**.
  — Increase the LEDs size for better appearance.
▷ **Step 4:**
  — Connect the **LED array** to **PORTD**.
▷ **Step 5:**
  — Define a new macro and name it **dih_ dih_ dih.**
▷ **Step 6:**
  — Add a **Loop** in the **dih_ dih_ dih** macro.
  — Set the loop to cycle three times.
▷ **Step 7:**
  — Send **148** to **PORTD** to **turn on** the LEDs attached to pins **D2**, **D4** and **D7**.
  — Note: sending a numeral 4 turns on LED on D2, sending a numeral 16 turns on LED on D4 and finally sending a numeral 128 turns on LED on D7. Therefore, to turn the three LEDs add up 4 + 16 + 128 = 148.
▷ **Step 8:**
  — Keep the LEDs **on** for **150 milliseconds**.
▷ **Step 9:**
  — Send **0** to **PORTD** to **turn off** the LEDs attached to pins **D2**, **D4** and **D7**.
▷ **Step 10:**
  — Keep the LEDs **off** for **150 milliseconds**.
▷ **Step 11:**
  — Call the **dih_ dih_ dih** macro to execute its contents.
▷ **Step 12:**
  — Do nothing for **300 milliseconds**.
▷ **Step 13:**
  — Define a new macro and name it **dah_ dah_ dah.**
▷ **Step 14:**
  — Copy all the contents in the **dih_ dih_ dih** macro.
▷ **Step 15:**
  — Paste everything into **dah_ dah_ dah** macro including the loop.

— Edit the two delays in the **dah_dah_dah** macro from **150 milliseconds** to **250 milliseconds**.

▷ **Step 16:**

— Switch to the Main program and call the **dah_dah_dah** macro.

▷ **Step 17:**

— Do nothing for **300 milliseconds**.

▷ **Step 18:**

— Again, call the **dih_dih_dih** macro.

▷ **Step 19:**

— Do nothing for **2 seconds**.

▷ **Step 20:**

— Simulate the program by clicking on the **Run** button and download it to the micro-controller on the PhasePlus development board.

Chapter 8

Project 5: 7-Segment Display

8.1. Objective

The purpose of this project is to demonstrate how to interface a 7-segment display to a microcontroller. A common requirement for many mechatronics systems is some form of numeric display for communication with the outside world. Generally, numeric displays serve as indicators which display information about the system, such as sensor reading or directives to the user. Basically, the main display components in mechatronics designs are; LEDs, 7-Segment displays, Liquid Crystal Displays (LCDs) and Graphical Liquid Crystal Displays (GLCDs) and of course of recent, the touch pad displays. This project is a primer to interfacing visual displays to mechatronics projects, although, LEDs have been introduced earlier.

Hardware

- ▷ 7-Segment LED Display
- ▷ 8 x 220Ω resistors
- ▷ PhasePlus PIC Development Board
- ▷ Connection wires

8.2. 7-Segment LED Display Overview

A 7-segment display is used mainly for display of numerical outputs. The display is divided into seven different regions or parts each containing an LED that can be switched on or off either individually or combined to produce simplified representations of the Arabic numerals. The display is widely used in digital clocks, electronic meters, and other electronic devices for displaying numerical information. In addition to the ten numerals, seven segment displays can be used to show letters of the Latin and Greek alphabets including punctuation.

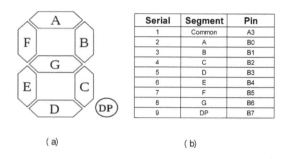

Figure 8.1. *7-Segment display schematic .*

The LEDs in a 7-segment display are not isolated from one another, rather, are interconnected in either a common cathode or a common anode configuration. In the common anode arrangement, Fig 8.2, all the anodes are connected together inside the package. When in use, they are connected to the positive power supply through a series protective resistor. Normally, the cathodes of all the LEDs are held at logic 1. To make a segment light, the cathode of that LED is connected to logic 0. This can be done by connecting the display directly to the output pins of a microcontroller or using a decoder/driver integrated circuit.

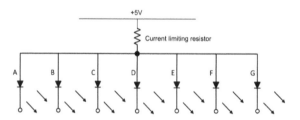

Figure 8.2. *7-Segment display schematic .*

In the common cathode configuration, Fig. 8.3 all the cathodes are connected together internally. In the circuit, they are connected to the GND through series resistors, normally, held at logic 0. Lightening a segment requires connecting it to logic 1.

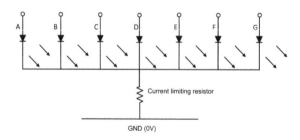

Figure 8.3. *7 Segment display schematic .*

8.3. Circuit Schematic

Figure 8.4 depicts the circuit schematic for this project. The seven LEDs making up the display segments A-G connect to pin B0-B7 of the microcontroller. The two common terminals of the display connect to pin D2.

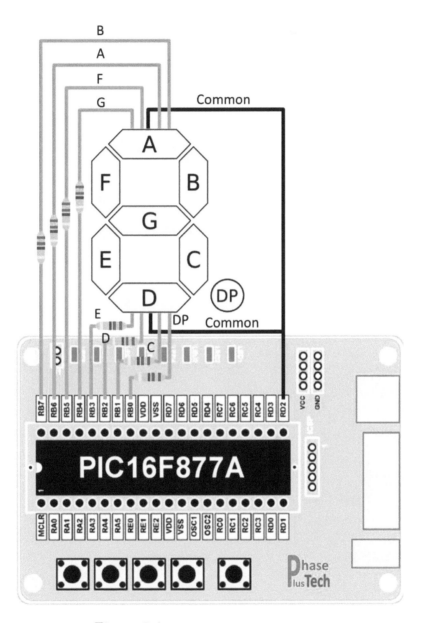

Figure 8.4. *Project 5 circuit schematic.*

8.4. Implementation Steps:

Project 5: Step 1

▷ Launch **Flowcode**.
▷ Select **Create a new Flowcode**, click **OK** and select **16F877A**.
▷ Click **OK**.

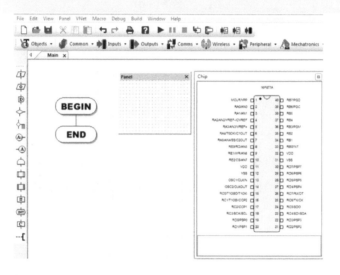

Figure 8.5. *An empty Flowcode project environment.*

Project 5: Step 2

▷ Insert a **Calculation** icon and double click on it.
▷ Double click on **Variables** to create a new variable of **Byte** type.
▷ In the **Name of new** variable field type **counter** and click **OK**.

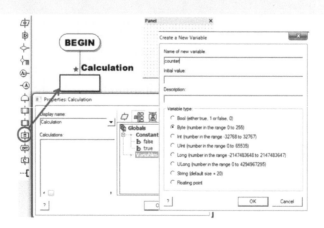

Figure 8.6. *Creating a variable.*

Project 5: Step 3

▷ In the **Calculations** field enter **counter = 0**.
▷ Click **OK**.

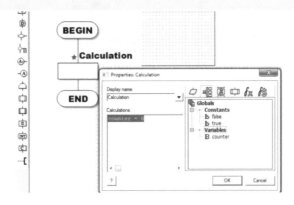

Figure 8.7. *Initializing a variable.*

Project 5: Step 4

▷ Insert a **Loop** icon.
▷ Click on the **Output** tab and select **7seg1** to insert a 7-segment display.

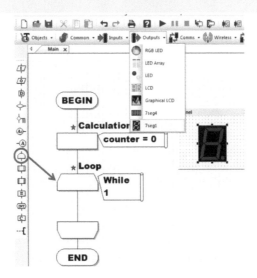

Figure 8.8. *Adding a loop and a 7-segement display component.*

Project 5: Step 5

▷ Right click on the **7-Segment Display** component and select **Connections**.
▷ Double check the **Display** is connected as indicated in **Fig. 8.9**.
▷ Click **Done**.

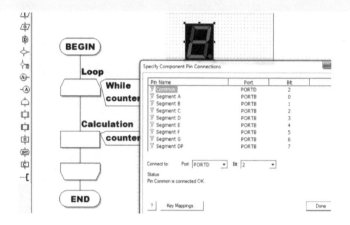

Figure 8.9. *Connecting the 7-segmant display to the output pins.*

Project 5: Step 6

▷ Insert a **Component Macro** icon and double click on it.
▷ Select **led7seg(0)** and **ShowDigit** in the **Component** and **Macro** field.
▷ Under **Expression** enter **counter** and **0**, click **OK**.

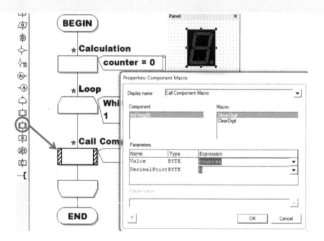

Figure 8.10. *Displaying a digit on the 7-segment display.*

Project 5: Step 7

▷ Insert a **Delay** icon double click on it.
▷ Set the delay time to **1 second**.
▷ Click **OK**.

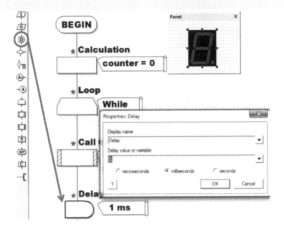

Figure 8.11. *Adding and configuring display.*

Project 5: Step 8

▷ Insert a **Decision** and double click on it.
▷ In the If field enter **counter > 9**.
▷ Click **OK**.

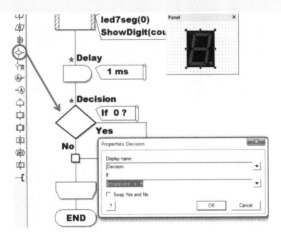

Figure 8.12. *Is the digit on the display greater than nine?*

Project 5: Step 9

▷ Insert a user-defined ***Macro Call*** icon and double click on it.
▷ Double click on ***Create a New Macro*** to create a new macro.

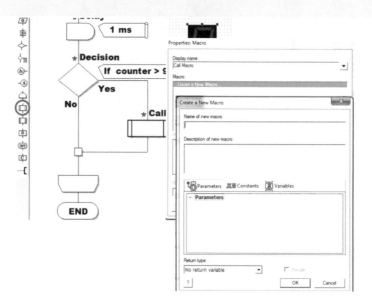

Figure 8.13. *Creating a user-defined macro.*

Project 5: Step 10

▷ In the ***Name of a New Macro*** field enter ***countDown***.
▷ Click ***OK*** and click ***OK & Edit*** tab to edit the new macro.

Figure 8.14. *Naming the macro created.*

Project 5: Step 11

▷ Insert a **Loop** icon and double click on it.
▷ Enter **counter > 0** in the **Loop while** field.
▷ Click **OK**.

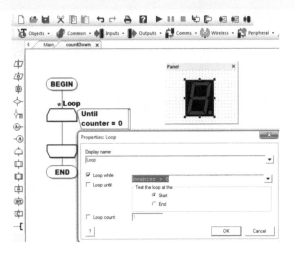

Figure 8.15. *Editing the countDown macro..*

Project 5: Step 12

▷ Insert a **Calculation** icon and double click on it.
▷ In the **Calculations** field enter **counter = counter - 1**.
▷ Click **OK**.

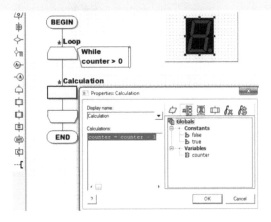

Figure 8.16. *Decrementing the counter variable.*

Project 5: Step 13

▷ Insert a *Component Macro* icon and double click on it.
▷ Select *led7seg(0)* in the *Component* field and *ShowDigit* in the *Macro* field.
▷ Under *Expression* type *counter* and *0*, click *OK*.

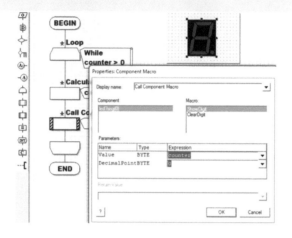

Figure 8.17. *Displaying a digit to the 7-segment display..*

Project 5: Step 14

▷ Insert a *Delay* icon double click on it.
▷ Set the delay time to *1 second*.
▷ Click *OK*.

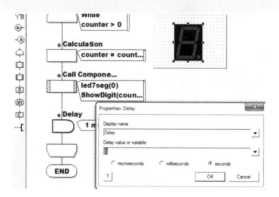

Figure 8.18. *Adding and configuring a delay.*

Project 5: Step 15

▷ Click on *Main* program tab and insert a *Calculation* icon.
▷ Double click on the *Calculation* icon.
▷ In the *Calculation* field enter *counter = counter + 1* and click *OK*.

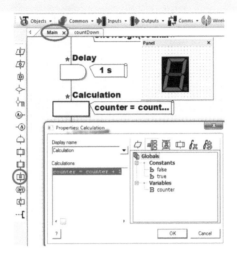

Figure 8.19. *Incrementing the counter variable.*

Project 5: Step 16

▷ Save the program and and click on *Run* to simulate it.

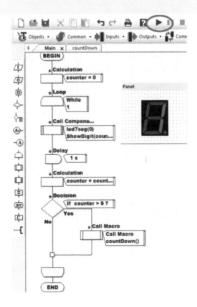

Figure 8.20. *Project completed ready for simulation and downloading.*

8.5. Program Description

This program implements a digital counter which counts up to the first ten digits and down to zero. In the program, a variable **counter** was declared an initialized to zero. The program runs in a continuous loop. On every cycle, the variable **counter** is incremented and displayed on the 7-segment display. However, the display is limited to showing only 0 to 9 digits. Therefore, when the value of the variable counter is greater than digit 9, the **countDown** macro is called to decrement the variable **counter**. The details of the program implementation step are listed below.

▷ **Step 1:**
▷ Launch **Flowcode** and start a new program.
▷ **Step 2:**
— Declare a **Byte** type variable and name it **counter**.
▷ **Step 3:**
— Initialize the variable **counter** to zero.
▷ **Step 4:**
— Add a **Loop** to make the program runs repeatedly.
— Also add a **7-segment** display.
▷ **Step 5:**
— Connect the **7-segment** display terminals as indicated below:
— Common to D2.
— Segment A to B0.
— Segment B to B1.
— Segment C to B2.
— Segment D to B3.
— Segment E to B4.
— Segment F to B5.
— Segment G to B6.
▷ **Step 6:**
— Display the current value of the variable **counter**.
▷ **Step 7:**
— Keep the digit on display for **one** second.
▷ **Step 8:**
— The display is only capable of displaying digits from zero to nine.
▷ **Step 9:**
— If the digit displayed is greater than **nine** create a macro to handle the situation.
▷ **Step 10:**
— Name the new macro **countDown** and edit it.
▷ **Step 11:**
— Add a loop to **countDown** macro and set the loop to repeat while the variable **counter** is greater than **zero**.
▷ **Step 12:**
— Decrement the variable **counter** on every cycle of the **countDown** macro.
▷ **Step 13:**
— Display the current value of the variable **counter**.

▷ **Step 14:**
  — Keep the digit on display for *one* second.
▷ **Step 15:**
  — Increment the variable *counter*.
▷ **Step 16:**
  — Simulate the program by clicking on the *Run* button and download it to the micro-controller on the PhasePlus development board.

Chapter 9

Project 6: Pedestrian Crossing Traffic Light System

9.1. Objective

The purpose of this project is to demonstrate how to build simple time-based pedestrians crossing traffic light system. Crossing a busy road at times can be hazardous particularly when the traffic volume is high and vehicles are moving at high speeds. Pedestrians crossing provide a clear and safe route to road users, reducing risks to pedestrians crossing the roads and ensuring unhindered vehicular flow. To protect pedestrians and to ensure smooth vehicular flow on busy roads, traffic lights incorporating pedestrians crossing option are installed at junctions or busy crossing points.

9.2. Traffic Light

Traffic lights are signalling devices positioned at road intersections, pedestrian crossings and other locations to control competing vehicular and human traffic flows. Traffic light was first introduced in the mid-eighteenth century in some industrialized nations, but are now found in most cities around the world. Basically, a traffic light controller regulates the right of way to road users by sequentially displaying lights of standard colours of red, yellow/amber and green.

9.3. Pedestrians Crossing

A pedestrian crossing or crosswalk is an area on a road where it is designated to serve as a converging point for the pedestrians to cross a road. Often, pedestrians crossings are found at road intersections or on busy roads where it becomes unsafe for a pedestrian to cross due to high volume of vehicles, high speeds or road size, such as shopping areas or where school children regularly cross.

9.4. The System Layout

The system is made up ten lights, labelled LED(0) - LED(9) and two switches as shown in the schematic (Fig.9.1). The road is modelled in such that vehicles flow from two directions namely north and south, referred to as northbound and southbound vehicles. Vehicular traffic lights are represented by three LEDs (red, yellow and green) for each direction, and two each (red and green) for the pedestrians crossing from either sides of the road. The pedestrians lights are operated by pressing either of the two momentary pushbutton switches located at the two crossing sides. The default working of the system is always passing the vehicular traffic. However, when a pedestrian wishes to cross, he presses the switch on his side and waits for a preset time for his turn.

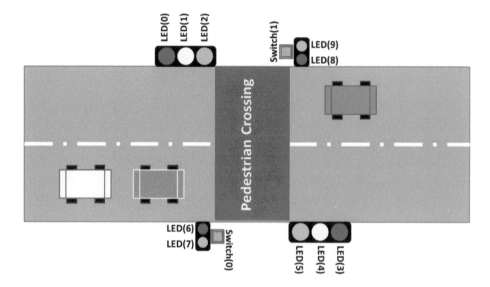

Figure 9.1. *Pedestrians crossing traffic light control - System Layout.*

Hardware

- ▷ 4 x Red LEDs
- ▷ 4 x Green LEDs
- ▷ 2 x Yellow LEDs
- ▷ 10 x 220Ω
- ▷ 2 x 2K resistor
- ▷ PhasePlus PIC Development Board
- ▷ Connection wires

9.5. Circuit Schematic

Figure 9.2 depicts the circuit schematic for this project. The cathodes of the seven LEDs on the 7-segment display connect to GND while the anodes connect to the output pins of the microcontroller via current limiting resistors. However, the terminals of the two pedestrians pushbutton switches connect to B0, C7, GND and +5V.

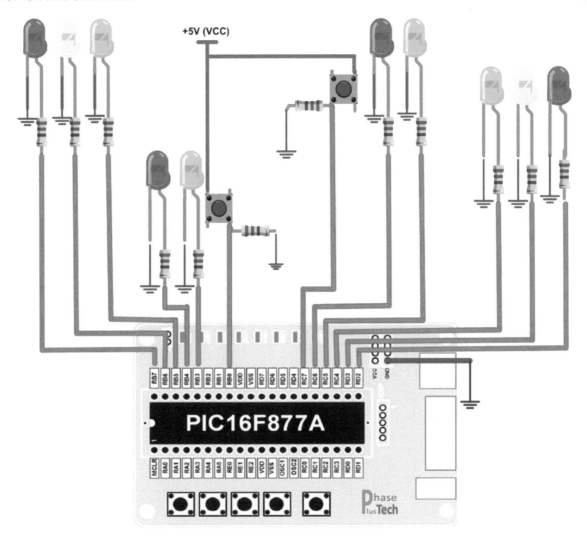

Figure 9.2. *Project 6 circuit schematic.*

9.6. Implementation Steps:

Project 6: Step 1

▷ Launch **Flowcode**.
▷ Select **Create a new Flowcode**, click **OK** and select **16F877A**.
▷ Click **OK**.

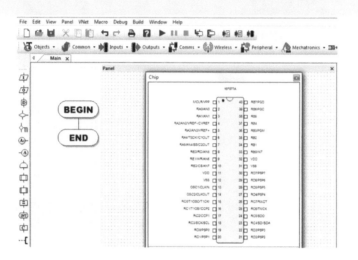

Figure 9.3. *An empty Flowcode program environment.*

Project 6: Step 2

▷ Click on the **Object** tab and select **Image**.
▷ Browse to **proj_ 6 folder** and select **road_ ped.jpg**.
▷ Click **Open** to load the image into the program.

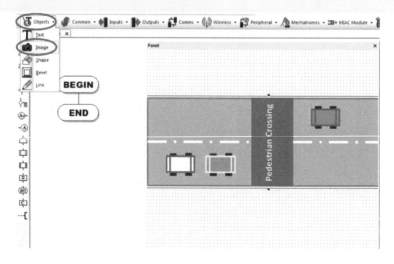

Figure 9.4. *Importing an image.*

Project 6: Step 3

▷ Click on the **Output** tab and select **LED**.

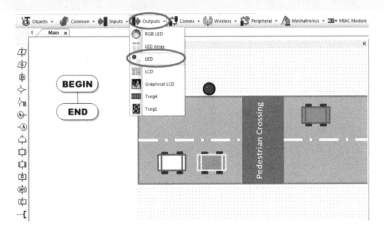

Figure 9.5. *Adding an LED component.*

Project 6: Step 4

▷ Right click on the **LED** and select **Ext Properties**.
▷ Draw the slide below the **LED** to increase its size to **35 x 35**.
▷ Click **OK**.

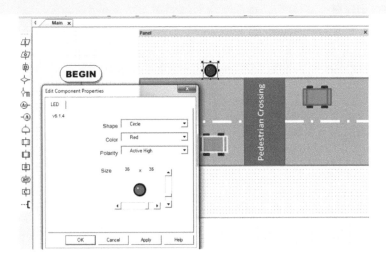

Figure 9.6. *Resizing the LED component.*

Project 6: Step 5

▷ Click on the **Object** tab and select **Text** to insert a **Text box**.
▷ Right click on the **Text box** and select **Properties**.
▷ In the **Caption** text field enter **LED(0)**.
▷ Drag the **Text box** and position it as shown in figure below.

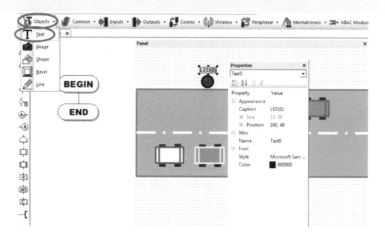

Figure 9.7. *labelling the LED component.*

Project 6: Step 6

▷ Insert two more **LEDs** and configure them as done in **Step 5**.
▷ Label the **Yellow LED** as **LED(1)** and **Green LED** as **LED(2)**.

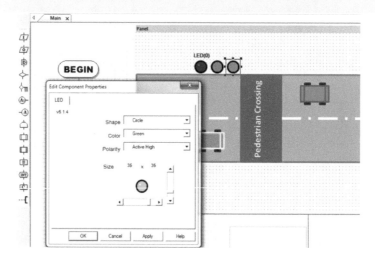

Figure 9.8. *Adding and configuring more LEDs.*

Project 6: Step 7

▷ Insert *three* other **LEDs** at the bottom right side as shown in **Fig. 9.9**.
▷ Configure the **LEDs** as done in previously.
▷ Label the **LEDs** as follows: Green- **LED(3)**, Yellow - **LED(4)** and Red - **(LED(5)**.

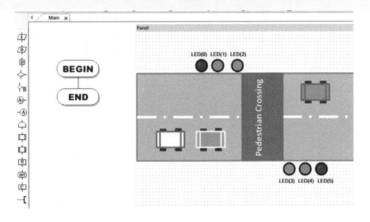

Figure 9.9. *Adding and configuring additional LEDs.*

Project 6: Step 8

▷ Insert four **LEDs** above and below the schematic as shown in **Fig. 9.10**.
▷ Label them as follows:
— Top LEDs: **Red** as **LED(6)** and **Green** as **LED(7)**.
— Bottom LEDs: **Red** as **LED(8)** and **Green** as **LED(9)**.

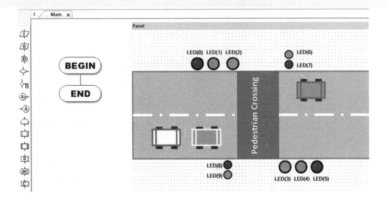

Figure 9.10. *Adding, configuring more LEDs.*

Project 6: Step 9

▷ Click on the **Input** tab and select **Switch**.
▷ Right click on the **Switch** and select **Ext Properties**.
▷ In the **Type** field choose **Pushbutton**.
▷ Select **Momentary** in the **Switch Operation** field and click **OK**.

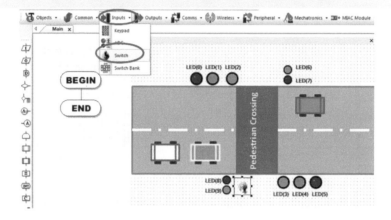

Figure 9.11. *Adding and configuring a switch component.*

Project 6: Step 10

▷ Insert another **Switch** and configure it as done in **Step 9**.
▷ Label the two switches as **Switch(1)** and **Switch(2)**.
▷ Position them as shown in **Fig. 9.12**.

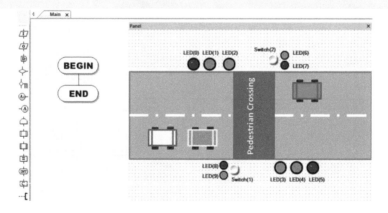

Figure 9.12. *Adding, configuring and labelling a switch component.*

Project 6: Step 11

▷ Right click on **LED(0)** and select **Connections**.
▷ In the **Port** menu select **PORTB** and **7** in the **Bit** field.
▷ Click **Done**.

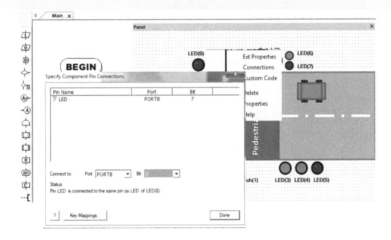

Figure 9.13. *Connecting LED to the microcontroller output pin.*

Project 6: Step 12

▷ Connect Other **LEDs** and **Switches** to the following **Ports** and **Bits**:
— **LED(1) PORTB Bit 6**
— **LED(2) PORTB Bit 5**
— **LED(3) PORTC Bit 4**
— **LED(4) PORTD Bit 3**
— **LED(5) PORTB Bit 2**
— **LED(6) PORTC Bit 5**
— **LED(7) PORTC Bit 6**
— **LED(8) PORTB Bit 4**
— **LED(9) PORTB Bit 3**
— **Switch(0) PORTB Bit 2**
— **Switch(1) PORTC Bit 7**

Project 6: Step 13

▷ Insert a **Loop** icon, click on the **Macro** tab and select **New**.
▷ In the **Name of new macro** field enter **vehiclesChance**.
▷ Click **OK** to edit the new macro.

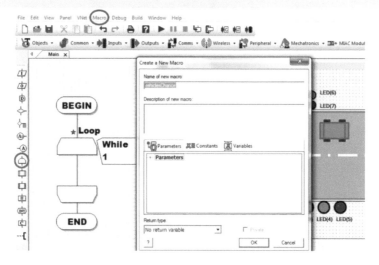

Figure 9.14. *Adding a loop and creating a user-defined macro.*

Project 6: Step 14

▷ Insert **ten Component Macro** icons into the empty **vehiclesChance** macro.
▷ Double click the first **Component Macro Call** item and configure it using **Table 9.1** as
  follows:
  — In the **Display** field enter: **led(0)_red**.
  — Under **Component** select **LED(0)**.
  — In the **Macro** field select **LEDOff**.
▷ Click **OK**.

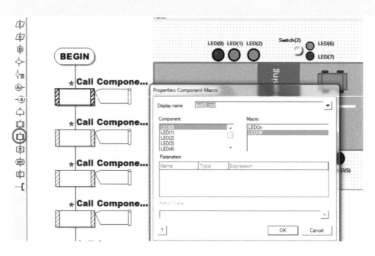

Figure 9.15. *Configuring LEDs.*

▷ NB = **Northbound.**
▷ SB = **Southbound.**
▷ S(1) = **Switch(1).**
▷ S(1) = **Switch(2).**
▷ peds(A)_red = **pedestrians(A)_red.**
▷ peds(A)_green = **pedestrians(A)_green.**
▷ peds(B)_red = **pedestrians(B)_red.**
▷ peds(B)_green = **pedestrians(B)_green.**

Table 9.1. *Pedestrians to vehicles switching*

	NB Vehicles		SB Vehicles		S(0)_peds		S(1)_peds	
Light	Display Name	State	Display Name	State	Display Name	State	Display Name	State
Red	led(0)_red	OFF	led(5)_red	OFF	peds(A)_red	ON	peds(B)_red	ON
Yellow	led(1)_yellow	OFF	led(4)_yellow	OFF	-	-	-	-
Green	led(2)_green	ON	led(3)_green	ON	peds(A)_green	OFF	peds(B)_green	OFF

Table 9.2. Vehicles turn

	NB Vehicles		SB Vehicles		S(0)_peds		S(1)_peds	
Light	Display Name	State	Display Name	State	Display Name	State	Display Name	State
Red	led(0)_red	OFF	led(5)_red	OFF	peds(A)_red	ON	peds(B)_red	ON
Yellow	led(1)_yellow	ON	led(4)_yellow	ON	-	-	-	-
Green	led(2)_green	OFF	led(3)_green	OFF	peds(A)_green	OFF	peds(B)_green	OFF

Table 9.3. Vehicles to pedestrians switching

	NB Vehicles		SB Vehicles		S(0)_peds		S(1)_peds	
Light	Display Name	State	Display Name	State	Display Name	State	Display Name	State
Red	led(0)_red	ON	led(5)_red	ON	peds(A)_red	OFF	peds(B)_red	OFF
Yellow	led(1)_yellow	OFF	led(4)_yellow	OFF	-	-	-	-
Green	led(2)_green	OFF	led(3)_green	OFF	peds(A)_green	ON	peds(B)_green	ON

Table 9.4. Pedestrians turn

	NB Vehicles		SB Vehicles		S(0)_peds		S(1)_peds	
Light	Display Name	State	Display Name	State	Display Name	State	Display Name	State
Red	led(0)_red	ON	led(5)_red	ON	peds(A)_red	ON	peds(B)_red	ON
Yellow	led(1)_yellow	OFF	led(4)_yellow	OFF	-	-	-	-
Green	led(2)_green	OFF	led(3)_green	OFF	peds(A)_green	OFF	peds(B)_green	OFF

Table 9.5. Safety

	NB Vehicles		SB Vehicles		S(0)_peds		S(1)_peds	
Light	Display Name	State	Display Name	State	Display Name	State	Display Name	State
Red	led(0)_red	OFF	led(5)_red	OFF	peds(A)_red	ON	peds(B)_red	ON
Yellow	led(1)_yellow	ON	led(4)_yellow	ON	-	-	-	-
Green	led(2)_green	OFF	led(3)_green	OFF	peds(A)_green	OFF	peds(B)_green	OFF

Project 6: Step 15

▷ Repeat the **Component Macro** configuration procedure used in **Step 14**.
▷ Configure the remaining **nine Component Macros**.

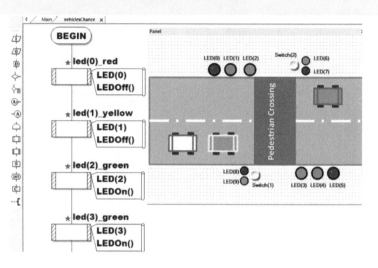

Figure 9.16. *Configuring more LEDs.*

Project 6: Step 16

▷ Create a new macro and name it **vehicles_to_peds_switching**.

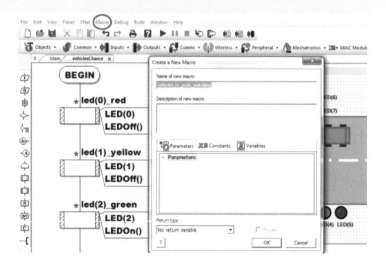

Figure 9.17. *Creating another user-defined macro.*

Project 6: Step 17

▷ Create **three** other user-defined **Macros** and name them:
1. pedestrians_turn.
2. safety.
3. pedestrians_to_vehicles_switching.

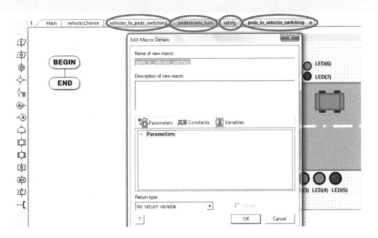

Figure 9.18. *Creating more user-defind macros.*

Project 6: Step 18

▷ Copy the ten **Component Macros** from **vehiclesChance** macro.
▷ Click on the **vehicles_ to _peds_ switching** macro tab.
▷ Paste the copied items.

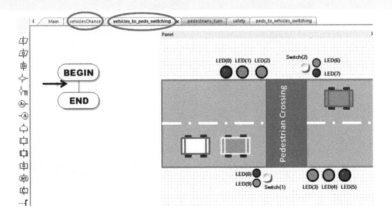

Figure 9.19. *Editing* **vehicles_ to _peds_ switching** *macro.*

Project 6: Step 19

▷ Configure all the **Component Macros** as done in **Step 16** using **Table 9.2**.
▷ Repeat **Step 18** for the remaining **Macros** using the following **Tables**:

1. pedestrians_turn: **Table 9.3**.
2. safety: **Table 9.4**.
3. pedestrians_to_vehicles_switching: **Table 9.5**.

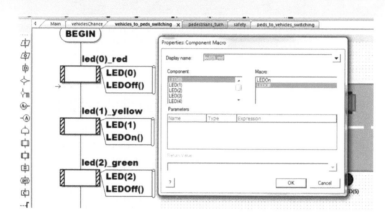

Figure 9.20. *Editing other user-defined macros.*

Project 6: Step 20

▷ Click on the **Main** program tab and insert a user-defined **Macro Call** icon.
▷ Double click on the **Macro Call** icon and select **vehiclesChance** macro.
▷ In the **Display** name field enter **Vehicle Turn** and click **OK**.

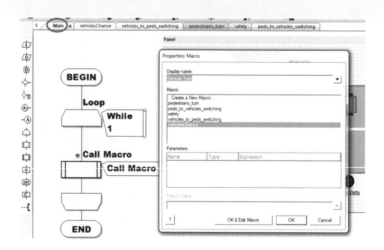

Figure 9.21. *Vehicle Turn macro call.*

Project 6: Step 21

▷ Insert a **Component Macro** icon and double click on it.
▷ Select **Switch(0)** and **ReadState** in the **Component** and **Macro** fields.
▷ Click on the arrow at the right of the **Return Value** field.

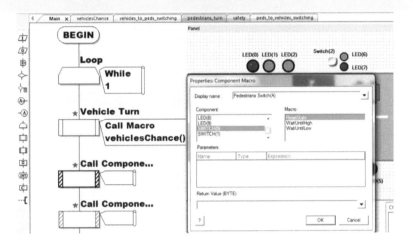

Figure 9.22. *Reading Switch(0) state.*

Project 6: Step 22

▷ Click on **Variables** to create a new variable.
▷ In the **Display name** field enter **Pedestrians Switch(A)**.
▷ Enter **switchA_press** in the **Name of new variable** field.
▷ Select **Bool** radio button under **Variable type** and click **OK**.

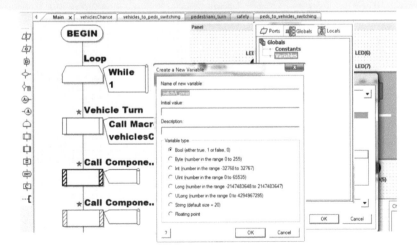

Figure 9.23. *Creating a variable to store the switch state.*

Project 6: Step 23

▷ Type *switchA_ press* in the ***Return Value*** field.
▷ Click ***OK***.

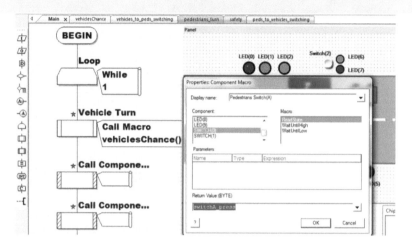

Figure 9.24. *Returning switch state to the main program.*

Project 6: Step 24

▷ Insert another ***Component Macro*** icon and configure as follows:
— Under Component select ***Switch(1)***.
— In the ***Display name*** field enter ***Pedestrians Switch(B)***.
— Create a variable ***switchB_ press*** and return it to the ***Main*** program.

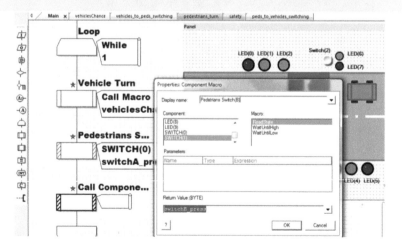

Figure 9.25. *Reading Switch(1) state.*

Project 6: Step 25

▷ Insert a **Decision** icon and double click on it.
▷ In the **If** field enter **switchA_press OR switchB_press = 1**.
▷ Click **OK**.

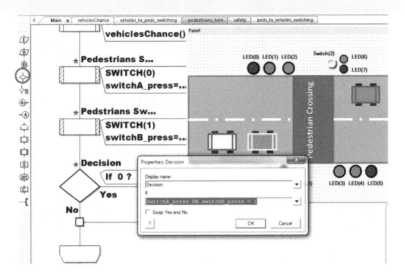

Figure 9.26. *Test to determine if the state of any of the switches has changed.*

Project 6: Step 26

▷ Copy and paste the **vehicleChance** macro to the **Yes** end of the **Decision** icon.

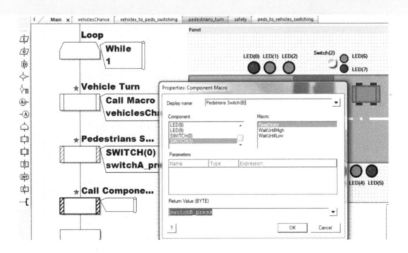

Figure 9.27. *Adding a user-defined macro call icon.*

Project 6: Step 27

▷ Insert a **Delay** icon double click on it.
▷ Set the delay time to **10 second**s.
▷ Click **OK**.

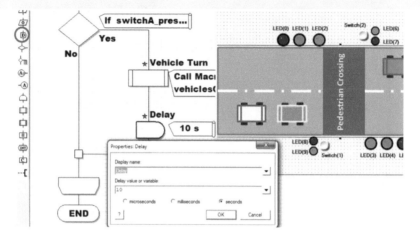

Figure 9.28. *Adding and configuring a delay.*

Project 6: Step 28

▷ Insert a user-defined **Macro** icon and double click on it.
▷ Select **vehicles_to_peds_switching** in the **Macro** field.
▷ In the **Display name** field enter **Switching Vehicle to Pedestrians** and click **OK**.

Figure 9.29. *Adding and configuring another user-defined macro call icon.*

Project 6: Step 29

▷ Insert a **Delay** icon double click on it.
▷ Set the delay time to **5 seconds**.
▷ Click **OK**.

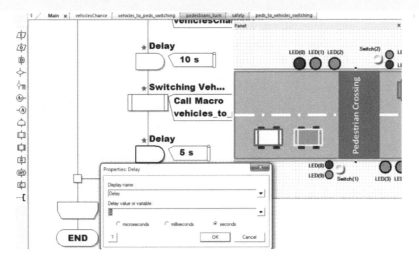

Figure 9.30. *Adding and configuring a delay.*

Project 6: Step 30

▷ Insert another user-defined **Macro** icon and double click on it.
▷ Select **safety** in the **Macro** field.
▷ In the **Display name** field enter **Safety** and click **OK**.

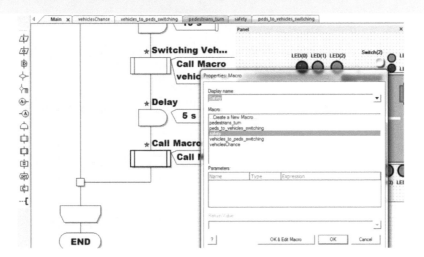

Figure 9.31. *Adding and configuring another user-defined macro call icon.*

Project 6: Step 31

▷ Insert a **Delay** icon double click on it.
▷ Set the delay time to **4 seconds**.
▷ Click **OK**.

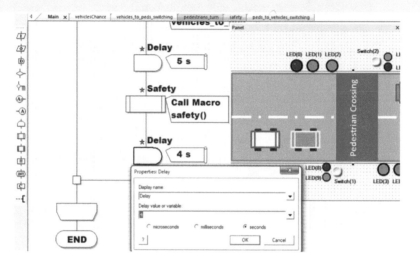

Figure 9.32. *Adding and configuring a delay.*

Project 6: Step 32

▷ Insert another user-defined **Macro Call** icon and double click on it.
▷ Select **pedestrians_ turn** in the **Macro** field.
▷ In the **Display name** field enter **Pedestrians Chance** and click **OK**.

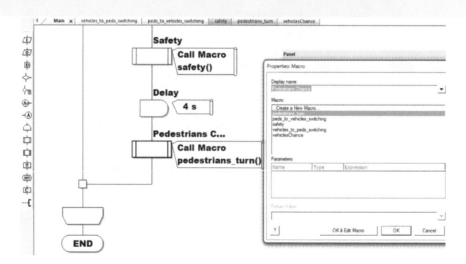

Figure 9.33. *Adding another user-defined macro call icon.*

Project 6: Step 33

▷ Insert a *Delay* icon double click on it.
▷ Set the delay time to *10 second*s.
▷ Click *OK*.

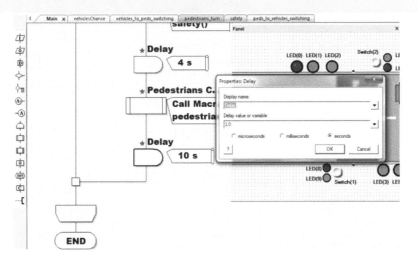

Figure 9.34. *Adding and configuring another user-defined macro call icon.*

Project 6: Step 34

▷ Copy the *Safety* macro and *4 seconds* delay icons.
▷ Paste the copied items to under the 10 seconds Delay icon. Fig. 9.35.

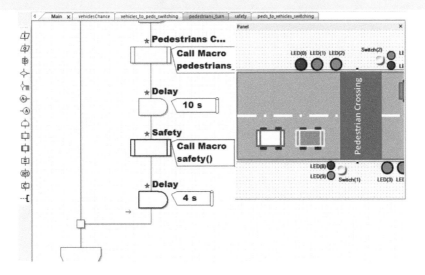

Figure 9.35. *Adding and configuring a delay.*

Project 6: Step 35

▷ Insert another user-defined *Macro Call* icon and double click on it.
▷ Select *peds_to_vehicle_switching* in the *Macro* field.
▷ In the *Display name* field enter *Switching Pedestrians to Vehicle* and click *OK*.

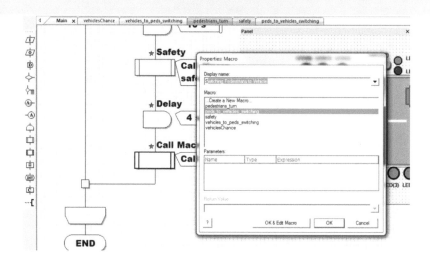

Figure 9.36. *Adding and configuring another user-defined macro call icon.*

Project 6: Step 36

▷ Insert a *Delay* icon double click on it.
▷ Set the delay time to *5 seconds*.
▷ Click *OK*.

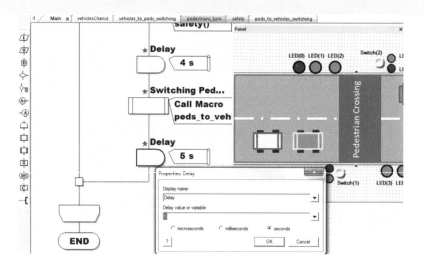

Figure 9.37. *Adding and configuring a delay.*

Project 6: Step 37

▷ Save the program and click **Run** to simulate it.

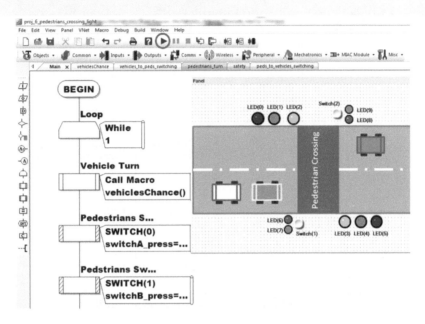

Figure 9.38. *Project completed ready for simulation and downloading.*

9.7. Program Description

This program implements a pedestrians crossing traffic light controller. The program is made up of the **Main** program and five other macros. The five macros are (1) **vehicleChance** (2) **vehicles_to_peds_switching** (3) **pedestrians_turn** (4) **safety** (5) **peds_to_vehicles_switching**. These macros implement the lights switching sequence.

The system default operation mode is continuous passing of vehicular traffic. However, when a pedestrian presses any of the switches, the system transfers right of way to the pedestrians after ten seconds. Switching from vehicular traffic chance to the pedestrians chance and back, follows a definite sequence. The sequence involves executing the two switching routines and a safety routine for every change. The listing below described in details the program implementation steps;

▷ **Step 1:**
— Launch **Flowcode** and start a new program.
▷ **Step 2:**
— Import the road layout as an image file (jpeg format).
▷ **Step 3:**
— Add a red **LED** for the Northbound vehicular traffic.
▷ **Step 4:**

— Increase the **LED** size to **35**x**35**.
▷ **Step 5:**
— Label the LED as **LED(0)**.
▷ **Step 6:**
— Add two LEDs for the green and yellow lights of the Northbound vehicular traffic.
— Change the LEDs colour from the default red to yellow and green.
— Label the LEDs as Follows:
  — Yellow LED - - **LED(1)**.
  — Green LED - **LED(2)**.
▷ **Step 7:**
— Add three more LEDs at the bottom right of the road layout for the eastbound vehicular traffic.
— Change the colour of two LEDs from the default **red** to **yellow** and **green**.
— Label the LEDs as Follows:
  — Green LED - **LED(3)**.
  — Yellow LED - **LED(4)**.
  — Red LED - **LED(5)**.
▷ **Step 8:**
— Add four LEDs for the pedestrians crossing, two on either sides of the road as depicted in Fig.9.10.
— Change the colour of the two LEDs from the default **red** to **green**.
— Label the LEDs as Follows:
  — Top LEDs
    — Green LED - **LED(6)**.
    — Red LED - **LED(7)**.
  — Bottom LEDs
    — Green LED - **LED(8)**.
    — Red LED - **LED(9)**.
▷ **Step 9:**
— Add a **Switch** component.
— Configure the switch to **Pushbutton** type and **Momentary** operation.
▷ **Step 10:**
— Add another **Switch** component.
— Label the two switches as **Switch(1)** and **Switch(2)**.
— Position the switches as depicted in Fig. 9.12.
▷ **Step 11:**
— Connect **LED(0)** to pin **B7**.
▷ **Step 12:**
— Connect other LEDs and switches as indicated below:
  — LED(1) to B6
  — LED(2) to B5
  — LED(3) to C4
  — LED(4) to D3
  — LED(5) to D2
  — LED(6) to C5

> — LED(7) to C6
> — LED(8) to B4
> — LED(9) to B3
> — Switch(1) to B0
> — Switch(2) to C7

▷ **Step 13:**
  — Add a *Loop* to make the program runs repeatedly.
  — Define a new macro and name it *vehiclesChance*.

▷ **Step 14:**
  — Edit the new macro.
  — Turn off the red LED for Northbound vehicles.

▷ **Step 15:**
  — Edit the remaining LEDs in the *vehiclesChance* macro as follows:
    — Northbound vehicles;
      — Turn off the yellow LED.
      — Turn on the green LED.
    — Eastbound vehicles;
      — Turn on the green LED.
      — Turn off the yellow LED.
      — Turn off the red LED.
    — Pedestrians;
      — Turn on the two green LEDs.
      — Turn off the two red LEDs.

▷ **Step 16:**
  — Define another macro and name it *vehicles_ to_ peds_ switching*.

▷ **Step 17:**
  — Define three other macros and name them:
    — *pedestrians_ turn*.
    — *safety*.
    — *pedestrians_ to_ vehicles_ switching*.

▷ **Step 18:**
  — Copy the ten *Component Macros* in the *vehiclesChance* macro.
  — Paste the copied items to *pedestrians_ to_ vehicles_ switching* macro.

▷ **Step 19:**
  — Use Tables 9.2 to 9.4 to edit the four user-defined macros as indicated below:
    — Table 9.2 - *vehicles_ to_ peds_ switching*.
    — Table 9.3 - *pedestrians_ turn*.
    — Table 9.4 - *safety*.
    — Table 9.5 - *pedes_ to_ vehicles_ switching*.

▷ **Step 20:**
  — Switch to the *Main* program.
  — Call the *vehicleChance* macro.
  — Note: This macro runs continuously passing vehicular traffic as long as no pedestrians switch is pressed.

▷ **Step 21:**

— Read the state of **Switch(0)**.

▷ **Step 22:**

— Declare a **Bool** type variable and name it **SwitchA_press**.

— Store the value read in step 21 to **SwitchA_press**.

▷ **Step 23:**

— Return the value of **SwitchA_press** to the **Main** program.

▷ **Step 24:**

— Read **Switch(1)** state.

— Return the value of **SwitchB_press** to the **Main** program.

▷ **Step 25:**

— Test if one of the switches is pressed.

▷ **Step 26:**

— If any of the switches is pressed, maintain vehicular traffic chance.

▷ **Step 27:**

— Do that for **ten** seconds.

▷ **Step 28:**

— Then call **vehicles_to_peds_switching** macro to perform a switching routine.

▷ **Step 29:**

— The switching routing lasts for **five** seconds.

▷ **Step 30:**

— Call **safety** macro to stop both vehicular traffic and pedestrians.

▷ **Step 31:**

— This macro turns on all the red LEDs for **four** seconds.

▷ **Step 32:**

— Call **pedestrians_turn** macro to pass the pedestrians.

▷ **Step 33:**

— Right of way remains with the pedestrians for **ten** seconds.

▷ **Step 34:**

— Run **safety** macro for four second to ensure road safety.

▷ **Step 35:**

— Call **peds_to_vehicle_switching macro** to perform the switching routine to vehicular traffic chance.

▷ **Step 36:**

— The switching routine takes **five** seconds.

▷ **Step 37:**

— Simulate the program by clicking on the **Run** button and download it to the microcontroller on the PhasePlus development board.

Chapter 10

Project 7: Door Alarm

10.1. Objective

The purpose of this project is to demonstrate how to build a door alarm system. A door alarm is signalling device typically placed near a building entrance and operated by pressing a button which activates an alarm inside the building. Its main purpose is to alert the building occupants of a visitor's presence.

Hardware

▷ Piezo sounder
▷ Push-button switch
▷ 10K resistor
▷ PhasePlus PIC Development Board
▷ Connection wires

10.2. Piezo Sounder

A Piezo buzzer is basically a sounding device which generates audible sounds for notification or alert. It is made from two conductors that are separated by Piezo crystals. When a voltage is applied to these crystals, they push on one conductor and pull on the other. The result of this push and pull is a sound wave http://www.ehow.com/audio amplifiers [5]. Piezo buzzes are used in many mechatronics applications such as time-elapse signalling, audible sounds on button press, sensor input and in alarm circuits.

10.3. Circuit Schematic

The circuit schematic for this project is shown Fig. 10.1. The Piezo sounder terminals connect to +5V and GND. One of the switch terminals connects to +5V, while the other connects to pin C5 of the microcontroller and GND via a 10K resistor.

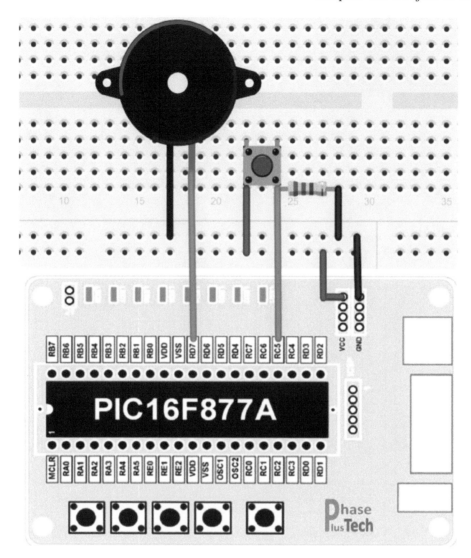

Figure 10.1. *Project 7 circuit schematic.*

10.4. Implementation Steps

Project 7: Step 1

▷ Launch *Flowcode*.
▷ Select *Create a new Flowcode*, click *OK* and select *16F877A*.
▷ Click *OK*.

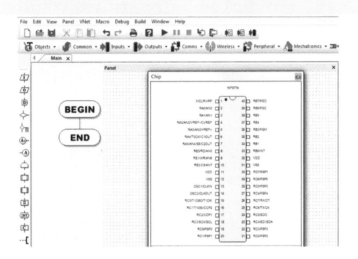

Figure 10.2. *An empty Flowcode environment.*

Project 7: Step 2

▷ Click on the *Input* tab and select *Switch*.
▷ Right click on the *Switch* and select *Ext Properties*.
▷ Select *Pushbutton* and *Momentary* in the *Type* and *Switch Operation* fields.
▷ Click *OK*.

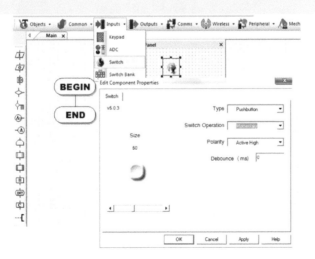

Figure 10.3. *Adding and configuring a switch component.*

Project 7: Step 3

▷ Right click on the *Switch* again and select *Connections*.
▷ From the *Port* and *Bit* menus select *PORTD* and bit *5*.
▷ Click *Done*.

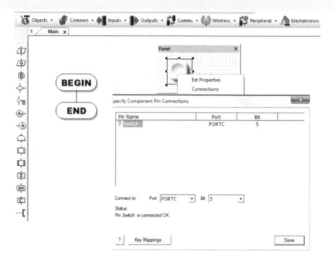

Figure 10.4. *Connecting a switch to an input pin.*

Project 7: Step 4

▷ Click on the *Output* tab and select *LED*.
▷ Right click on the *LED* and select *Connections*.
▷ From the *Port* and *Bit* menus select *PORTD* and bit *7*, click *Done*.

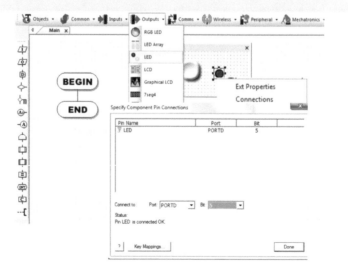

Figure 10.5. *Adding and connecting an LED to the output pin.*

Project 7: Step 5

▷ Insert a **Calculation** icon and double click on it.
▷ Double click on **Variables** to create a new variable of **Bool** type.
▷ Type **buttonPress** in the **Name of new variable** field and click **OK**.

Figure 10.6. *Creating a variable.*

Project 7: Step 6

▷ In the **Calculations** field enter: **buttonPress = 0**.
▷ Click **OK**.

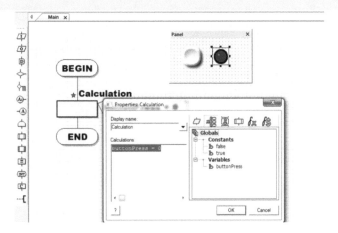

Figure 10.7. *Initializing a variable.*

Project 7: Step 7

▷ Insert a **Loop** icon, **Component Macro** icon and double click on it.
▷ Select **Switch(0)** and **ReadState** in the **Component** and **Macro** fields.
▷ Type **buttonPress** in the **Return Value** field and click **OK**.

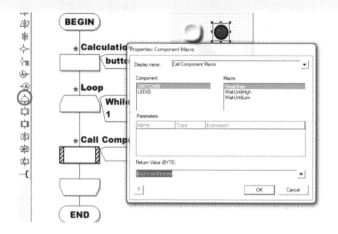

Figure 10.8. *Adding a loop and reading a switch state.*

Project 7: Step 8

▷ Insert a **Decision** icon and double click on it.
▷ In the **If** field enter **buttonPress = 1**.
▷ Click **OK**.

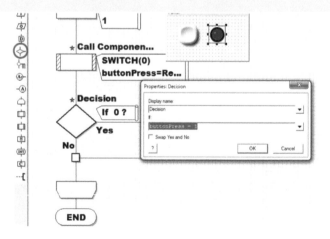

Figure 10.9. *Adding a decision to monitor if the switch state has changed.*

Project 7: Step 9

▷ Insert a user-defined **Macro Call** icon and double click on it.
▷ Enter **Sound Alarm**.in the **Display name** field.
▷ Click **Create a New Macro** to create a new macro.

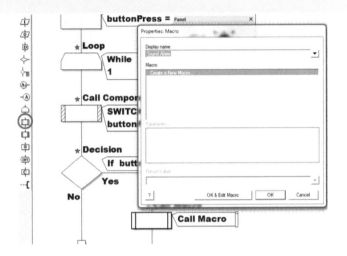

Figure 10.10. *Creating a user-defined macro.*

Project 7: Step 10

▷ In the **Name of new macro** field type **door_ alarm_ sounder**.
▷ Click **OK**.
▷ Click **OK & Edit Macro**.

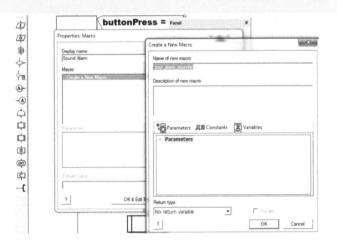

Figure 10.11. *Naming a user-defined macro.*

Project 7: Step 11

▷ Insert a *Loop* icon and double click on it.
▷ Check the *Loop count* box and enter *10* in its field.
▷ Click *OK*.

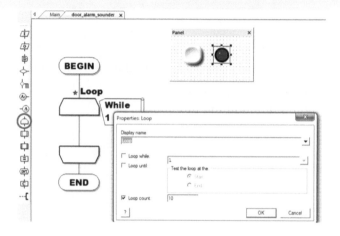

Figure 10.12. *Adding and setting its number of cycles.*

Project 7: Step 12

▷ Insert a *Component Macro* icon and double click on it.
▷ In the *Display name* field type *sounder_on*
▷ Select *LED(0)* and *LEDOn* in the *Component* and *Macro* fields, click *OK*

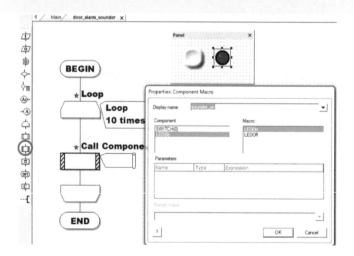

Figure 10.13. *Sending a high logic level to the output pin.*

Project 7: Step 13

▷ Insert a **Delay** icon and double click on it.
▷ Set the delay time **400 milliseconds**.
▷ Click **OK**.

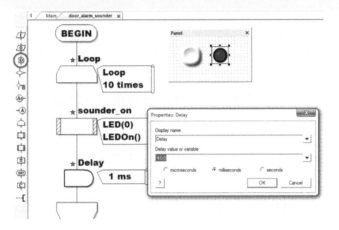

Figure 10.14. *Adding and configuring a delay.*

Project 7: Step 14

▷ Insert a **Component Macro** icon and double click on it.
▷ In the **Display name** field type **sounder_ on**
▷ Select **LED(0)** and **LEDOff** in the **Component** and **Macro** fields, click **OK**

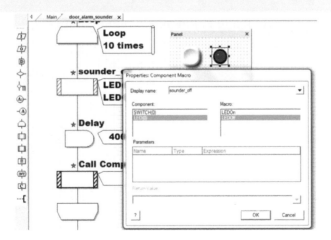

Figure 10.15. *Sending a low logic level to the output pin..*

Project 7: Step 15

▷ Insert a **Delay** icon and double click on it.
▷ Set the delay time **200 milliseconds**.
▷ Click **OK**.

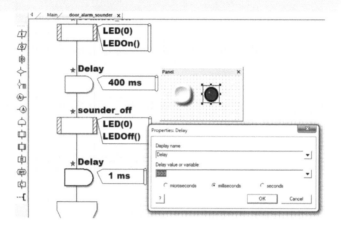

Figure 10.16. *Adding and configuring a delay.*

Project 7: Step 16

▷ Save the program and click **Run** for simulation.

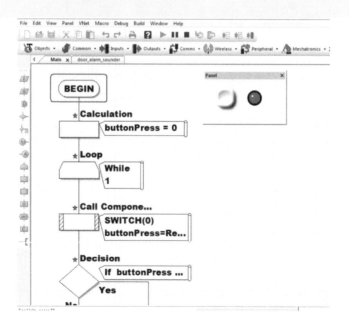

Figure 10.17. *Program completed ready for simulation and downloading.*

10.4.1. Program Description

This program implements a simple door alarm system. The program continuously checks the state of the switch attached to the microcontroller input pin. Anytime the switch state changes, implies a visitor has pressed the switch, an alarm then sounds inside the building to notify the occupants of someone presence at the building entrance. The details of the program implementation steps are listed below;

▷ **Step 1:**
▷ Launch *Flowcode* and start a new program.
▷ **Step 2:**
 — Add a *Switch* component.
 — Configure the *Switch* to *Pushbutton* type.
▷ **Step 3:**
 — Connect the *Switch* component to pin *C5* of the microcontroller.
▷ **Step 4:**
 — Add an *LED* component to represent the *Piezo sounder* as Flowcode does not have a *Buzzer* in its component library.
 — Connect the *LED* to pin *D7* of the microcontroller.
▷ **Step 5:**
 — Declare a *Bool* type variable and name it *buttonPress*.
▷ **Step 6:**
 — Initialize the variable to *zero*.
▷ **Step 7:**
 — Add a *Loop* to make the program runs repeatedly.
 — Read the state of the *Switch* through pin *D2*.
 — Store the state of the switch in the variable *buttonPress*.
▷ **Step 8:**
 — Test if *buttonPress* has changed from *zero* to *one*.
▷ **Step 9:**
 — Define a new macro and edit it.
▷ **Step 10:**
 — Name the macro *door_ alarm_ sounder*.
▷ **Step 11:**
 — Add a *Loop* and set it to cycle ten times.
▷ **Step 12:**
 — Sound an alarm if *step 8* evaluates *True*.
▷ **Step 13:**
 — Keep it on for *400 millisecond*.
▷ **Step 14:**
 — Turn *off* the LED.
▷ **Step 15:**
 — Keep it off for *200* milliseconds.
▷ **Step 16:**
 — Simulate the program by clicking on the *Run* button and download it to the microcontroller on the PhasePlus development board.

Chapter 11

Project 8: Intruder Motion Detection Alarm

11.1. Objective

The purpose of this project is to demonstrate how to build an intruder motion detection system based on a passive infrared (PIR) sensor. A PIR sensor is one of the most commonly used motion sensor in mechatronics applications requiring motion sensing. The concept in this project can be extended to building sophisticated custom security systems.

Hardware

- ▷ PIR sensor
- ▷ Piezo sounder
- ▷ 10K resistor
- ▷ Connection wires
- ▷ PhasePlus PIC Development Board

11.2. PIR Sensor

Passive infrared sensing is a motion detection technique in which motion is detected by measuring changes in human or animal body heat to signal a change in the environment. A basic PIR sensor module, Fig. 11.1, detects motion by taking images on two sensors at different times. When the images differ, it implies a motion.

Figure 11.1. *An empty Flowcode environment.*

In home security devices, each time a PIR sensor detects a significant change in a nearby object's infrared or heat energy in relation to the rest of the room or environment, an alarm is triggered [7]. The sensor detects motion when a body moves in or out of the sensor's range. The sensor's output pin goes to *Low* if it detects a motion and *High* if there is no motion. The signal pin of the sensor is an open-collector. The term open-collector typically refers to a transistor output where the collector (output) of a transistor is not connected to a positive voltage [9]. In the off state, i.e. when motion is detected, the terminal supplies a path to ground. However, in the on state, when there is no motion, the terminal floats. Hence the need for the pull-up resistor to drive the pin high when no motion is detected.

PIR sensors are commonly used in home security devices such as motion detectors and security lights. However, Flowcode does not have PIR sensor in its components library. Therefore, a push-button switch will be used to simulate the sensor.

11.3. Circuit Schematic

Figure 11.2 depicts the circuit schematic for this project. The sensor's output terminal connects to pin D2 of the microcontroller through a 10K pull-up resistor and the power terminals connect to the +5V and GND. The buzzer terminals connect +5V and GND.

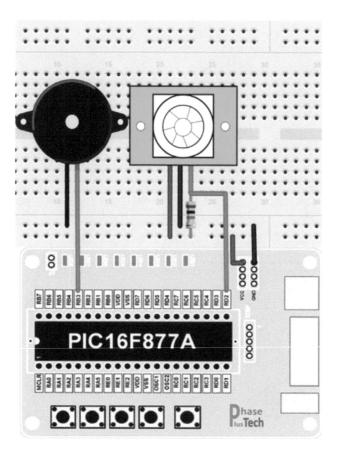

Figure 11.2. *Adding a loop and a switch component.*

11.4. Implementation Steps

Project 8: Step 1

▷ Launch **Flowcode**.
▷ Select **Create a new Flowcode**, click **OK** and select **16F877A**.
▷ Click **OK**.

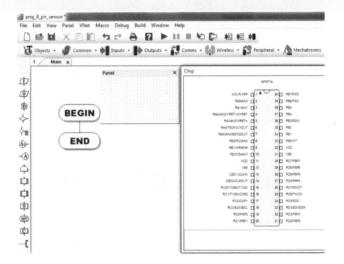

Figure 11.3. *An empty Flowcode environment.*

Project 8: Step 2

▷ Insert a **Loop icon** and click on the **Input** tab and select **Switch**.

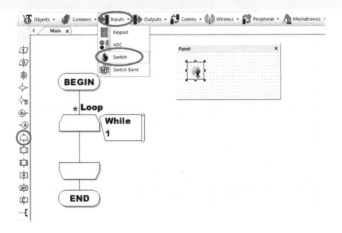

Figure 11.4. *Adding a loop and a switch component.*

Project 8: Step 3

▷ Right click on the **Switch** and select **Ext Properties**.
▷ Select **Pushbutton** in the **Type** field.
▷ In the **Polarity** field select **Active High** and click **OK**.

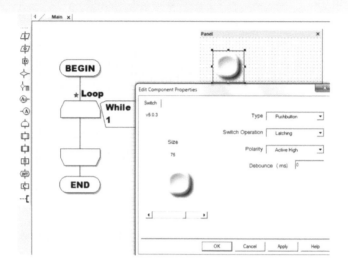

Figure 11.5. *Configuring the switch component.*

Project 8: Step 4

▷ Right click on the **Switch** again and select **Connections**.
▷ From **Port** and **Bit** menus select **PORTD** and Bit **2**.
▷ Click **Done**.

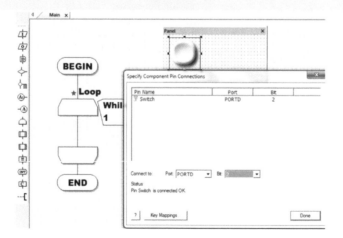

Figure 11.6. *Connecting a switch to an input pin.*

Project 8: Step 5

▷ Click on the **Output** tab and select **LED**.
▷ Right click on the **LED** and select **Connections**.
▷ From the **Port** and **Bit** menus select **PORTB** and Bit **3** respectively, click **Done**.

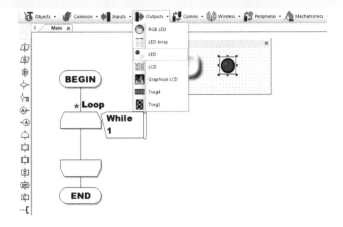

Figure 11.7. *Adding and connecting an LED to output pin.*

Project 8: Step 6

▷ Insert an **Input** icon and double click on it.
▷ Select **PORTD** in the **Port** menu.
▷ Select **Single bit** under **Input from** and choose **2** from its drop menu.

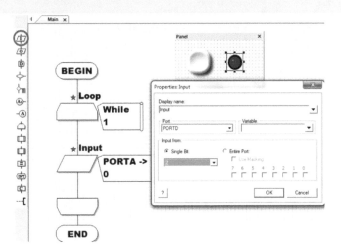

Figure 11.8. *Connecting an input device to an input pin.*

Project 8: Step 7

▷ Click on the **arrow** at the right of the **Variable** field.
▷ Double click on **Variables** and enter **pirSensor** in the **Name of new variable** field.
▷ Select **Bool** under **Variable type** and click **OK**.

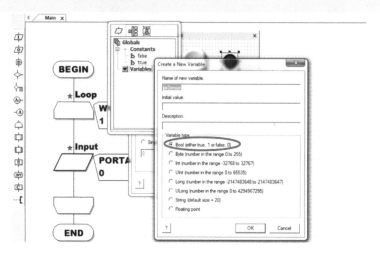

Figure 11.9. *Creating a variable.*

Project 8: Step 8

▷ In the **Variable** field type **pirSensor**.
▷ Click **OK**.

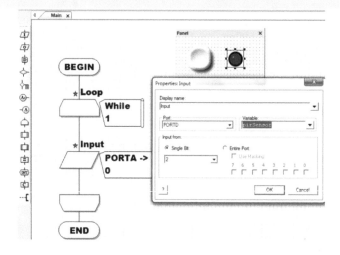

Figure 11.10. *Assigning an input value to a variable.*

Project 8: Step 9

▷ Insert a *Calculation* icon and double click on it.
▷ In the *Calculations* field type *pirSensor = 1*.
▷ Click *OK*.

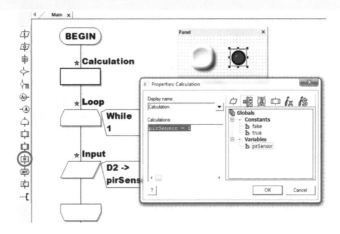

Figure 11.11. *Initializing a variable.*

Project 8: Step 10

▷ Insert a *Decision* icon and double on it.
▷ In the *If* field enter *pirSensor = 0*.
▷ Click *OK*.

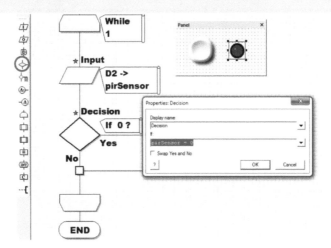

Figure 11.12. *Checking if the state of the input pin has changed.*

Project 8: Step 11

▷ Insert a *Component Macro* icon and double click on it.
▷ Select *LED(0)* and *LEDOff* in the *Component* and fields.
▷ Click *OK*.

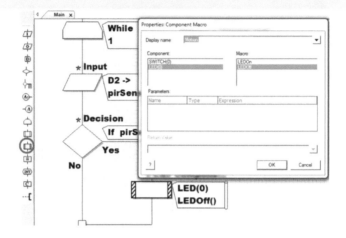

Figure 11.13. *Sending a low logic value to the output pin.*

Project 8: Step 12

▷ Insert another *Component Macro* icon on to the *No* end of the *Loop*.
▷ Select *LED(0)* and *LEDOn* in the *Component* and fields.
▷ Click *OK*.

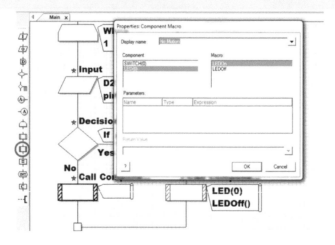

Figure 11.14. *Sending a high logic value to the output pin.*

Project 8: Step 13

▷ Save the program and click **Run** for simulation.

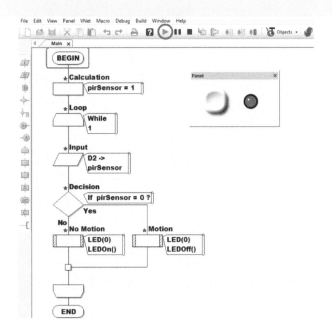

Figure 11.15. *Project is completed ready for simulation and downloading.*

11.5. Program Description

This program implements an intruder motion detection alarm. The sensor detects motion when its output terminal changes from high to low. The system repeatedly checks for when the sensor's signal will change from high to low. When this happens, it implies that motion is detected and the buzzer connected to the system sounds a warning alert. The listing below describes in details the program implementation steps;

▷ **Step 1:**
▷ Launch **Flowcode** and start a new program.
▷ **Step 2:**
   — Add a **Loop** to make the program runs repeatedly.
   — Add a **Switch** component to represent the **PIR** sensor as Flowcode does not have a **PIR** sensor in its component library.
▷ **Step 3:**
   — Configure the **Switch** component to **Pushbutton** type
   — Set its polarity to **Active High**.
▷ **Step 4:**
   — Connect the **Switch** component to pin **D2** of the microcontroller.
▷ **Step 5:**

— Add an **LED** component to represent the **Buzzer** as Flowcode does not have a **Buzzer** in its component library.

— Connect the **LED** to pin **B3**.

▷ **Step 6:**

— Read the state of the **Switch** through pin **D2**.

▷ **Step 7:**

— Declare a **Bool** type variable and name it **pirSensor**.

▷ **Step 8:**

— Store the **Switch** state in the declared variable.

▷ **Step 9:**

— Initialized the variable **pirSensor** to **one**.

▷ **Step 10:**

— Test whether **pirSensor** has changed state from **one** to **zero**.

▷ **Step 11:**

— If **pirSensor** changes from **one** to **zero** turn **on** the **Buzzer** (motion is detected).

▷ **Step 12:**

— Otherwise, turn **off** the **Buzzer**.

▷ **Step 13:**

— Simulate the program by clicking on the **Run** button and download it to the microcontroller on the PhasePlus development board.

Chapter 12

Project 9: LCD and Keypad interfacing to microcontroller

12.1. Objective

The purpose of this project is to demonstrate how to interface a character LCD and a matrix keypad to a microcontroller for building interactive mechatronics systems. Most mechatronics systems require some kind of user interface and data input means for human-machine interaction. For instance, a user can view numerical, textual, or graphical information on the screen of the system. Also, certain applications may require a user to enter data, such as password, selection of operation mode, changing system settings, etc. Therefore, this project aims to introduce the concept of building human-machine interactive systems.

Hardware

- ▷ Character-based LCD (16x2)
- ▷ Keypad (3x4)
- ▷ Connection wires
- ▷ PhasePlus PIC Development Board
- ▷ 10K resistor (optional)
- ▷ Rotary potentiometer (optional)

12.2. Input/Output Devices

The most basic input/output devices used in building mechatronics systems are the character-based LCD and matrix keypad. However, if the application does not require complex display, a 7-segment display can be used. On the other hand, if the application display requirement cannot be satisfied by a 7-segment display unit, like displaying some alphanumeric text, then LCD Module is always an alternative.

12.2.1. LCD

LCDs come in various sizes and for different requirements. In this project, a 16x2 character LCD model is used. It displays 2 lines of 16 characters. Other models are 16x4, 20x4, 8x1, 8x2 etc. The most commonly used character LCDs are based on Hitachi's HD44780 controller or those that are compatible with HD44580.

LCD Interface to Microcontroller

Most LCDs come with one row of 16 pins. The first 14 pins are used to control the display and the last two are for adjusting display brightness. Fig. 12.1 depicts a schematic of 16x2 character LCD, while Table 12.1 contains details of the LCD pins assignment.

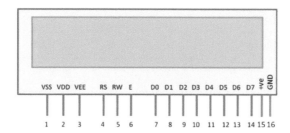

Figure 12.1. *Project 9- Character-based LCD module.*

Table 12.1. *Character LCD Pins Function*

Pin	Designation	Function
1	VSS	Ground (GND)
2	VDD	+5V
3	VEE	Connects to +5V and GND through 10K Pot for display contrast
4	RS	LOW for and HIGH for characters
5	RW	LOW for write and HIGH for read
6	E	Operation (data read/write) enable signal
7-14	D0-D14	Data pins
15	LED +ve	Back-light +ve
16	LED GND	Back-light GND

12.2.2. Keypad

Keypad enables data input aspect of Human-Machine Interface (HMI). It plays an important role in mechatronics systems where human-machine interaction or human input is needed to operate a system. Matrix keypad is the most commonly used keypad in mechatronics applications. It has a simple architecture and ease of interfacing to a microcontroller. This project utilizes a 4x3 matrix keypad.

Keypad Interface to Microcontroller

There are many techniques upon which a keypad can be interfaced to a microcontroller. However, the logic is the same in any of the methods. The basic logic is to make the columns serve as input and drive the rows making the output. This is procedure is called *keypad scanning.*

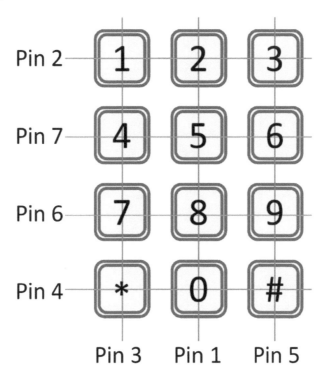

Figure 12.2. *Project 9- Matrix keypad layout.*

Figure 12.2 depicts a matrix keypad layout. The buttons on this particular keypad are setup in a 3 × 4 matrix format so only 7 pins are required to detect the pressing of 12 keys. For instance, when number 5 is pressed Pins 7 and 1 are connected, number 9 connects Pins 4 and 5, e.t.c. The row pins (3, 5, 6 & 7) are connected to the microcontroller through a resistor to 5V supply and to digital pins on the microcontroller. The resistors can range from 1K to 10K ohm.

12.3. Circuit Schematic

Figure 12.3 depicts the circuit schematic for this project. The seven terminals of the keypad connect to pins C4-C6 and D4-D7 of the microcontroller all via 10K pull-down resistor. While, the LCD terminals connect to the microcontroller as follows;

▷ Data lines (D1-D3) connect to PORTB pins RB0 - RB3.
▷ Enable, read/write and RS pins connect to B5, GND and B4 respectively.
▷ The LCD back light pins, A and K connect to VCC via a 220 resistor and GND.

Adding a potentiometer is optional if the LCD's back-light is not required.

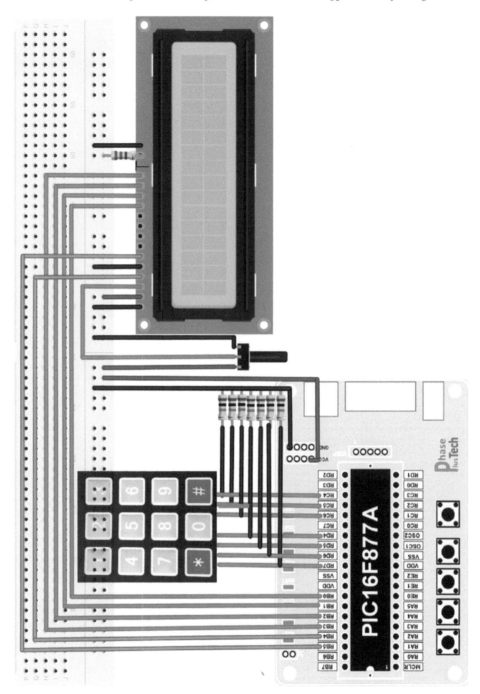

Figure 12.3. *Project 9 circuit schematic.*

12.4. Implementation Steps

Project 9: Step 1

▷ Launch *Flowcode*.
▷ Select *Create a new Flowcode*, click *OK* and select *16F877A*.
▷ Click *OK*.

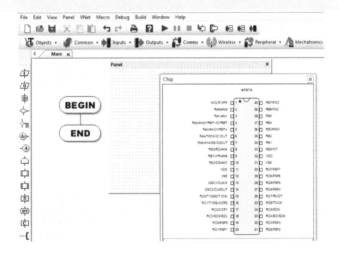

Figure 12.4. *An empty Flowcode environment.*

Project 9: Step 2

▷ Click on the *Output* tab and select *LCD*.
▷ Right click on the *LCD* select *Connections*.
▷ Double check the LCD is connected to *PORTB* and click *Done*.

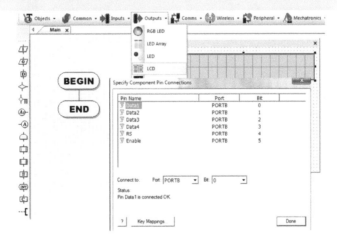

Figure 12.5. *Adding and connecting an LCD component to the output pins.*

Project 9: Step 3

▷ Click on the **Input** tab and select **Keypad**.
▷ Right click on the **Keypad** and select **Connections**.
▷ Highlight **Column1** and select **PORTD** from the **Port** menu.
▷ Then highlight **Row A** and select **PORTD** from the **Port** menu, click **Done**.

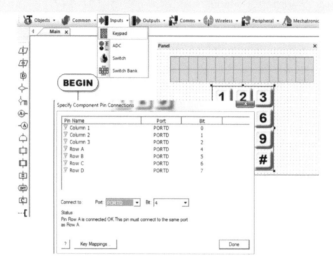

Figure 12.6. *Adding and connecting a keypad to the input pins.*

Project 9: Step 4

▷ Insert a **Component Macro** icon and double click on it.
▷ Select **LCD(0)** and **Start** in the **Component** and **Macro** fields.
▷ Click **OK**.

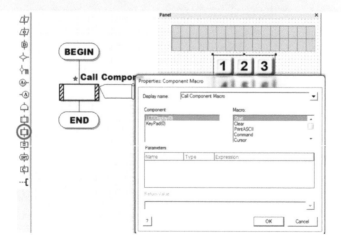

Figure 12.7. *Initializing the LCD component.*

Project 9: Step 5

▷ Insert a **Delay** icon and double click on it.
▷ Set the delay time to **100 milliseconds**.
▷ Click **OK**.

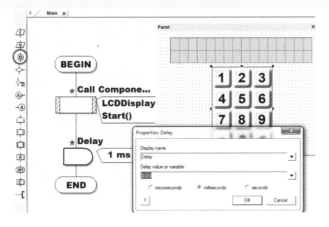

Figure 12.8. *Adding and configuring a delay.*

Project 9: Step 6

▷ Insert a **Loop** icon.
▷ Then insert a **Component Macro** icon and double click on it.
▷ Select **LCDDisplay(0)** and **Cursor** in the **Component** and **Macro** fields.
▷ In the **x** and **y** fields enter **0** and **0**, click **OK**.

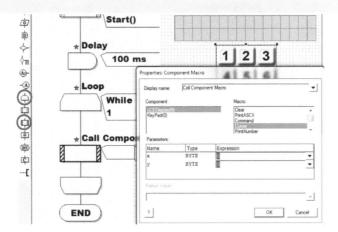

Figure 12.9. *Setting the LCD cursor position.*

Project 9: Step 7

▷ Insert a **Component Macro** icon and double click on it.
▷ Select **LCDDisplay(0)** and **Print ASCII** in the **Component** and **Macro** fields.
▷ Enter **"How old are you?"** in the **Expression** field and click **OK**.

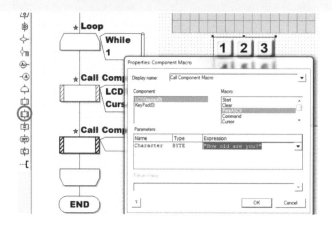

Figure 12.10. *Printing a string constant to the LCD.*

Project 9: Step 8

▷ Insert a **Component Macro** icon and double clcik on it.
▷ Select **Keypad(0)** in the **Component** field.
▷ In the **Macro field** select **GetKeypadNumber**.

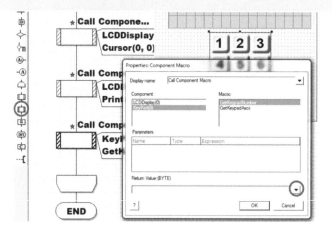

Figure 12.11. *Receiving a number from the keypad.*

Project 9: Step 9

▷ Click on the **arrow** right of **Return value** field to create a new variable.
▷ In the **Name of new variable** field enter **keyPress**.
▷ Click **OK**.

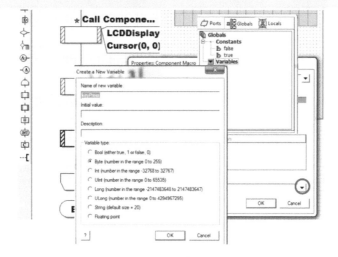

Figure 12.12. *Creating a new variable.*

Project 9: Step 10

▷ In the **Return value** field type **keyPress**.
▷ Click **OK**.

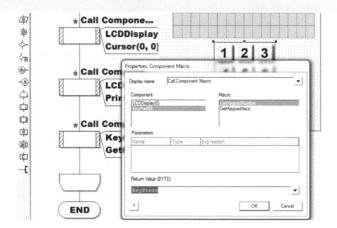

Figure 12.13. *Returning a variable to the main program.*

Project 9: Step 11

▷ Insert a **Decision** icon and double click on it.
▷ Enter **keyPress = 255** in the **If** field.
▷ Click **OK**.

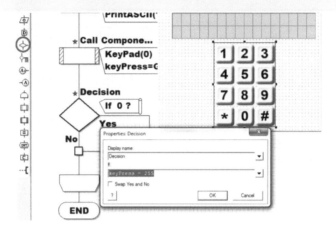

Figure 12.14. *Program flow direction conditional test.*

Project 9: Step 12

▷ Declare a **Connection** point above the **GetKeyPress Macro Call** icon.
▷ Insert a **Jump to Connection** point icon at **Yes** side of the **Decision** icon.

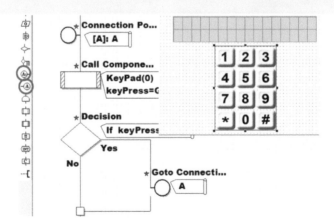

Figure 12.15. *Adding a jump to connection point for breaking.*

Project 9: Step 13

▷ Insert a **Calculation** icon and double click on it.
▷ Double click on **Variables**, create two variables **digitOne** and **digitTwo**.
▷ Click **OK**.

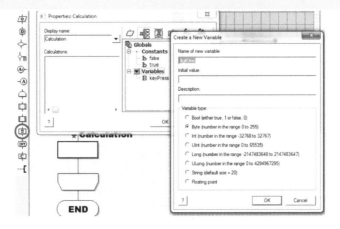

Figure 12.16. *Creating more variables.*

Project 9: Step 14

▷ In the **Calculations** field enter **digitOne = keyPress**.
▷ Click **OK**.

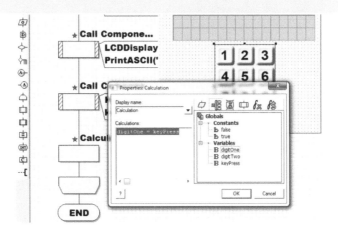

Figure 12.17. *Assigning value to a variable.*

Project 9: Step 15

▷ Insert a *Component Macro* icon and double click on it.
▷ Select *Keypad(0)* and *GetKeypadNumber* in the *Component* and Macro fields.
▷ Enter *keyPress* in the *Return value* field and click *OK*.

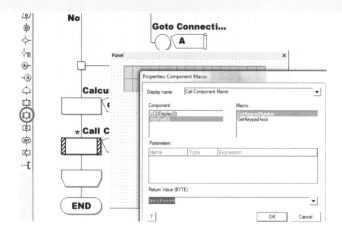

Figure 12.18. *Receiving a variable from keypad and returning the variable to the main program.*

Project 9: Step 16

▷ Insert a *Decision* icon and double click on it.
▷ Enter *keyPress = 255* in the *If* field.
▷ Click *OK*.

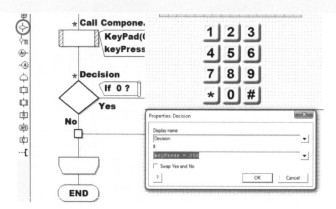

Figure 12.19. *Program flow direction conditional test.*

Project 9: Step 17

▷ Declare a **Connection** point above the **GetKeyPress Macro**.
▷ Insert a **Jump to Connection Point** icon at **Yes** side of the **Decision** icon.
▷ Double click on the **Jump to Connection Point** icon and **B:B** and click **OK**.

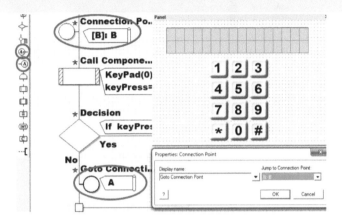

Figure 12.20. *Adding a jump to connection point for breaking from a loop.*

Project 9: Step 18

▷ Insert a **Component Macro** icon and double click on it.
▷ Select **LCD(0)** in the **Component** field and **Cursor** in the **Macro field**.
▷ Enter **0** in the **x** field **and** 1 in the **y** field, click **OK**.

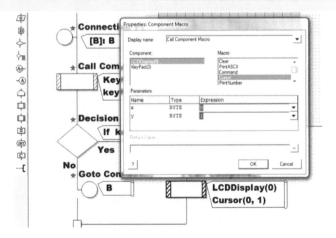

Figure 12.21. *Setting the LCD display cursor.*

Project 9: Step 19

▷ Insert a ***Component Macro*** icon and double click on it.
▷ Select ***LCD(0)*** in the ***Component*** field and ***PrintNumber*** in the ***Macro field***.
▷ In the ***Expression*** field type ***digitOne*** and click ***OK***.

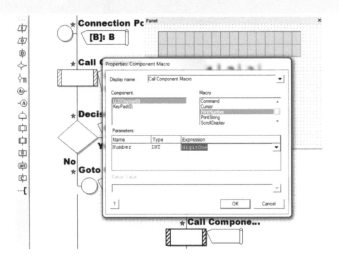

Figure 12.22. *Printing a variable of int type to the LCD.*

Project 9: Step 20

▷ Insert a ***Component Macro*** icon and double click on it.
▷ Select ***Keypad(0)*** and ***GetKeypadNumber*** in the ***Component*** and Macro fields.
▷ Enter ***keyPress*** in the ***Return value*** field and click ***OK***.

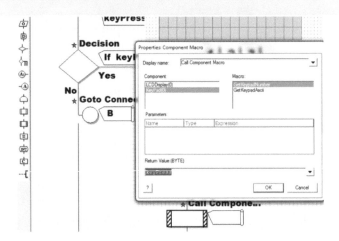

Figure 12.23. *Receiving a variable from keypad and returning the variable to the main program.*

Project 9: Step 21

▷ Insert a **Decision** icon and double click on it.
▷ Enter **keyPress = 255** in the **If** field.
▷ Click **OK**.

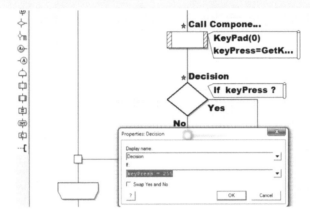

Figure 12.24. *Program flow direction conditional test.*

Project 9: Step 22

▷ Declare a **Connection** point above the **GetKeyPress Macro** icon.
▷ Insert a **Jump to Connection Point** icon at **Yes** end of the **Decision** icon.
▷ Double click on the **Jump to Connection** point icon and select **C:C**.
▷ Click **OK**.

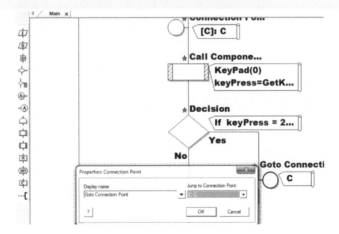

Figure 12.25. *Adding a jump to connection point for breaking from loop.*

Project 9: Step 23

▷ Insert a **Calculation** icon at the **No** end of the **Decision** and double click on it.
▷ In the Calculations field enter **digitTwo = keyPress**.
▷ Click **OK**.

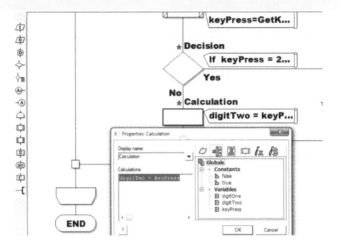

Figure 12.26. *Assigning value to a variable.*

Project 9: Step 24

▷ Insert a **Component Macro** icon and double click on it.
▷ Select **Keypad(0)** and **GetKeypadNumber** in the **Component** and Macro fields.
▷ Enter **keyPress** in the **Return value** field and click **OK**.

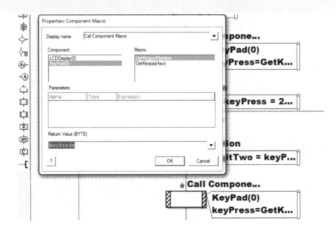

Figure 12.27. *Receiving a variable from keypad and returning the variable to the main program.*

Project 9: Step 25

▷ Insert a **Decision** icon and double click on it.
▷ Enter **keyPress = 255** in the **If** field.
▷ Click **OK**.

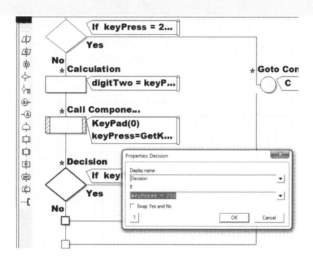

Figure 12.28. *Program flow direction conditional test.*

Project 9: Step 26

▷ Declare Connection point above the **GetKeyPress Macro** icon.
▷ Insert a **Jump to Connection Point** icon at **Yes** end of the **Decision** icon.
▷ Double click on the **Jump to Connection Point** icon and select **D:D**.
▷ Click **OK**.

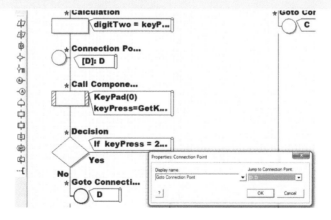

Figure 12.29. *Adding a jump to connection point for breaking from a loop.*

Project 9: Step 27

▷ Insert a **Component Macro** icon and double click on it.
▷ Select **LCD(0)** in the **Component** field and **PrintNumber** in the **Macro field**.
▷ In the **Expression** field enter **digitTwo** and click **OK**.

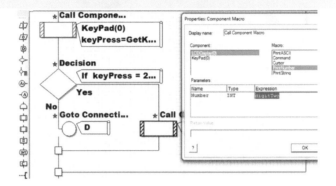

Figure 12.30. *Printing a variable of int type to the LCD.*

Project 9: Step 28

▷ Insert another **Component Macro** icon and double click on it.
▷ Select **LCD(0)** in the **Component** field and **PrintAscii** in the **Macro field**.
▷ In the **Expression** field type **"yrs"** and click **OK**.

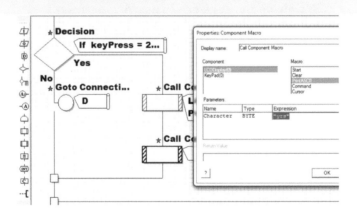

Figure 12.31. *Printing a string constant to the LCD.*

Project 9: Step 29

▷ Insert a **Delay** icon and double click on it.
▷ Set the delay time to **2 seconds**.
▷ Click **OK**.

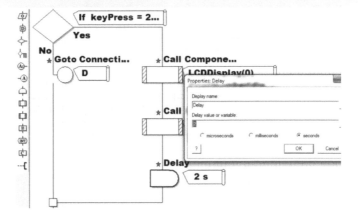

Figure 12.32. *Adding and configuring a delay function.*

Project 9: Step 30

▷ Insert a user-defined **Macro Call** icon and double click on it.
▷ Double click on the **Create a New Macro** to create a new macro.

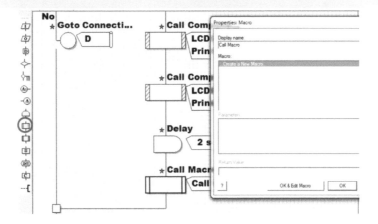

Figure 12.33. *Adding a user-defined macro.*

Project 9: Step 31

▷ In the **Name of new macro** field type **response**.
▷ Click **OK**.
▷ Then click **OK & Edit Macro** to edit the new macro.

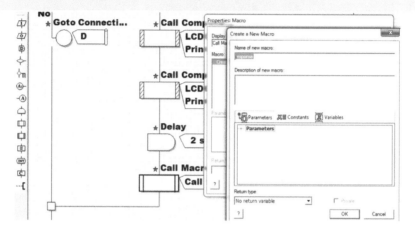

Figure 12.34. *Creating a new macro.*

Project 9: Step 32

▷ Insert a **Decision** icon and double click on it.
▷ Enter **digitOne = 1** in the **If** field.
▷ Click **OK**.

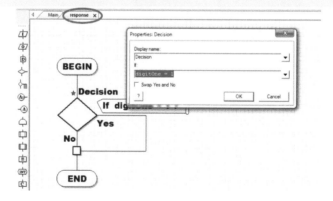

Figure 12.35. *Program flow direction conditional test.*

Project 9: Step 33

▷ Insert a **Component Macro** icon and double click on it.
▷ Select **LCD(0)** in the **Component** field.
▷ In the **Macro** field select **Clear** and click **OK**.

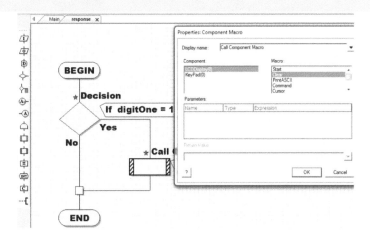

Figure 12.36. *Clearing the LCD screen.*

Project 9: Step 34

▷ Insert another **Component Macro** icon and double click on it.
▷ Select **LCD(0)** in the **Component** field and **PrintASCII** in the **Macro** field.
▷ Type **"Whao! too young"** in the **Expression** field and click **OK**.

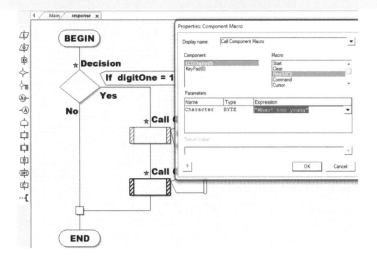

Figure 12.37. *Printing a string constant to the LCD.*

Project 9: Step 35

▷ Insert a **Delay** icon double click on it.
▷ Set the delay time to **4 seconds**.
▷ Click **OK**.

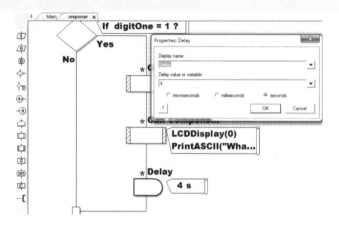

Figure 12.38. *Adding and configuring a delay function.*

Project 9: Step 36

▷ Insert a **Component Macro** icon and double click on it.
▷ Select **LCD(0)** in the **Component** field.
▷ In the **Macro** field select **Clear** and click **OK**.

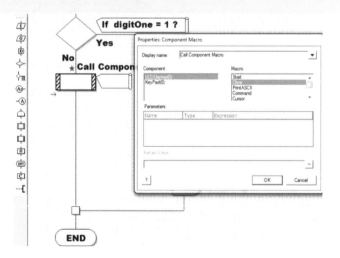

Figure 12.39. *Clearing the LCD screen.*

Project 9: Step 37

▷ Insert another **Component Macro** icon and double click on it.
▷ Select **LCD(0)** in the **Component** field and PrintAscii in the **Macro** field.
▷ Type *"a bit matured"* in the **Expression** field and click **OK**.

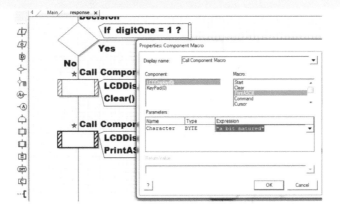

Figure 12.40. *Printing a string constant to the LCD.*

Project 9: Step 38

▷ Insert a **Delay** icon double click on it.
▷ Set the delay time to *4 seconds*.
▷ Click **OK**.

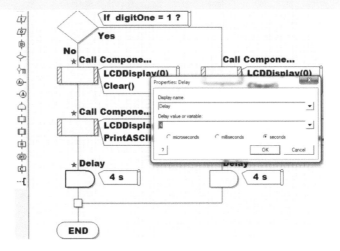

Figure 12.41. *Adding and configuring a delay function.*

Project 9: Step 39

▷ Figure 12.42 depicts the layout of the **response** macro.

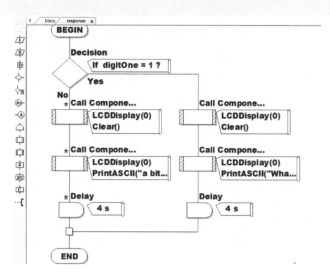

Figure 12.42. *Layout of the* **response** *macro.*

Project 9: Step 40

▷ Save the program and click **Run** for simulation.

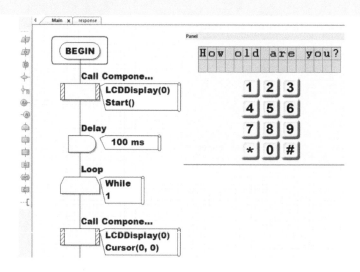

Figure 12.43. *Project is completed ready for simulation and downloading.*

12.5. Program Description

This program implements a human-machine interactive medium by interfacing character LCD and matrix keypad to a microcontroller. The program is intended for people above nine years old. Its prompts a user to input his age (a two digits number). If the user is a teenager, that is less than 20 years old, a message *"Whao! too young"* appears on the LCD. However, for a user above 20 years old, a message *"a bit matured"* pops up on the screen. The listing below described in details the program implementation steps:

▷ **Step 1:**
— Launch *Flowcode* and start a new program.

▷ **Step 2:**
— Add an *LCD* and connect it to to *PORTB*.

▷ **Step 3:**
— Add a *KeyPad* component.
— Connect the *KeyPad* terminals to the following pins of the microcontroller:
— Column 1 to D0
— Column 2 to D1
— Column 3 to D2
— Row A to D3
— Row B to D4
— Row C to D5

▷ **Step 4:**
— Initialized the *LCD*.

▷ **Step 5:**
— Wait for *100 milliseconds* to allow the completion of the *LCD* initialization process.

▷ **Step 6:**
— Add a *Loop* to make the program runs repeatedly.
— Set the *LCD* cursor to the beginning of the display.

▷ **Step 7:**
— Print the string *"How old are you?"* to the *LCD*.

▷ **Step 8:**
— Read the state of the *KeyPad* and store it in a *Byte* type variable.

▷ **Step 9:**
— Declare a new variable.
— Name the variable *keyPress*.

▷ **Step 10:**
— Return the variable *keyPress* to the *Main* program.

▷ **Step 11:**
— If the variable *keyPress* is equal to *255*, no key is pressed.

▷ **Step 12:**
— Declare a *Connection* point to keep the program looping until a key is pressed.

▷ **Step 13:**
— Declare a variable *digitOne* to store the numeric value of the pressed key.

▷ **Step 14:**
— Assign the variable *keyPress* to *digitOne*.

▷ **Step 15:**
— Read the state of the **KeyPad** again to confirm the pressed key has been released.

▷ **Step 16:**
— The pressed key is released when **keyPress** equals **255**, otherwise the key is still pressed.

▷ **Step 17:**
— Declare a **Connection** point to keep the program looping until the pressed key is released.

▷ **Step 18:**
— Set the **LCD Cursor** to position $x = 0$ and $y = 1$.

▷ **Step 19:**
— Print the variable **digitOne** to the **LCD** (which is the first digit of the user's age).

▷ **Step 20:**
— Read the state of the **KeyPad** and store it in the variable **keyPress**.

▷ **Step 21:**
— Test whether the pressed key has been pressed.

▷ **Step 22:**
— Declare a **Connection** point to keep the program looping until a key is pressed.

▷ **Step 23:**
— Declare a variable digitTwo and store the numeric value of the second key press.

▷ **Step 24:**
— Read the state of the **KeyPad** and store it in the variable **keyPress**.

▷ **Step 25:**
— Test if the pressed key has been released.

▷ **Step 26:**
— Declare a **Connection** point to keep the program looping until the pressed key is released.

▷ **Step 27:**
— Print the variable **digitTwo** to the **LCD** (which is the second digit of the user's age).

▷ **Step 28:**
— Print the string **"yrs"** to right of **digitTwo**.

▷ **Step 29:**
— Keep the display on for **two seconds** to allow the user views his entry.

▷ **Step 30:**
— Define a new **Macro**.

▷ **Step 31:**
— Name the new macro **response** and edit it.

▷ **Step 32:**
— In the macro **response**, test the first digit of user's entry.
— If the user's first entry is equal to **1**.

▷ **Step 33:**
— Prepare the **LCD** screen for display.

▷ **Step 34:**
— Print the string **"Whao! too young"** to the **LCD**.

▷ **Step 35:**

— Keep the string displayed in *step 34* for *four seconds*.

▷ **Step 36:**

— Prepare the *LCD* screen for another display.

▷ **Step 37:**

— However, if step 32 evaluates *False*, print the string *"a bit matured"*.

▷ **Step 38:**

— Keep the string displayed in *step 37* for *four seconds*.

▷ **Step 39:**

— A figure showing the layout of the macro *response*.

▷ **Step 40:**

— Simulate the program by clicking on the *Run* button and download it to the micro-controller on the PhasePlus development board.

Chapter 13

Project 10: Distance Sensing Device

13.1. Objective

The purpose of this project is to demonstrate how to build a digital distance sensing device using ultrasonic sensor and character LCD. The concept in this project can be employed in applications such as robot obstacle avoidance, vehicle reverse guidance system, automatic door system, among others.

Hardware

- Ultrasonic range sensor
- Character-based LCD (16x2)
- Connection wires
- Potentiometer (optional)
- 10K resistor (optional)

13.2. Ultrasonic Range Sensor Overview

Ultrasonic range finder is a transducer commonly used for motion detection, robotics and sensing applications. It uses a vibrating material (typically *Piezo* ceramic/composite) that vibrates between 20,000 - 40,000+ times a second (20-40+kHz) to create a vibrating motion of sound traveling at a certain distance. When sound wave travels towards an object it is either absorbed or deflected. In the case of ultrasonic sensor, when the ultrasonic sound travels towards a solid object such as a wall, it bounces back towards the source of the sound. In order to determine the distance of a solid object, the time frame of the echo is calculated. So, if the sound travels longer towards the wall, then the time frame of the echo is longer meaning longer distance. A faster echo equals shorter distance from the wall.

There are numerous brands of ultrasonic sensors in the market, most popular among them are SensComp, Parallax's PING and LV-MaxSonar among others. Many of these have excellent performance. However, this project will utilize the LV-MaxSonar ultrasonic range sensor.

13.2.1. Features of Maxbotix Ultrasonic Sensor

The LV-MaxSonar ultrasonic range finder sensor (Fig. 13.1) requires 2.5V - 5.5V to operate. It provides very short to long-range detection and ranging. The sensor detects objects from zero inch to 254 inches (6.45-meters) and provides sonar range information from six inches to up to 254 inches with an inch resolution. The sensor output formats are pulse width, analogue voltage and serial digital outputs.

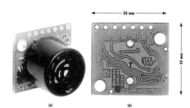

Figure 13.1. *LV-MaxSonar (a) Side view (Rear view).*

The sensor outputs analogue voltage with a scaling factor of (Vcc/512) per inch. A supply of 5V yields approximately 9.8mV/in. and 3.3V yields approximately 6.4mV/in. The output is buffered and corresponds to the most recent range data. The following relation converts the sensor output from inch to meter and scales it to the appropriate range:

$$Distance_{centimeters} = \frac{254}{1024} \times 2 \times Sensor_{Reading} \times 2.54 \qquad (13.1)$$

13.3. Circuit Schematic

Figure 13.2 depicts the circuit schematic for this project. The sensor's output terminal connects to the microcontroller analogue pin An0 with the power terminal connecting to +5V and GND. The listing below indicates how the LCD connects to the microcontroller;

▷ Data lines (D1-D3) connect to PORTB pins RB0 - RB3.
▷ Enable, read/write and RS pins connect to B5, GND and B4 respectively.
▷ The LCD back light pins, A and K connect to VCC via a 220 resistor and GND.

Note: Flowcode does not have an ultrasonic sensor in its components library. Therefore, an ADC component will be used to simulate the ultrasonic sensor. The PIC16F877A has a 10 bit ADC module with resolution of $2^{10} = 1023$. In which 0V represents 0 ADC value and 5V equals to 1023 ADC value.

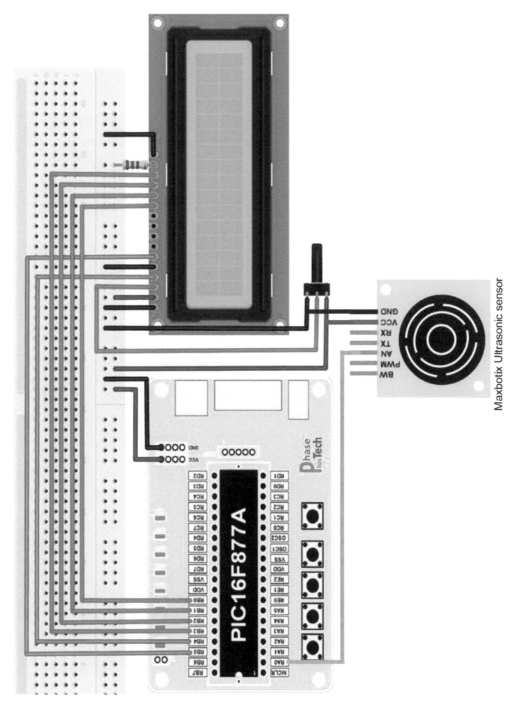

Figure 13.2. *Project 10 circuit schematics.*

13.4. Implementation Steps

Project 10: Step 1

▷ Launch *Flowcode*
▷ Select *Create a new Flowcode*, click *OK* and select *16F877A*
▷ Click *OK*

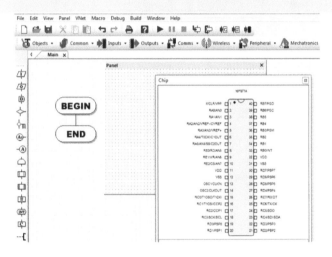

Figure 13.3. *An empty Flowcode environment.*

Project 10: Step 2

▷ Click on the *Input* tab and select *ADC*
▷ Right click on the *ADC* and select *Ext Properties*

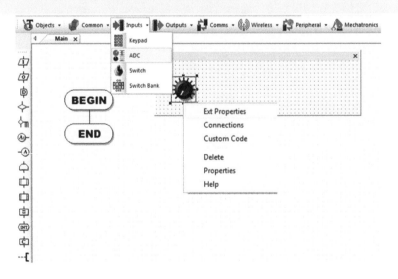

Figure 13.4. *Adding an ADC component.*

Project 10: Step 3

▷ From the **Type** menu select **Slider**
▷ Increase the **Slider** size to **145** by clicking on the arrow indicated in Fig. 13.5
▷ Click **OK**

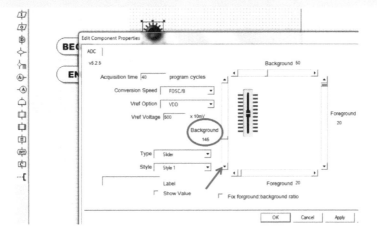

Figure 13.5. *Configuring the ADC component.*

Project 10: Step 4

▷ Right click on the **ADC** again and select **Connections**
▷ Double check **An0** is selected in the **ADC** menu
▷ Click **Done**

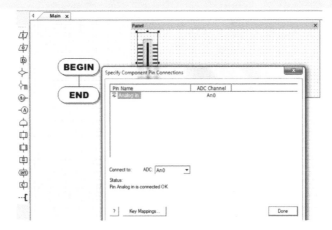

Figure 13.6. *Connecting ADC component to analogue input pin.*

Project 10: Step 5

▷ Click on the **Output** tab and select **LCD**
▷ Right click on the **LCD** and select **Connection**
▷ Double check the **LCD** is connected to **PORTB** as shown in Fig. 13.7
▷ Click **Done**

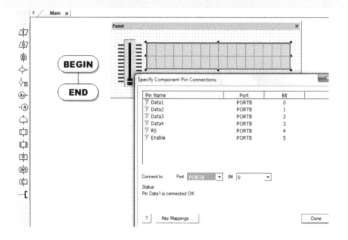

Figure 13.7. *Adding an LCD and connecting it to PORTB.*

Project 10: Step 6

▷ Insert a **Component Macro** icon and double click on it
▷ In the **Component** field select **LCDDisplay(0)**
▷ In the **Macro** field select **Start** and click **OK**

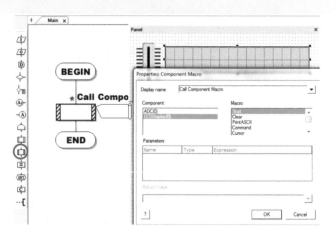

Figure 13.8. *Initializing the LCD.*

Project 10: Step 7

▷ Insert a *Loop* icon, a *Component Macro* and double click on it
▷ Select *ADC(0)* and *ReadAsInt* in the *Component* and *Macro* fields
▷ Double click on the *arrow* right of *Return Value* field

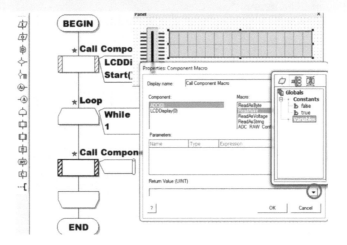

Figure 13.9. *Adding a loop and reading an int value from an analogue device.*

Project 10: Step 8

▷ Double click on *Variables*
▷ Enter *sensorValue* in the *Name of new variable* field
▷ Select *ULong* under *Variable type* and click *OK*

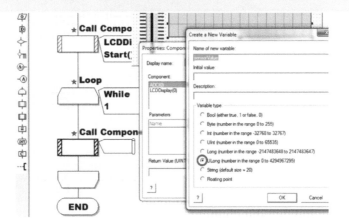

Figure 13.10. *Creating a new variable.*

Project 10: Step 9

▷ In the **Return Value** field enter *sensorValue*
▷ Click **OK**

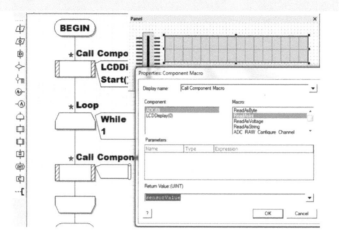

Figure 13.11. *Returning a variable to the Main program.*

Project 10: Step 10

▷ Insert a **Delay** icon and double click on it
▷ Set the delay time to **100 milliseconds**
▷ Click **OK**

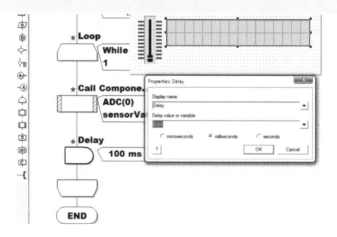

Figure 13.12. *Adding and configuring a delay.*

Project 10: Step 11

▷ Insert a *Calculation* icon and double click on it
▷ Double click on *Variables* and create a *ULong* type variable
▷ Enter *distance_inch* in the *Name of new variable* field and click *OK*

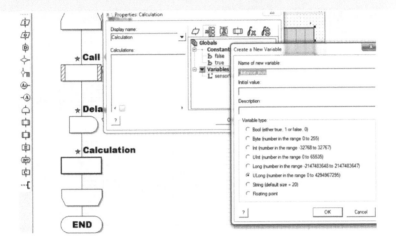

Figure 13.13. *Creating a ULong type variable.*

Project 10: Step 12

▷ Create another variable name *distance_meter*
▷ Select *ULong* under *Variable type*
▷ Click *OK*

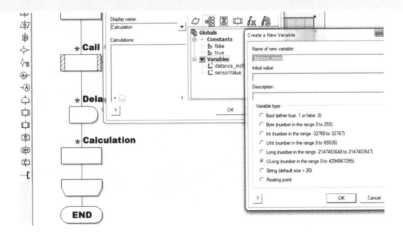

Figure 13.14. *Creating another ULong type variable.*

Project 10: Step 13

▷ In the **Calculations** field type:
— **distance_inch** $= (254.0/1024.0) * 2.0 * sensorValue$
— **distance_centimetre** $= (254.0/1024.0) * 2.0 * sensorValue$
▷ Click **OK**

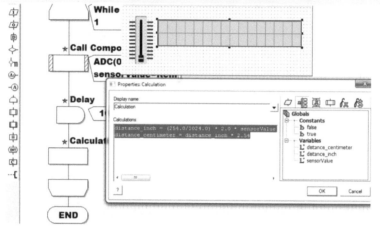

Figure 13.15. *Evaluating variables.*

Project 10: Step 14

▷ Insert a **Component Macro** icon and double click on it
▷ In the **Component** field select **LCDDsiplay(0)**
▷ In the **Macro** field select **Clear** and click **OK**

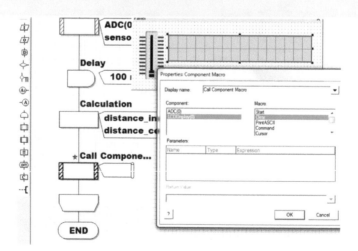

Figure 13.16. *Clearing the LCD display.*

Project 10: Step 15

▷ Insert a **Component** Macro icon and double click on it
▷ Select **LCDDisplay(0)** and **Cursor** in the **Component** and **Macro** fields
▷ In the **x** and **y** fields enter **0** and **0**, click **OK**

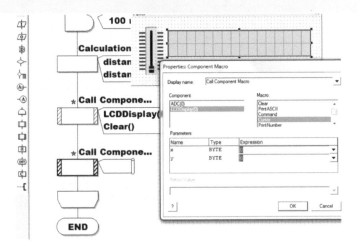

Figure 13.17. *Setting the LCD cursor position.*

Project 10: Step 16

▷ Insert another **Component Macro** icon and double click on it
▷ Select **LCDDisplay(0)** and **PrintNumber** in the **Component** and **Macro** fields
▷ Enter **distance_ centimetre** in the **Expression** field and click **OK**

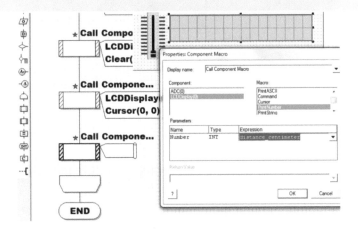

Figure 13.18. *Printing an **int** type variable to the LCD.*

Project 10: Step 17

▷ Insert a **Component** Macro icon and double click on it
▷ Select **LCDDisplay(0)** and **Cursor** in the **Component** and **Macro** fields
▷ In the x and y fields enter **4** and **0**, click **OK**

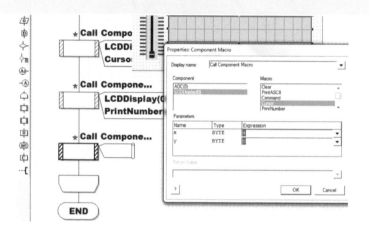

Figure 13.19. *LCD's cursor positioning.*

Project 10: Step 18

▷ Insert another **Component Macro** icon and double click on it
▷ Select **LCDDsiplay(0)** and **PrintNumber** in the **Component** and **Macro** fields
▷ Type *"cm"* in the **Expression** field and click **OK**

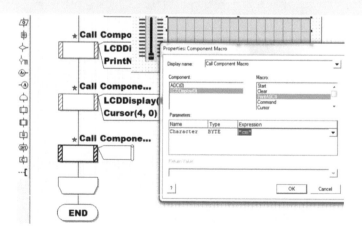

Figure 13.20. *Printing a string constant to the LCD.*

Project 10: Step 19

▷ Insert a **Delay** icon and double click on it
▷ Set the delay time to **2 seconds**
▷ Click **OK**

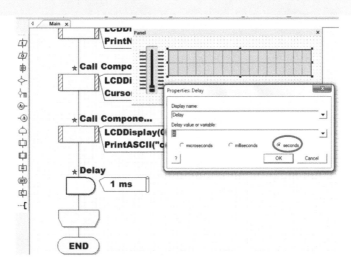

Figure 13.21. *Adding and configuring a delay.*

Project 10: Step 20

▷ Save the program and click **Run** to simulate it

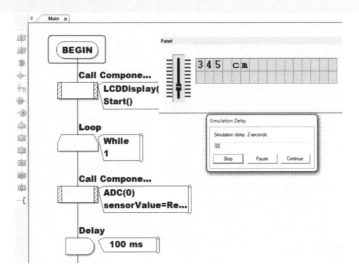

Figure 13.22. *Program completed, ready for simulation and downloading.*

13.5. Program Description

This project implements a digital distance sensing device using an ultrasonic sensor. The sensor transmits sound wave and listens to receive the reflection of the transmitted waves. If no reflection is received, that means there is no any object within the sensor's range (6.5m). However, if there is an object in the sensor's range, the object's distance is computed and displayed on the LCD. The microcontroller reads the sensor signal pin through one of its analogue pins, and then carries out an analogue to digital conversion before evaluating the object's distance in centimetre. Below are the detailed descriptions of the implementation steps;

▷ **Step 1:**
— Launch **Flowcode** and start a new program.

▷ **Step 2:**
— Add an **ADC** component to represent the ultrasonic sensor as **Flowcode** does not have an ultrasonic sensor in its component library.

▷ **Step 3:**
— Select a slider type **ADC** and increase its size to **145**.

▷ **Step 4:**
— Connect the **ADC** component to pin **An0** of the microcontroller.

▷ **Step 5:**
— Add an **LCD** component and connect it to **PORTB** as shown in Fig. 13.7.

▷ **Step 6:**
— Initialized the **LCD** component.

▷ **Step 7:**
— Add a **Loop** to make the program runs repeatedly and read the sensors output terminal as an **int** variable

▷ **Step 8:**
— Declare a variable **sensorValue** of **ULong** type and assign it to the value read in step 7.

▷ **Step 9:**
— Return the variable **sensorValue** to the **Main** program.

▷ **Step 10:**
— Slow the program for **100 milliseconds** to allow the analogue-digital conversion completes.

▷ **Step 11:**
— Declare a variable **distance_inch** of **ULong** type.

▷ **Step 12:**
— Declare another variable **distance_centimetre** of **ULong** type.

▷ **Step 13:**
— Evaluate the variables **distance_inch** and **distance_centimetre** form variable **sensorValue**.

▷ **Step 14:**
— Clear the **LCD** display.

▷ **Step 15:**
— Set the **LCD Cursor** to position $x = 0$ and $y = 0$.

▷ **Step 16:**
   — Print the variable *distance_centimetre* to the **LCD**.

▷ **Step 17:**
   — Set the **LCD Cursor** to position $x = 4$ and $y = 0$.

▷ **Step 18:**
   — Print the string constant *"cm"* to the **LCD**

▷ **Step 19:**
   — Slow down the program by *2 seconds* in every cycle.

▷ **Step 20:**
   — Simulate the program by clicking on the **Run** button and download it to the micro-controller on the PhasePlus development board.

Chapter 14

Project 11: Obstacle detection - Infrared (IR) Sensor

14.1. Objective

The purpose of this project is to demonstrate how to interface an IR sensor to a microcontroller for obstacle detection applications. The concept in this project can be extended to building mechatronics systems such as speed measurement for objects moving at very high speeds, tachometers, proximity sensing among others.

14.2. Infrared (IR) Sensor Overview

An infrared sensor is an electronic device that emits and/or detects infrared radiation in order to sense some aspects of its surroundings. Infrared sensors can measure the heat of an object, as well as detect motion. Many of these types of sensors only measure infrared radiation, rather than emitting it, and thus are known as passive infrared (PIR) sensors(see Project 8).

14.2.1. IR Detector

IR detectors are devices specially designed for modulated Infrared light, not suitable at detecting visible light. They have a demodulator inside that looks for modulated IR between 38 - 56kHz. If an IR LED is lit, it will not be detected by an IR detector. The LED has to be pulse width modulated (PWM), i.e blinking at the detector's frequency. IR detector outputs a digital signal, either detecting the modulated frequency say 38kHz IR signal and outputs **Low** (0V) or detecting nothing and outputs **High** (5V).

Hardware Required

- ▷ TSOP11 IR Receiver Module
- ▷ TSFF5410 IR Emitting Diode
- ▷ Red LED
- ▷ 220Ω resistor
- ▷ Connection wires

14.3. IR Receiver Module - TSOP11

The TSOP11 IR receiver module, Fig. 14.1(b) is a miniaturized receiver that can be used in applications such as infrared remote control systems, proximity sensor, e.t.c. It consists of photo detector and preamplifier in one package. The receiver has an internal filter for Pulse Code Modulation (PCM) frequency and improved shielding against electrical field disturbance. The demodulated output signal can directly be decoded by a microcontroller.

TSOP11 IR sensor is sensitive only to infrared light that is modulated in the 38kHz frequency. Meaning, the sensor detects only an IR light which turns on and off 38000 times in one second, filtering out any other frequency. There are other IR sensors that detect frequencies up to 56kHz. TSOP11 IR sensor outputs a HIGH signal when it does not detect a 38kHz modulated light and LOW when it detects the appropriate signal. The IR emitter is programmed to generate the 38kHz signal. Both the sensor and emitter are positioned side by side (Fig. 14.2) in such away when a 38kHz light is emitted, and there is an obstacle perpendicular to it, the emitted light will be deflected back and detected by the sensor.

14.4. IR Light Emitting Diode - TSFF5410

TSFF5410, Fig. 14.1(a) is an infrared, 870nm emitting diode with high radiant power and high speed, moulded in a clear, untinted plastic package. It can be used for infrared video data transmission, free air data transmission system or other related applications requiring high modulation frequencies or high data transmission rates.

Figure 14.1. *Project 11 - (a)* SFF5410 is an infrared, 870 nm emitting diode (b) TSOP11 IR receiver module.

14.5. Circuit Schematic

Figure 14.2 depicts the circuit schematic for this project. Positive terminal of the IR emitting diode connects to pin D7 of the microcontroller via a 220Ω current limiting resistor, while the negative terminals connects to GND. Positive and negative terminals of the IR receiver connect to +5V and GND. The sensing terminal of the receiver, pin 3 connects to Pin B0 of the microcontroller. The Piezo sounder terminals connect to pin D2 of the microcontroller and GND.

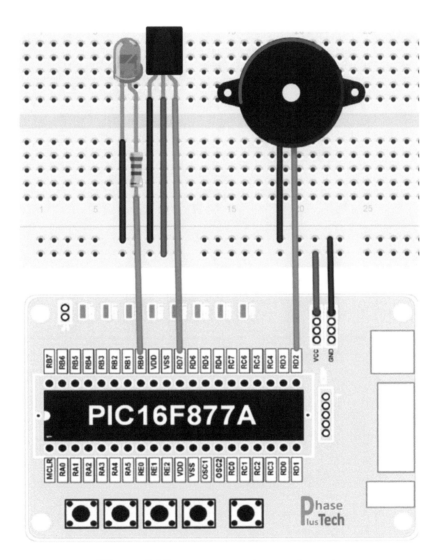

Figure 14.2. Project 11 circuit schematic.

14.6. Project Implementation Steps

Project 11: Step 1

▷ Launch *Flowcode*
▷ Select *Create a new Flowcode*, click *OK* and select *16F877A*
▷ Click *OK*

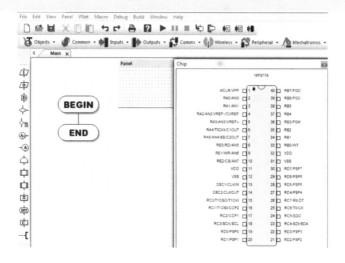

Figure 14.3. *An empty Flowcode project environment.*

Project 11: Step 2

▷ Insert a *Loop* icon.
▷ Click on *Output* tab and select *LED*.
▷ Right click on the *LED* and select *Ext Properties*.

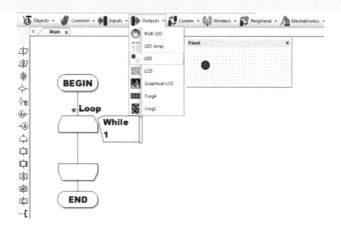

Figure 14.4. *Adding a loop and an LED component.*

Project 11: Step 3

▷ Under the **Color** menu select **Green**.
▷ Increase the **LED** size by drawing the horizan6tal slide to right.
▷ Click **OK**.

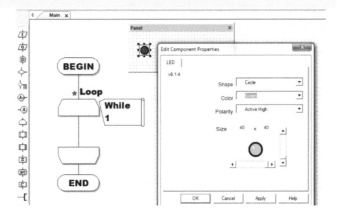

Figure 14.5. *LED resizing and colour selection.*

Project 11: Step 4

▷ Right click on the **LED** and select **Connections**.
▷ Select **PORTD** and **Bit 7**.
▷ Click **Done**.

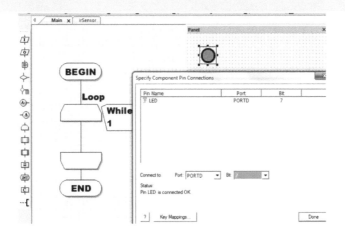

Figure 14.6. *Connecting the LED component to an output pin.*

Project 11: Step 5

▷ Insert a user-defined **Macro** icon and double click on it.
▷ Select **Create a New Macro**.
▷ Type **irSensor** in the **Name of new macro** field and click **OK**.

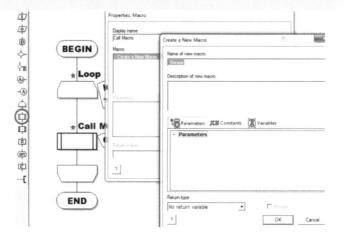

Figure 14.7. *Creating a macro.*

Project 11: Step 6

▷ Insert a **Calculation** icon and double click on it.
▷ Double click on **Variable** and type **counter** in the **Name of new variable** field.
▷ Select **Uint** under **Variable type** and click **OK**.

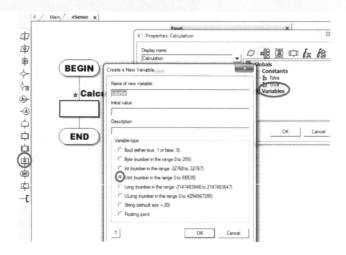

Figure 14.8. *Variable declaration.*

Project 11: Step 7

▷ In the *Calculations* field enter *counter = 0*.
▷ Click *OK*.

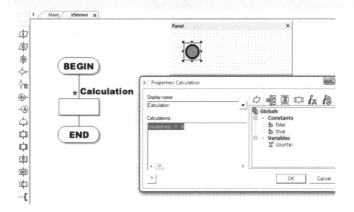

Figure 14.9. *Initializing a variable.*

Project 11: Step 8

▷ Insert a *Loop* icon and double click on it.
▷ In the *Loop while* field enter: *counter <= 384*.
▷ Click *OK*.

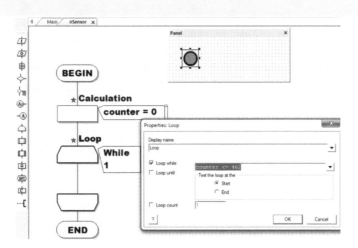

Figure 14.10. *Adding and configuring a loop.*

Project 11: Step 9

▷ Insert a **Component Macro** icon and double click on it.
▷ In the **Display name** field enter **ir_ emitter**.
▷ Select **LED(0)** and **LEDOn** and click **OK**.

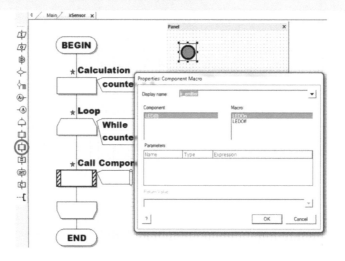

Figure 14.11. *Sending a high logic to the output pin.*

Project 11: Step 10

▷ Insert a **C code** *icon* and double click on it.
▷ In the **C code** text box enter **delay_ us(13);**.
▷ Click **OK**.

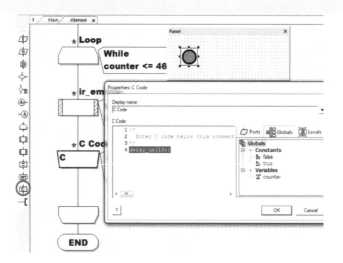

Figure 14.12. *Adding a microseconds delay.*

Project 11: Step 11

▷ Insert another **Component Macro** icon and double click on it.
▷ In the **Display name** field enter **ir_emitter**.
▷ Select **LED(0)** and **LEDOn** and click **OK**.

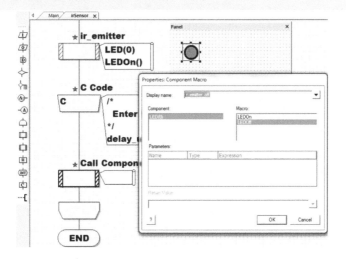

Figure 14.13. *Sending a low logic to the output pin.*

Project 11: Step 12

▷ Insert another **C code icon** and double click on it.
▷ In the **C code** text box enter **delay_us(13);**.
▷ Click **OK**

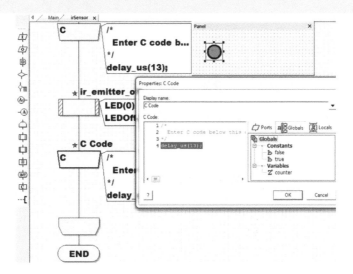

Figure 14.14. *Adding another microseconds delay.*

Project 11: Step 13

▷ Click on **Input** tab, select **Switch** and click on it.
▷ From **Type** menu select **Pushbutton**.
▷ Select **Momentary** from **Switch Operation** menu and click **OK**.

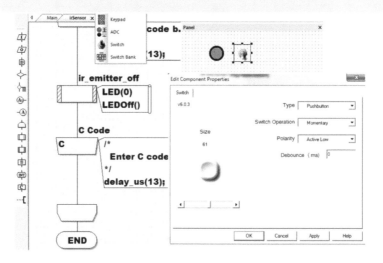

Figure 14.15. *Adding and configuring a switch component.*

Project 11: Step 14

▷ Insert an **Input** *icon* and double click on it.
▷ From the **Port** menu choose **PORTB** and select **Single Bit 0** button.
▷ Double click on **Variables**.

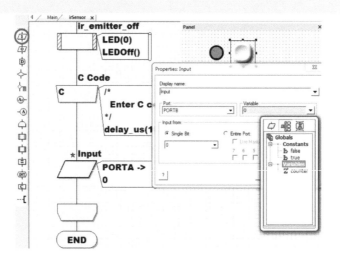

Figure 14.16. *Setting a pin for input.*

Project 11: Step 15

▷ In the **Name of variable field** enter: **irReceiver**.
▷ Under **Variable type** select **Bool**.
▷ Click **OK**.

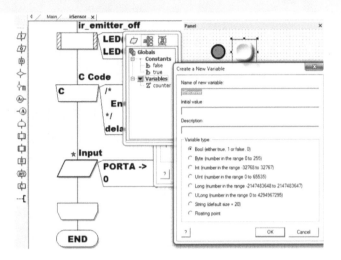

Figure 14.17. *Declaring a variable.*

Project 11: Step 16

▷ In the **Variable** field type **irReceiver**.
▷ Click **OK**.

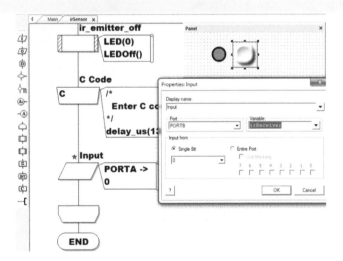

Figure 14.18. *Assigning a value to a variable.*

Project 11: Step 17

▷ Insert a **Decision** icon.
▷ Enter: **irReceiver == 0** in the **If** field.
▷ Click **OK**.

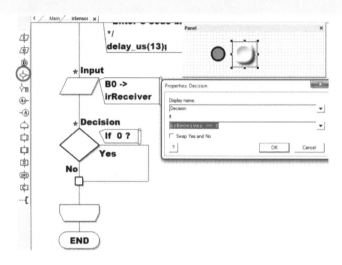

Figure 14.19. *Adding a decision for condition test.*

Project 11: Step 18

▷ Click on the **Output** tab and select **LED**.
▷ Right click on the **LED** and select **Connections**.
▷ Select **PORTD** and **Bit 2**, click **OK**.

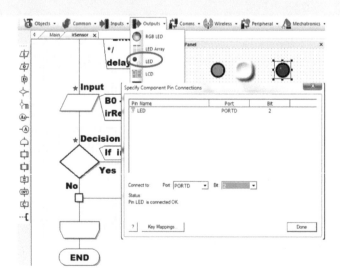

Figure 14.20. *Adding and connecting an LED to an output pin.*

Project 11: Step 19

▷ Insert a **Component Macro** icon and double click on it.
▷ In the **Display name** filed enter **Alert_ON**.
▷ Select **LED(1)** and **LEDOn**, click **OK**.

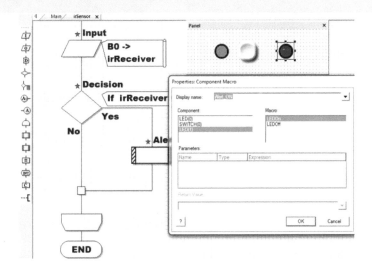

Figure 14.21. *Sending a high logic to the output pin.*

Project 11: Step 20

▷ Insert another **Component Macro** icon and double click on it.
▷ In the **Display name** filed enter **Alert_OFF**.
▷ Select **LED(1)** and **LEDOff**, click **OK**.

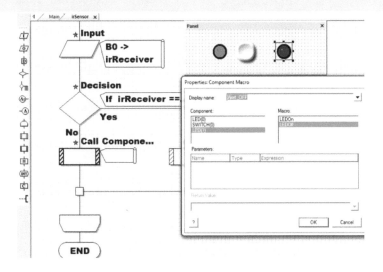

Figure 14.22. *Sending a low logic to the output pin.*

Project 11: Step 21

▷ Switch to the **Main** program by clicking on its tab.
▷ Insert a **Delay** icon and double click on it.
▷ Set the delay time to **100 milliseconds** and click **OK**.

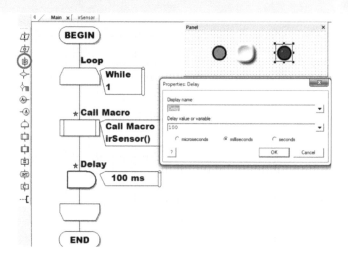

Figure 14.23. *Adding and configuring a delay.*

Project 11: Step 22

▷ Insert a **Calculation** item and double click on it.
▷ In the **Calculations** field enter: **counter = counter + 1**.
▷ Click **OK**.

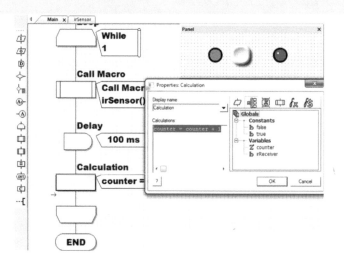

Figure 14.24. *Incrementing a counter variable.*

Project 11: Step 23

▷ Save the Program and click **Run** for simulation.

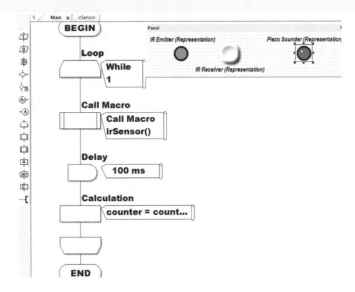

Figure 14.25. *Program is completed ready for simulation and downloading.*

14.7. Program Description

This program implements an obstacle detection system using an IR emitter and receiver. The IR emitter flashes a modulated IR light 38000 times in a second for 10 milliseconds and the IR receiver detects and demodulates the signal. The receiver's output terminal is always High (+5V) when it detects the emitted IR light, that is when nothing is obstructing the light. However, when the emitted IR light is not seen by the receiver its output terminal goes Low (0V), implying an obstacle is detected and the alarm attached to the system sounds. Although, in the simulation, a red LED was used to represent the Piezo sounder as Flowcode does have the sounder in its components library.

NOTE: The LED's on and off time is determined by dividing one second with 38000 to give 0.000026 seconds (0.026 milliseconds or 26 microseconds). The IR emitter (green LED in Flowcode simulation) is turned on for half of 26 microseconds and turned off for the other half resulting in a 50% duty cycle. Also, the 10 milliseconds is divided by 0.026 milliseconds to obtain the number of times the IR emitter will be flashed, which gives 384. The details of the program implementation steps are listed below.

▷ **Step 1:**
— Launch **Flowcode** and start a new program.
▷ **Step 2:**
— Add a loop to make the program runs repeatedly.

— Also add an **LED** to represent the IR emitter in the simulation as **Flowcode** does not have IR emitter in its component library.

▷ **Step 3:**

— Configure the **LED** by changing its colour from the default **red** to **green**.

— Increase the **LED** size for better appearance.

▷ **Step 4:**

— Connect the **LED** to *pin* **D7**.

▷ **Step 5:**

— Define a new macro and name it **irSensor**.

▷ **Step 6:**

— Declare a new variable of **integer** type and name it **counter**.

▷ **Step 7:**

— Initialize the variable **counter** to **zero**.

▷ **Step 8:**

— Add a loop and set the loop count to **384** times.

— Use the variable **counter** for storing the the loop count.

▷ **Step 9:**

— Send a high logic to the IR emitter LED to turn it **on**.

▷ **Step 10:**

— Keep it **on** for **13 microseconds**. Although, **Flowcode** in-built delay does not provide microseconds delay. Therefore, creating a microseconds delay involves embedding a **C code** within the **Flowcode** program. This is done using a **C code** icon.

▷ **Step 11:**

— Send a low logic to the IR emitter LED to turn it **off**.

▷ **Step 12:**

— Keep it **on** for **13 microseconds**.

▷ **Step 13:**

— Add a switch and configure it to; **Pushbutton**, **Momentary** and **Active Low**.

▷ **Step 14:**

— Set pin **B0** for data input.

▷ **Step 15:**

— Declare a **Bool** type variable and name it **irReceiver**.

▷ **Step 16:**

— Assign the value received on pin **B0** to the variable **irReceiver**

▷ **Step 17:**

— Monitor when the variable **irReceiver** will be zero.

▷ **Step 18:**

— Add another **LED** and connect it to pin **D2** to represent the **Piezo sounder**.

▷ **Step 19:**

— Send a high logic to the **Piezo sounder** (red LED) to sound an alarm when the step 17 evaluates **True**.

— This implies and obstacle is detected.

▷ **Step 20:**

— Otherwise, send a low logic to the **Piezo sounder** (red LED) turning **off** the alarm if step 17 evaluates **False**.

▷ **Step 21:**

— Switch to the **Main** program.

— Update the state of the variable **irReceiver** every **100 milliseconds**.

▷ **Step 22:**

— Increment the variable **counter** on every main program cycle.

▷ **Step 23:**

— Simulate the program by clicking on the **Run** button and download it to the microcontroller on the PhasePlus development board.

Chapter 15

Project 12: Analogue Temperature Sensor

15.1. Objective

The purpose of this project is to demonstrate how to interface an analogue temperature sensor to a microcontroller for applications requiring temperature monitoring and control such as oven controllers, remote temperature sensing, incubators and any other temperature sensing applications. A number of these sensors are available from various manufacturers. However, this project utilizes the LM35 analogue temperature sensor.

Hardware

- ▷ LM35 Analogue temperature sensor
- ▷ Character-based LCD (16x2)
- ▷ Piezo sounder
- ▷ Connection wires
- ▷ PhasePlus PIC16F877A development board
- ▷ Potentiometer (optional)
- ▷ 10K resistor (optional)

15.2. Analogue Temperature Sensor Overview

An analogue temperature sensor is a device that measures the ambient temperature. This sensor does not use a bimetallic strip, thermistor or mercury (like with other thermometers), rather, it uses solid-state technology to sense temperature. Using a solid state technique to measure temperature is based on the fact that as temperature increases, the voltage drop between the base and emitter (V_{BE}) of a diode also increases at a known rate. Therefore, an analogue signal that is directly proportional to temperature can easily be generated if the voltage is amplified. This sensor does not have moving parts, hence; it is precise, does not require calibration and works under varying environmental conditions. Again, it is inexpensive, does not wear out and interfaces easily to a microcontroller.

15.2.1. LM35 Centigrade Temperature Sensor

The LM35 temperature sensor depicted in Fig. 15.1, is a precision integrated-circuit temperature sensor whose output voltage is linearly proportional to the Celsius (Centigrade) temperature. It does not require any external calibration or trimming to provide typical accuracies of over its full -55 to $+150^0$C temperature range. The sensor's low output impedance, linear output, and precise inherent calibration make interfacing to a microcontroller easy. It can be used with single power supplies, or with polarized supplies. It draws only 60μA from its supply having very low self-heating, less than 0.1^0C in still air. There are several manufacturers of this popular part and each has LM35 sensor specifications, datasheets and other free LM35 downloads.

Figure 15.1. *LM35 Centigrade temperature sensor.*

The sensor output is linearly calibrated directly to degree Celsius (Centigrade) and operates on 4-30VDC with accuracy of roughly 0.50^0C. The following formula converts the sensor output to a temperature reading in degree Celsius;

$$Temperature = Sensor_{Reading} \times 100 \qquad (15.1)$$

15.3. Circuit Schematic

Circuit schematic for this project is shown in Fig. 15.2. The sensor's signal terminal connects to analogue pin An0 of the microcontroller and the power terminals connect to the +5V and GND. While, the Piezo sounder terminals connect to D2 and GND. The listing below indicates how the LCD connects to the microcontroller;

▷ Data lines (D1-D3) connect to PORTB pins RB0 - RB3.
▷ Enable, read/write and RS pins connect to B5, GND and B4 respectively.
▷ The LCD back light pins, A and K connect to VCC via a 220 resistor and GND.

However, Flowcode does not have the LM35 sensor in its components library. Therefore, an ADC component will be used to simulate the sensor.

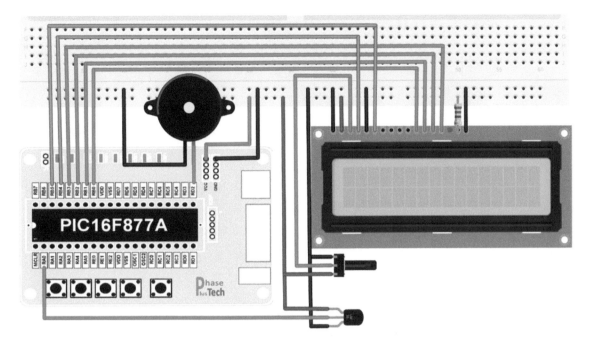

Figure 15.2. Project 12 circuit schematic.

15.4. Project Implementation Steps:

Project 12: Step 1

▷ Launch **Flowcode**.
▷ Select **Create a new Flowcode**, click **OK** and select **16F877A**.
▷ Click **OK**.

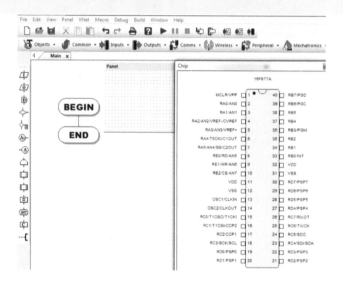

Figure 15.3. *An empty Flowcode project environment.*

Project 12: Step 2

▷ Click on the **Output** tab and select **LCD**.
▷ Insert a **Component Macro** icon and double click on it.
▷ Select **LCDDisplay(0)** and **Start** in the **Component** and **Macro** fields.
▷ Click **OK**.

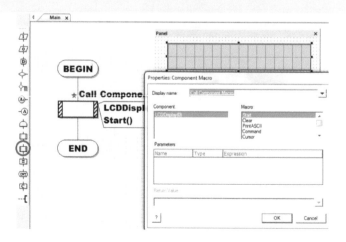

Figure 15.4. *Adding and initializing an LCD component..*

Project 12: Step 3

▷ Insert a **Loop** icon, click on the **Input** tab and select **ADC**.
▷ Right click on the **ADC** and select **Ext Properties**.
▷ From the **Size** menu select **Slider** and click **OK**.

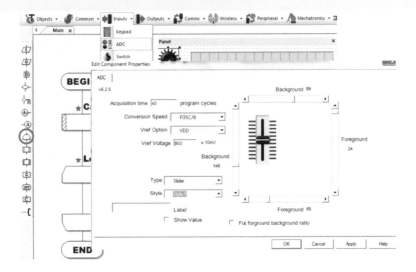

Figure 15.5. *Adding a Loop, an ADC device and configuring the ADC.*

Project 12: Step 4

▷ Insert a **Component Macro** icon and double click on it.
▷ Select **ADC(0)** and **ReadAsVoltage** in the **Component** and **Macro** fields.
▷ Click on the **arrow** at the right end of the **Return Value** field.

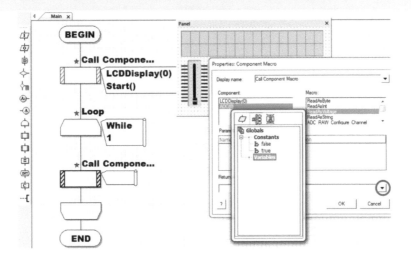

Figure 15.6. *Reading analogue signal from an analogue device.*

Project 12: Step 5

▷ Double click on *Variables* to create a new variable.
▷ In the *Name of new variable* field enter *sensorValue*.
▷ Under *Variable Type* select *Float* and click *OK*.

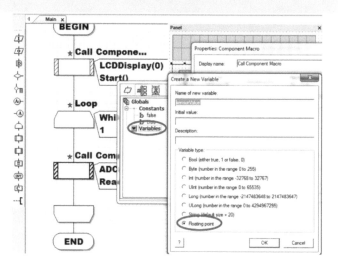

Figure 15.7. *Creating a float type variable.*

Project 12: Step 6

▷ Type *sensorValue* in the *Return value* field.
▷ Click *OK*.

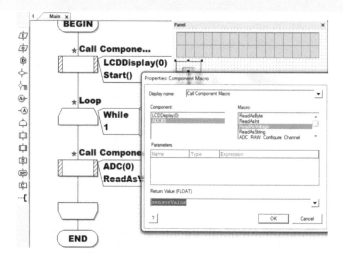

Figure 15.8. *Returning a variable to the main program.*

Project 12: Step 7

▷ Insert a **Calculation** icon and double click on it.
▷ Double click on **Variables** to create another variable of **Float** type.
▷ In the **Name of new variable** field enter **temp** and click **OK**.

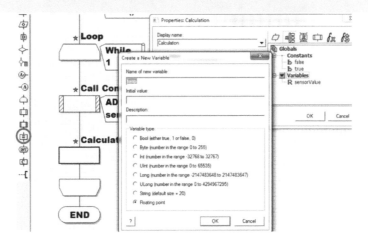

Figure 15.9. *Creating another float variable.*

Project 12: Step 8

▷ Double click on **Variables** again and create another variablev
▷ In the **Name of new variable** field enter **tempString[4]**.
▷ Under **Variable type** select **String** and click **OK**.

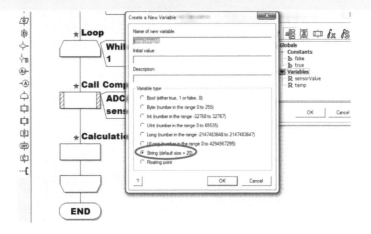

Figure 15.10. *Adding a loop and an LED component.*

Project 12: Step 9

▷ In the **Calculations** field enter the following;
— $temp = fmul(sensorValue; 100)$.
— $tempString = FloatToString\$(temp)$.
▷ Click **OK**.

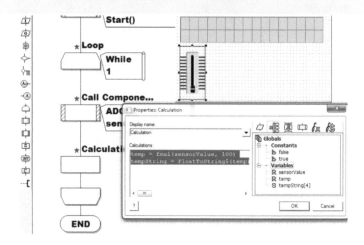

Figure 15.11. *Assigning value to variables.*

Project 12: Step 10

▷ Insert a **Component Macro** icon and double click on it.
▷ Select **LCDDisplay(0)** and **Cursor** in the **Component** and **Macro** fields.
▷ In the **x** and **y** fields enter **2** and **0**, click **OK**.

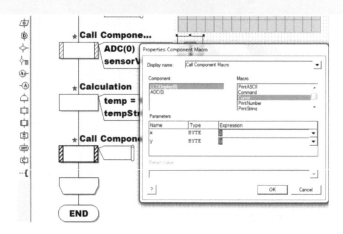

Figure 15.12. *Setting LCD display cursor*

Project 12: Step 11

▷ Insert another **Component Macro** icon and double click on it.
▷ Select **LCDDisplay(0)** and **PrintString** in the **Component** and **Macro** fields.
▷ Type **"Temperature"** in the **Expression** field and click **OK**.

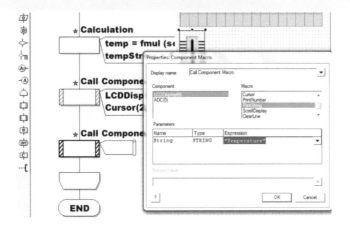

Figure 15.13. *Printing a string constant to LCD.*

Project 12: Step 12

▷ Insert a **Component** Macro icon and double click on it.
▷ Select **LCDDisplay(0)** and **Cursor** in the **Component** and **Macro** fields.
▷ In the **x** and **y** fields enter **4** and **1**, click **OK**.

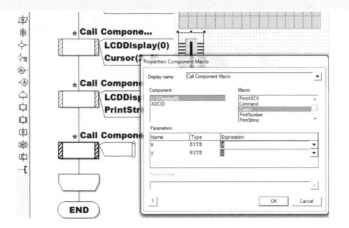

Figure 15.14. *Setting LCD display cursor.*

Project 12: Step 13

> ▷ Insert another ***Component Macro*** icon and double click on it.
> ▷ Select ***LCDDisplay(0)*** and ***PrintString*** in the ***Component*** and ***Macro*** fields.
> ▷ Enter ***tempString*** in the ***Expression*** field and click ***OK***.

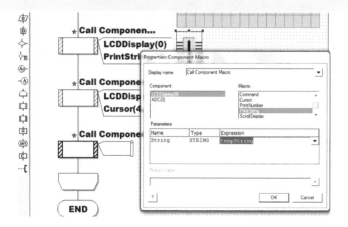

Figure 15.15. *Printing a string variable to LCD.*

Project 12: Step 14

> ▷ Insert a ***Component*** Macro icon and double click on it.
> ▷ Select ***LCDDisplay(0)*** and ***Cursor*** in the ***Component*** and ***Macro*** fields.
> ▷ In the ***x*** and ***y*** fields enter ***9*** and ***1***, click ***OK***.

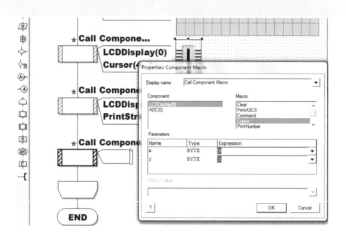

Figure 15.16. *Setting LCD display cursor.*

Project 12: Step 15

▷ Insert another **Component Macro** icon and double click on it.
▷ Select **LCDDisplay(0)** and **PrintString** in the **Component** and **Macro** fields.
▷ Enter **"C"** in the **Expression** field and click **OK**.

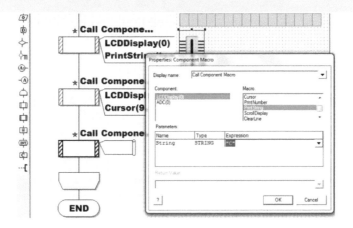

Figure 15.17. *Printing a string constant to LCD.*

Project 12: Step 16

▷ Insert a **Decision** icon and double click on it.
▷ Enter **temp > 40** in the **If** field.
▷ Click **OK**.

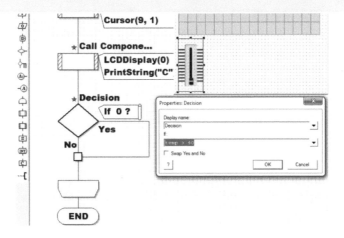

Figure 15.18. *Program flow direction conditional test.*

Project 12: Step 17

▷ Click on the *Output* tab and select *LED*.
▷ Right click on the *LED* and select *Connections*.
▷ Select *PORTD* and *Bits 2*, click *OK*.

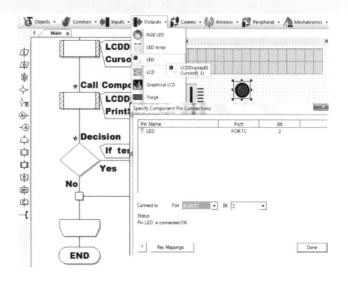

Figure 15.19. *Adding and connecting an LED to the output pin.*

Project 12: Step 18

▷ Insert a *Component Macro* icon and double click on it.
▷ In the *Display name* filed enter *Alert_ON*.
▷ Select *LED(0)* and *LEDOn* in the *Component* and *Macro* fields, click *OK*.

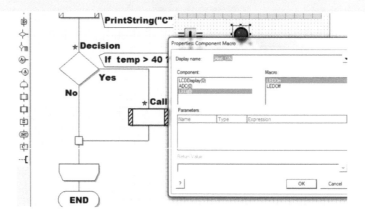

Figure 15.20. *Setting an output pin HIGH.*

Project 12: Step 19

▷ Insert a *Component Macro* icon and double click on it.
▷ In the *Display name* filed enter *Alert_OFF*.
▷ Select *LED(0)* and *LEDOff* in the *Component* and *Macro* fields, click *OK*.

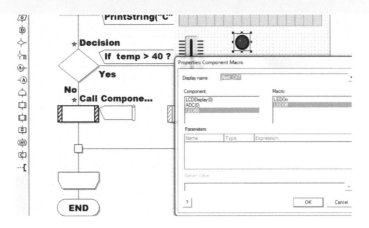

Figure 15.21. *Setting an output pin LOW.*

Project 12: Step 20

▷ Insert a *Delay* icon and double click on it.
▷ Set the delay time to *1 second*.
▷ Click *OK*.

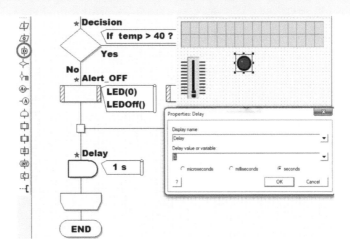

Figure 15.22. *Adding and configuring a delay.*

Project 12: Step 21

▷ Save the Program and click **Run** for simulation.

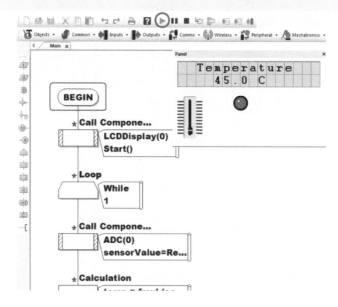

Figure 15.23. *Program is completed ready for simulation and downloading.*

15.5. Program Description

This project implements a temperature sensing and alerting system using an analogue temperature sensor. The sensor senses the ambient temperature and displays the value in degree Celsius to the LCD. However, anytime the temperature exceeds 40^0 an alarm is sounded to indicate high temperature. The sensor has an output voltage that is linearly proportional to the centigrade temperature. Therefore, the sensing terminal of the sensor is read through the ADC of the microcontroller and converted to temperature in degree Celsius. ,. However, for the simulation, an ADC device is used to represent the sensor as Flowcode does not have an analogue temperature sensor in its components library. The details of the program implementation steps are listed below.

▷ Launch **Flowcode** and start a new program.
▷ **Step 2:**
  — Add an **LCD** and initialized it.
▷ **Step 3:**
  — Add a loop to make the program runs repeatedly.
  — Also add an **ADC** component to represent the analogue temperature.
  — Connect the **ADC** component to pin **An0** of the microcontroller.
▷ **Step 4:**
  — Read the voltage level at the sensor's output terminal.

▷ **Step 5:**
— Declare a new variable of *float* type,
— Name the variable *sensorValue.*
— Store the voltage level at the sensor's terminal into the variable *sensorValue.*

▷ **Step 6:**
— Return the variable *sensorValue* to the *Main* program.

▷ **Step 7:**
— Declare a new variable of *float* type.
— Name the variable *temp*.

▷ **Step 8:**
— Declare another variable of *string* type.
— Name the variable *tempString*.

▷ **Step 9:**
— Evaluate *temp* and *tempString* from *sensorValue*.

▷ **Step 10:**
— Set the *LCD Cursor* to position $x = 2$ and $y = 0$.

▷ **Step 11:**
— Print the string constant *"Temperature"* to the *LCD*.

▷ **Step 12:**
— Set the *LCD Cursor* to position $x = 4$ and $y = 1$.

▷ **Step 13:**
— Print the string variable *tempString* to the *LCD*.

▷ **Step 14:**
— Set *LCD Cursor* to position $x = 9$ and $y = 1$.

▷ **Step 15:**
— Print the string constant *"C"* to the *LCD*

▷ **Step 16:**
— Ensure that the temperature does not exceed 40^0C.

▷ **Step 17:**
— Add an *LED* component to represent the *Piezo sounder* (for Flowcode simulation).
— Connect the LED to pin *D2*

▷ **Step 18:**
— Sound an alarm if the temperature exceeds 40^0C.

▷ **Step 19:**
— Otherwise, turn *off* the alarm.

▷ **Step 20:**
— Update the temperature state after every *100 milliseconds*.

▷ **Step 21:**
— Simulate the program by clicking on the *Run* button and download it to the microcontroller on the PhasePlus development board.

Chapter 16

Project 13: Digital Temperature Sensor

16.1. Objective

The purpose of this project is to demonstrate how to interface a digital temperature sensor to a microcontroller. Digital temperature sensors are more accurate than their analogue counterparts. These sensors are used mostly in applications requiring precision temperature sensing and control such as in medical instrumentation and test equipment. There are numerous types of digital temperature sensors featuring different serial interfaces for communication with microcontrollers or other peripherals. However, this project utilizes the TMP102 manufactured by Texas Instruments.

Hardware

- TMP102 digital temperature sensor
- Character-based LCD (16x2)
- 3.3V voltage regulator
- Piezo sounder
- Connection wires
- PhasePlus PIC16F877A development board
- Potentiometer (optional)
- 1x10K resistor (optional)

16.2. Digital Temperature Sensor Overview

A digital temperature sensor is a device which measures temperature and outputs precise digital representation of the measured quantity. It does not require external signal conditioning or conversion to a digital value. These sensors work on the principle that when two identical transistors are operated at a constant ratio of collector current densities, the difference in their base-emitter voltage is proportional to absolute temperature. Although, there are other classes of the sensors that work based on the behaviour of the base-emitter voltage, V_{BE}, of the diode-connected to the transistor, which varies inversely with its temperature. The rate at which this voltage varies is a very consistent $-2mV/°C$. However, the absolute value of V_{BE} varies from transistor to transistor.

16.2.1. TMP102 Digital Temperature Sensor

The temperature sensor TMP102 shown in Fig. 16.1, is a digital sensor operating with a voltage of between 1.4 to 3.6VDC. Communication with the TMP102 is achieved through a two-wire serial interface (I2C). The sensor is capable of reading temperatures to a resolution of 0.00625^0C changes between -25 and $+85^0C$, with accuracy of 0.5^0C, consuming only 10μA. On the overall, the sensor is specified for operation over a temperature range of -40 to +125°C.

Figure 16.1. *Sparkun breakout board for TMP102 digital temperature sensor.*

The sensor has five terminals; serial data (SDA), serial clock (SCL), power (3.3VDC and GND), address pin (ADD0) and alert pin (Alt). SDA is for data communication and SCL provides the communication timing. Pin ADDo is used to change the sensor's address. Connecting the pin to GND sets the sensor on address 72 (0x48 hex), while connecting it to 3.3VDC sets the address to 73 (0×49 hex). The pin is useful when more than one of this sensor is used. The alert pin can be left unconnected. The following relation converts the sensor's output to a temperature reading in degree Celsius;

$$Temperature = Sensor_{Reading} \times 0.0625 \quad\quad\quad (16.1)$$

16.2.2. I2C Serial Interface Overview

I2C (pronounced I-squared-C) created by Philips Semiconductors and commonly written as 'I2C' stands for Inter-Integrated Circuit and allows communication of data between I2C devices over two wires. It sends information serially using one line for data (SDA) and one for clock (SCL). Although, there is a need for power, +5V and GND. The devices on the I2C bus are either masters or slaves. The master is always the device that drives the SCL clock line. The slaves are devices that respond to the master. A slave cannot initiate a transfer over the I2C bus; only a master can do that. There can be multiple slaves on the I2C bus with normally a singe master.

16.2.3. The I2C Basic Command Sequence

A basic master to slave read sequence for I2C follows the following order:

1. Send the START bit.
2. Send the slave address.
3. Send the Read.

4. Wait for an acknowledge bit.
5. Receive the data byte (8 bits).
6. Send acknowledge bit.
7. Send the STOP bit.

16.3. Circuit Schematic

The circuit schematic for this project is shown in Fig. 15.2. The two terminals of the sensor, SDA and SCL connect to pins C3 and C4 of the microcontroller. The sensor's power terminals connect to the output of the 3.3V regulator and GND. While, the Piezo sounder pins connect to pin D2 of the microcontroller and GND. The listing below indicates how the LCD connects to the microcontroller;

▷ Data lines (D1-D3) connect to PORTB pins RB0 - RB3.
▷ Enable, read/write and RS pins connect to B5, GND and B4 respectively.
▷ The LCD back light pins, A and K connect to VCC via a 220 resistor and GND.

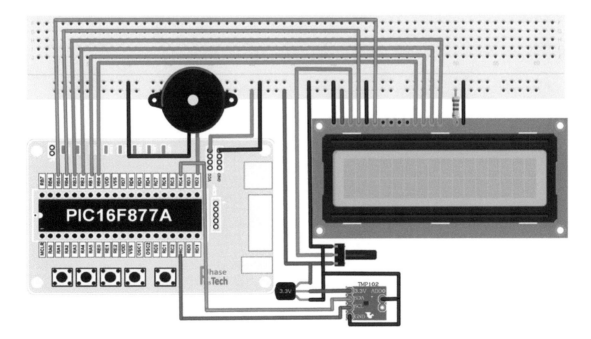

Figure 16.2. Project 13 circuit schematic.

16.4. Implementation Steps:

Project 13: Step 1

▷ Launch *Flowcode*.
▷ Select *Create a new Flowcode*, click *OK* and select *16F877A*.
▷ Click *OK*.

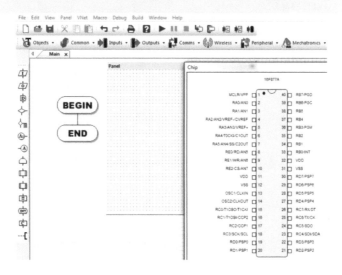

Figure 16.3. *An empty Flowcode project environment.*

Project 13: Step 2

▷ Click on the *Output* tab and select *LCD*.
▷ Right click on the *LCD* and select *Connections*.
▷ Double check the *LCD* is connected as shown in Fig. 16.4 and click *OK*.

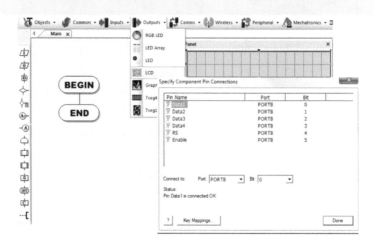

Figure 16.4. *Adding and initializing an LCD component..*

Project 13: Step 3

▷ Insert a **Component Macro** icon and double click on it.
▷ Select **LCDDisplay(0)** and **Start** in the **Component** and **Macro** fields.
▷ Click **OK**.

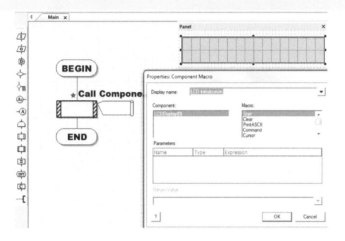

Figure 16.5. *Initializing the LCD display component.*

Project 13: Step 4

▷ Click on the **Comms** tab and select **I2C Master**.

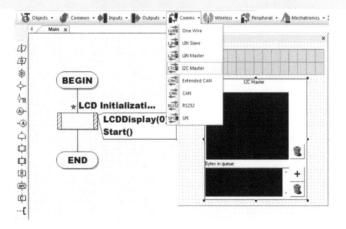

Figure 16.6. *Adding an I2C device.*

Project 13: Step 5

▷ Insert a **Component Macro** icon and double click on it.
▷ Select **I2C_ Master(0)** and **MI2C_ Init** in the **Component** and **Macro** fields.
▷ Click **OK**.

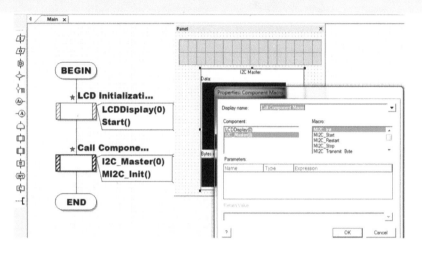

Figure 16.7. *Initializing the I2C device.*

Project 13: Step 6

▷ Insert a **Loop** icon.
▷ Also insert a **Component Macro** icon and double click on it.
▷ Select **I2C_ Master(0)** and **MI2C_ Start** in the **Component** and **Macro** fields.
▷ Click **OK**.

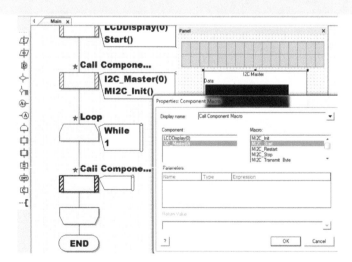

Figure 16.8. *Adding a loop and starting the I2C device.*

Project 13: Step 7

▷ Insert a **Component Macro** icon and double click on it.
▷ Select **I2C_Master(0)** and **MI2C_Transmit_Byte** in the **Component** and **Macro** fields.
▷ Type 0×48 in the **Expression** field and click **OK**.

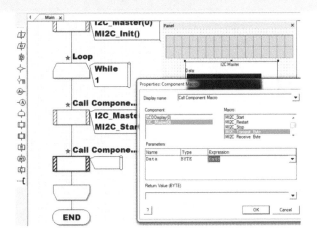

Figure 16.9. *Transmitting the I2C external device address.*

Project 13: Step 8

▷ Insert a **Component Macro** icon and double click on it.
▷ Select **I2C_Master(0)** and **MI2C_Transmit_Byte** in the **Component** and **Macro** fields.
▷ Enter 0×01 in the **Expression** field and click **OK**.

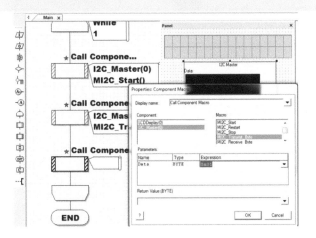

Figure 16.10. *Transmitting the I2C internal device address.*

Project 13: Step 9

▷ Insert a *Component Macro* icon and double click on it.
▷ Select *I2C_Master(0)* and *MI2C_Restart* in the *Component* and *Macro* fields.
▷ Click *OK*.

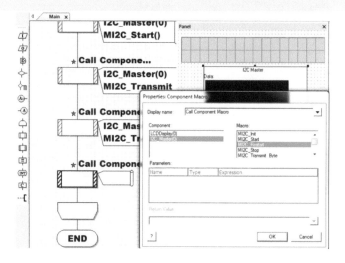

Figure 16.11. *Restarting the I2C device.*

Project 13: Step 10

▷ Insert a *Component Macro* icon and double click on it.
▷ Select *I2C_Master(0)* and *MI2C_Transmit_Byte* in the *Component* and *Macro* fields.
▷ Enter 0 × 91 in the *Expression* field and click *OK*.

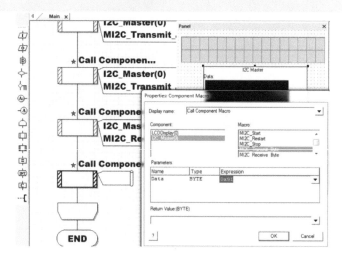

Figure 16.12. *Transmit the I2C external device address to receive the main significant byte of the data.*

Project 13: Step 11

▷ Insert a **Component Macro** icon and double click on it.

▷ Select **I2C_Master(0)** and **MI2C_Receive_Byte** in the **Component** and **Macro** fields.

▷ Click on the arrow at the right end of the **Return value** field.

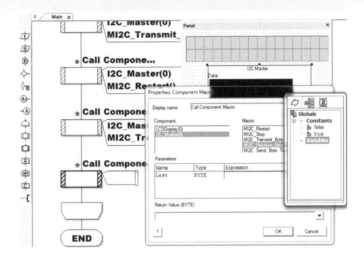

Figure 16.13. *Receiving the main significant byte of data from I2C device.*

Project 13: Step 12

▷ Double click on **Variables**.

▷ Enter **msb** in the **Name of new variable** field.

▷ Under **Variable type** select **Byte** and click **OK**.

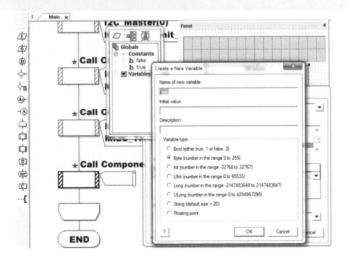

Figure 16.14. *Creating a variable to store the data received from I2C device.*

Project 13: Step 13

▷ In the *Expression* field enter0 × 91.
▷ Enter *msb* in the *Return value* field.
▷ Click *OK*.

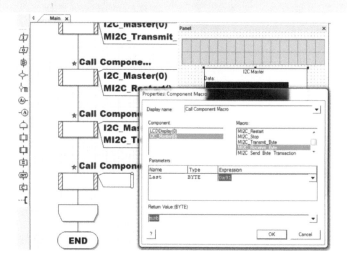

Figure 16.15. *Storing the data into the variable msb.*

Project 13: Step 14

▷ Insert a *Delay* icon and double click on it.
▷ Set the delay time to *5 milliseconds*.
▷ Click *OK*.

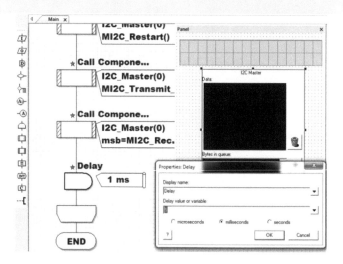

Figure 16.16. *Adding and initializing a delay.*

Project 13: Step 15

▷ Insert a *Component Macro* icon and double click on it.
▷ Select *I2C_Master(0)* and *MI2C_Transmit_Byte* in the *Component* and *Macro* fields.
▷ Enter 0 × 48 in the *Expression* field and click *OK*.

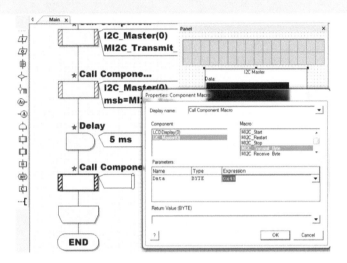

Figure 16.17. *Transmitting the I2C external device address.*

Project 13: Step 16

▷ Insert a *Component Macro* icon and double click on it.
▷ Select *I2C_Master(0)* and *MI2C_Transmit_Byte* in the *Component* and *Macro* fields.
▷ Enter 0 × 02 in the *Expression* field and click *OK*.

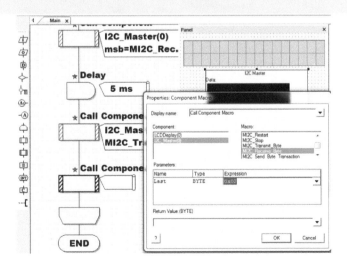

Figure 16.18. *Transmitting the I2C internal device address.*

Project 13: Step 17

▷ Insert a **Component Macro** icon and double click on it.
▷ Select **I2C_ Master(0)** and **MI2C_ Restart** in the **Component** and **Macro** fields.
▷ Click **OK**.

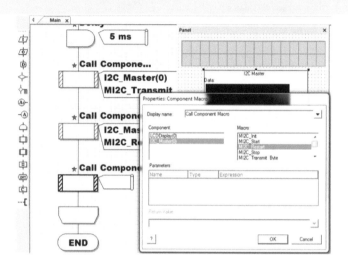

Figure 16.19. *Restarting the I2C device.*

Project 13: Step 18

▷ Insert a **Component Macro** icon and double click on it.
▷ Select **I2C_ Master(0)** and **MI2C_ Transmit_ Byte** in the **Component** and **Macro** fields.
▷ Enter 0×91 in the **Expression** field and click **OK**.

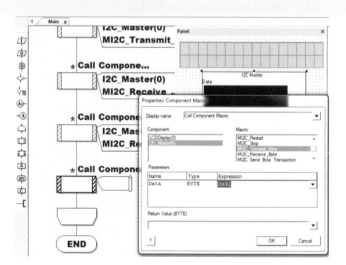

Figure 16.20. *Transmitting the I2C external device address to receive the least significant byte of the data.*

Project 13: Step 19

▷ Insert a **Component Macro** icon and double click on it.
▷ Select **I2C_Master(0)** and **MI2C_Receive_Byte** in the **Component** and **Macro** fields.
▷ Click on the **arrow** at the right end of the **Return value** field.

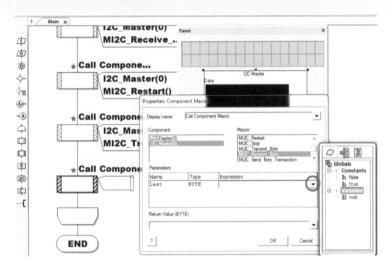

Figure 16.21. *Receiving the main significant byte of data from I2C device.*

Project 13: Step 20

▷ Double click on **Variables**.
▷ Enter **lsb** in the **Name of new variable** field.
▷ Under **Variable type** select **Byte** and click **OK**.

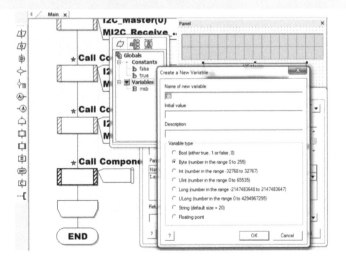

Figure 16.22. *Creating a variable to store the data received from I2C device.*

Project 13: Step 21

▷ Enter 0 × 91 in the ***Expression*** field.
▷ In the ***Return value*** field, enter ***lsb***.
▷ Click ***OK***.

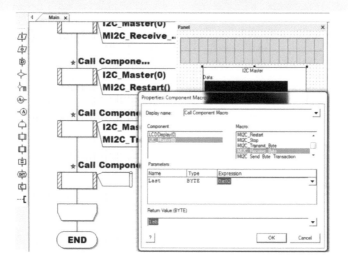

Figure 16.23. *Storing the data into the variable lsb.*

Project 13: Step 22

▷ Insert a ***Component Macro*** icon and double click on it.
▷ Select ***I2C_Master(0)*** and ***MI2C_Stop*** in the ***Component*** and ***Macro*** fields.
▷ Click ***OK***.

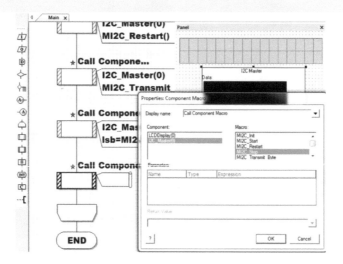

Figure 16.24. *Stopping the I2C device.*

Project 13: Step 23

▷ Insert a user-defined *Macro Call* icon and double click on it.

▷ Enter *computeTemp* in the *Name of new macro* field.

▷ Click *OK* and *OK & Edit Macro* button to edit the new macro.

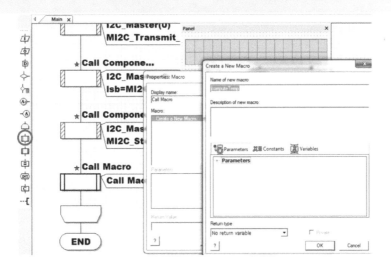

Figure 16.25. *Adding and editing a user-defined macro call icon.*

Project 13: Step 24

▷ Insert a *Calculation* icon and double click on it.

▷ Double click on *Variables* to create a new variable of *UInit* type.

▷ Enter *temp* in the *Name of new variable* field and click *OK*.

Figure 16.26. *Creating a new variable.*

Project 13: Step 25

▷ Create two other variables as follows:
  — Variable name **celsiusTemp**, type **Float**.
  — Variable name **stringTemp**, type **String**.

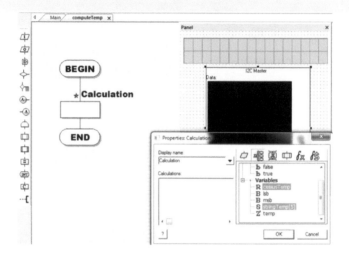

Figure 16.27. *Creating more variables.*

Project 13: Step 26

▷ Enter the following expressions into the **Calculations** field:
  — $temp = ((msb << 8) \; lsb) >> 4$
  — $celsiusTemp = int2float(temp)$.
  — $celsiusTemp = fmul(celsiusTemp, 0:0625)$.
  — $stringTemp = FloatToString\$(celsiusTemp)$.
  — Click **OK**.

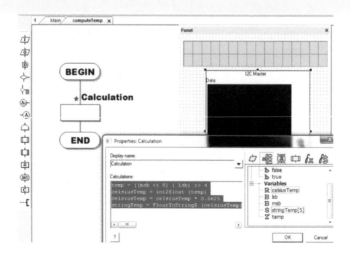

Figure 16.28. *Assigning values to variables.*

Project 13: Step 27

▷ Click on the *Macro* tab and select *New* to create a new macro.
▷ Enter *tempDisplay* in the *Name of new macro* field.
▷ Click *OK* to edit new macro.

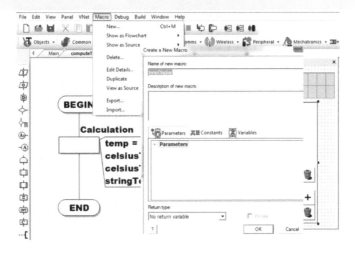

Figure 16.29. *Creating a user-defined macro.*

Project 13: Step 28

▷ Insert a *Component Macro* icon and double click on it.
▷ Select *LCDDisplay(0)* and *Cursor* in the *Component* and *Macro* fields.
▷ Enter *2* and *0* in the *x* and *y* fields, click *OK*.

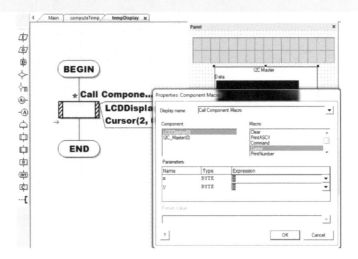

Figure 16.30. *Setting the LCD display cursor.*

Project 13: Step 29

▷ Insert another **Component Macro** icon and double click on it.

▷ Select **LCDDisplay(0)** and **PrintString** in the **Component** and **Macro** fields.

▷ Enter *"Temperature"* in the **Expression** field and click **OK**.

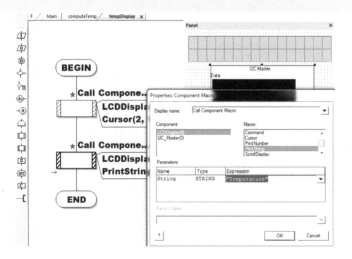

Figure 16.31. *Printing a string constant to the LCD.*

Project 13: Step 30

▷ Insert another **Component Macro** icon and double click on it.

▷ Select **LCDDisplay(0)** and **Cursor** in the **Component** and **Macro** fields.

▷ Enter *4* and *1* in the *x* and *y* fields, click **OK**.

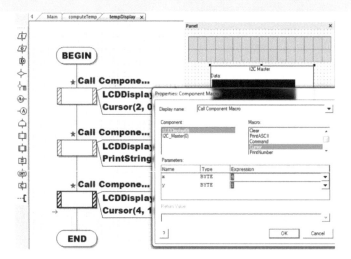

Figure 16.32. *Setting the LCD display cursor.*

Project 13: Step 31

▷ Insert another **Component Macro** icon and double click on it.
▷ Select **LCDDisplay(0)** and **PrintString** in the **Component** and **Macro** fields.
▷ Enter **"tempString"** in the **Expression** field and click **OK**.

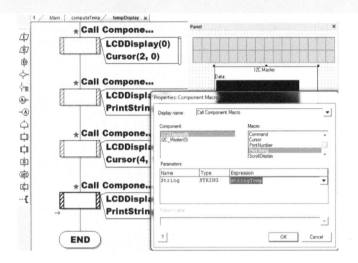

Figure 16.33. *Printing a string variable to the LCD.*

Project 13: Step 32

▷ Insert another **Component Macro** icon and double click on it.
▷ Select **LCDDisplay(0)** and **Cursor** in the **Component** and **Macro** fields.
▷ Enter **9** and **1** in the **x** and **y** fields, click **OK**.

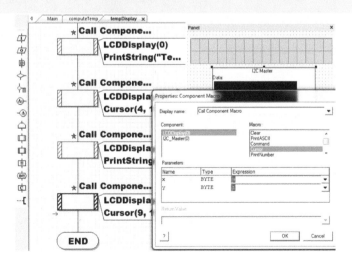

Figure 16.34. *Setting the LCD display cursor.*

Project 13: Step 33

▷ Insert another **Component Macro** icon and double click on it.
▷ Select **LCDDisplay(0)** and **PrintString** in the **Component** and **Macro** fields.
▷ Enter **"C"** in the **Expression** field and click **OK**.

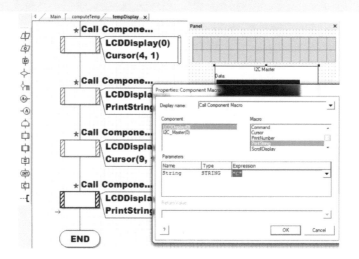

Figure 16.35. *Printing a string constant to the LCD.*

Project 13: Step 34

▷ Insert a **Decision** icon.
▷ Enter **temp > 40** in the **If** field.
▷ Click **OK**.

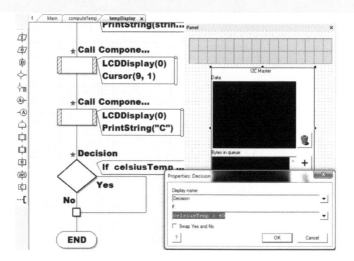

Figure 16.36. *Defining a condition to determine the flow direction.*

Project 13: Step 35

▷ Click on the *Output* tab and select *LED*.
▷ Right click on the *LED* and select *Connections*.
▷ Select *PORTD* and *Bits 2*, click *Done*.

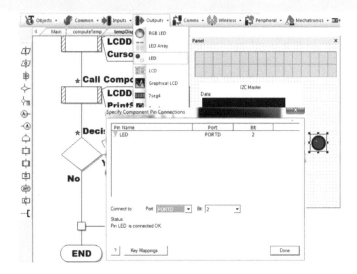

Figure 16.37. *Adding an LED component and connecting the LED to the output pin.*

Project 13: Step 36

▷ Insert a *Component Macro* icon and double click on it.
▷ Enter *blowAlarm_ On* in the *Display name* field.
▷ Select *LED(0)* and *LEDOn*, click *OK*.

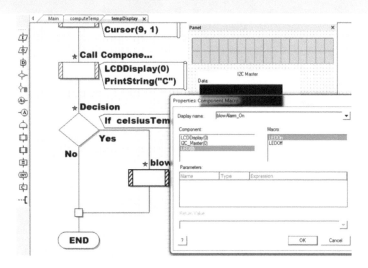

Figure 16.38. *Sending a high logic to the microcontroller output pin.*

Project 13: Step 37

▷ Insert a **Delay** icon and double click on it.
▷ Set the delay time to **150 millisecond**s.
▷ Click **OK**.

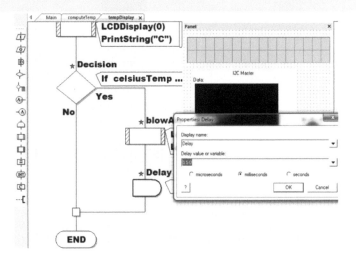

Figure 16.39. *Adding and configuring a delay.*

Project 13: Step 38

▷ Insert a **Component Macro** icon and double click on it.
▷ Enter **blowAlarm_ On** in the **Display name** field.
▷ Select **LED(0)** and **LEDOff**, click **OK**.

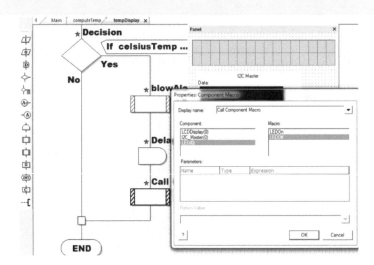

Figure 16.40. *Sending a low logic to the microcontroller output pin.*

Project 13: Step 39

▷ Insert a **Delay** icon and double click on it.
▷ Set the delay time to **150 milliseconds**.
▷ Click **OK**.

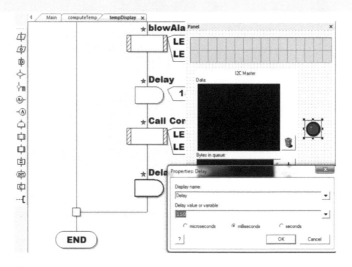

Figure 16.41. *Adding and configuring a delay.*

Project 13: Step 40

▷ Insert a **Component Macro** icon and double click on it.
▷ Enter **Alarm_Off** in the **Display name** field.
▷ Select **LED(0)** and **LEDOff**, click **OK**.

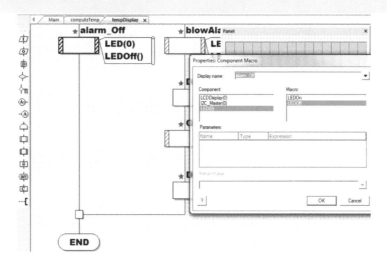

Figure 16.42. *Sending a low logic to the microcontroller output pin.*

Project 13: Step 41

▷ Insert a **Delay** icon and double click on it.
▷ Set the delay time to **600 milliseconds**.
▷ Click **OK**.

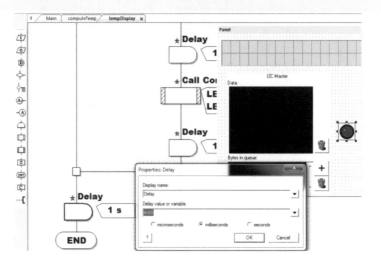

Figure 16.43. *Adding and configuring a delay.*

Project 13: Step 42

▷ Insert a user-defined **Macro Call** icon and double click on it.
▷ In the **Macro** filed select **tempDisplay** macro.
▷ Click **OK**.

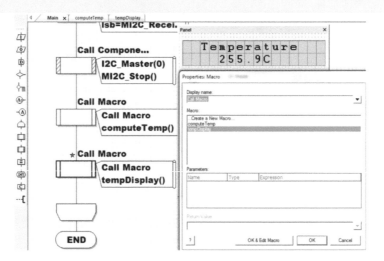

Figure 16.44. *Adding user-defined macro call icon.*

Project 13: Step 43

▷ Save the program and click on **Run** for simulation.

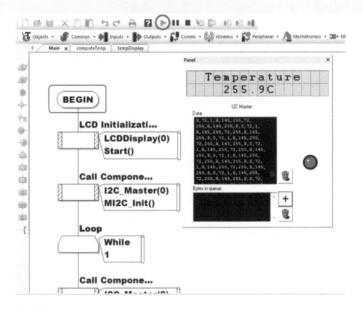

Figure 16.45. *Program is completed ready for simulation and downloading.*

16.5. Program Description

This program implements an ambient temperature monitoring system using a digital temperature sensor. The sensor measures and transmits the ambient temperature to a microcontroller via an I2C bus. The microcontroller evaluates and displays the ambient temperature in degree Celsius to the LCD. However, if the temperature goes beyond 40^0C, an alarm is raised. Details of the programme implementation steps are listed below;

Note: The **I2C device** referred to in the program represents the TMP102 digital temperature sensor or any other I2C temperature sensor used to implement the project.

▷ **Step 1:**
— Launch **Flowcode** and start a new program.
▷ **Step 2:**
— Add an **LCD** component.
— Connect the **LCD** to **PORTB**.
▷ **Step 3:**
— Initialize the **LCD**.
▷ **Step 4:**
— Add an **I2C** master device from **comms** tab.
▷ **Step 5:**

— Initialize the *I2C* device.

▷ **Step 6:**

— Start the *I2C* device.

   — This makes the device to start listening to the I²C bus.

▷ **Step 7:**

— Transmit the external address of the *I2C* device.

   — This sets the sensor's address for reading data.

▷ **Step 8:**

— Transmit the internal address of the *I2C* device.

   — This enables the device and set it to read mode.

▷ **Step 9:**

— Restart the *I2C* device.

▷ **Step 10:**

— Transmit the external address of the *I2C* device to receive the ***main significant byte*** of the data.

▷ **Step 11:**

— Declare a variable to store the ***main significant byte*** of the data.

▷ **Step 12:**

— Name the variable *msb*.

▷ **Step 13:**

— Return the variable *msb* to the **Main** program.

▷ **Step 14:**

— Wait for ***50 milliseconds*** to finish receiving the data.

▷ **Step 15:**

— Transmit the external address of the *I2C* device again.

   — This sets the address of the device to read data from.

▷ **Step 16:**

— Transmit the internal address of the *I2C* device again.

   — This enables the device and set it to read mode.

▷ **Step 17:**

— Restart the *I2C master* device again.

▷ **Step 18:**

— Transmit the external address of the *I2C* device to receive the ***least significant byte*** of the data.

▷ **Step 19:**

— Declare a variable to store the ***least significant byte*** of the data.

▷ **Step 20:**

— Name the variable *lsb*.

▷ **Step 21:**

— Return the variable *lsb* to the **Main** program.

▷ **Step 22:**

— Stop the *I2C* device.

▷ **Step 23:**

— Define and call a **Macro** to evaluate the sensor's ambient temperature based on ***Equation 16.1***.

— Name the macro **computeTemp** and edit the macro.

▷ **Step 24:**
— Declare an **unsigned** integer variable.
— Name the variable **temp**.

▷ **Step 25:**
— Declare **float** and **string** type variables.
— Name the **float** variable **celsiusTemp** and the **string** variable **stringTemp**.

▷ **Step 26:**
— Evaluate the three variables as follows:
— temp = ((msb << 8)lsb) >> 4.
— celsiusTemp = int2float(temp).
— celsiusTemp = fmul(celsiusTemp, 0. 0625).
— stringTemp = FloatToString\$(celsiusTemp).

▷ **Step 27:**
— Define a new user-defined macro.
— Name the macro **tempDisplay**.

▷ **Step 28:**
— Set the LCD display cursor to **column two** and **row zero**.

▷ **Step 29:**
— Print the string constant **"Temperature"** to the **LCD**.

▷ **Step 30:**
— Set the LCD display cursor to **column four** and **row one**.

▷ **Step 31:**
— Print the string variable **tempString** to the **LCD**.
— The variable **tempString** is the sensor's ambient temperature.

▷ **Step 32:**
— Set the LCD display cursor to **column nine** and **row one**.

▷ **Step 33:**
— Print the string constant **"C"** to the **LCD**.

▷ **Step 34:**
— Monitor the ambient temperature.
— Do not allow the ambient temperature exceeds 40^0C.

▷ **Step 35:**
— Add an **LED** component to represent a Piezo sounder.
  — Note: Flowcode does have a Piezo sounder in its components library.
— Connect the **LED** pin **D2** of the microcontroller.

▷ **Step 36:**
— Send a high logic to pin **D2** of the microcontroller to turn **on** the **LED** (blow the sounder) connected to the pin once the ambient temperature exceeds 40^0C.

▷ **Step 37:**
— Keep the **LED on** (alarm on) for **150 milliseconds**.

▷ **Step 38:**
— Turn the **LED off**.

▷ **Step 39:**
— Keep the **LED off** (alarm on) for **150 milliseconds**.

▷ **Step 40:**

— However, always turn *off* the LED (the alarm) when the ambient temperature is below *40*^0C.

▷ **Step 41:**

— Update the ambient temperature every 60*0 milliseconds*.

▷ **Step 42:**

— Switch to the *Main* program and add a user-defined *Macro Call* icon.

— Call the *tempDisplay* macro to handle the LCD display tasks.

▷ **Step 43:**

— Simulate the program by clicking on the *Run* button and download it to the microcontroller on the PhasePlus development board.

Chapter 17

Project 14: Humidity Measurement

17.1. Objective

The purpose of this project is to demonstrate how to interface a humidity sensor to a micro-controller for humidity sensing and control. The concept in this project can be extended to building a wide variety of mechatronics systems requiring humidity monitoring and control such HVAC (Heating, ventilation and Air Conditioning) systems and incubators. Humidity sensors are available from various manufacturers. However, this project utilizes the HIH-4030 Honeywell.

Hardware

- ▷ HIH-4030 humidity sensor
- ▷ Character-based LCD (16x2)
- ▷ Piezo sounder
- ▷ Connection wires
- ▷ PhasePlus PIC16F877A development board
- ▷ Potentiometer (optional)
- ▷ 10K resistor (optional)

17.2. Humidity Sensor Overview

A humidity sensor does not measure absolute humidity; rather it measures relative humidity. Relative humidity expressed as a percentage; is the ratio of actual moisture in the air to the highest amount of moisture the air can contain at a given temperature. The warmer the air is, the more moisture it can hold, so relative humidity changes with fluctuations in temperature. The measure of how much moisture is actually present in the air is called a dew point. A reading of 100 percent relative humidity means that the air is totally saturated with water vapour and cannot hold any more.

17.2.1. HIH-4030 Sensor

The HIH-4030 is a humidity sensor capable of measuring relative humidity (%RH) and delivers it as an analogue output voltage. Its output can be connected directly to the ADC pin on a microcontroller. The sensor works with between 4 to 6VDC consuming about 200mA. It delivers a stable near linear output having a fast response time and low drift performance. The sensor is used in applications such as refrigeration equipment, HVAC equipment, medical equipment drying, meteorology and battery-powered systems, etc.

Figure 17.1. *Sparkun breakout board for HIH 4030 humidity sensor.*

The following expression converts the sensor's output to a relative humidity (%RH):

$$Relative\_Humidity = \frac{Sensor_{Reading} \times 196}{6} \qquad (17.1)$$

17.3. Project Circuit Schematic

The circuit schematic for this project is shown in Fig. 17.2. The sensor's signal terminal connects to the analogue pin An0 of the microcontroller and the power terminals connect to the +5V and GND. Two terminals of the Piezo sounder connect to pin D2 of the microcontroller and GND. The listing below indicates how the LCD connects to the microcontroller;

▷ Data lines (D1-D3) connect to PORTB pins RB0 - RB3.
▷ Enable, read/write and RS pins connect to B5, GND and B4 respectively.
▷ The LCD back light pins, A and K connect to VCC via a 220 resistor and GND.

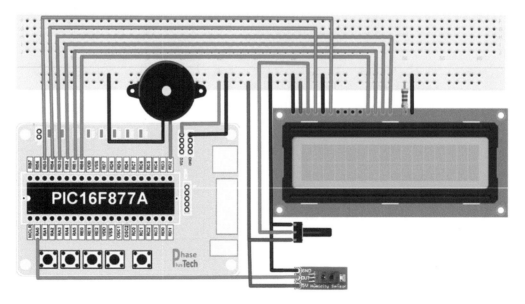

Figure 17.2. Project 14 circuit schematic.

17.4. Implementation Steps:

Project 14: Step 1

▷ Launch **Flowcode**.
▷ Select **Create a new Flowcode**, click **OK** and select **16F877A**.
▷ Click **OK**.

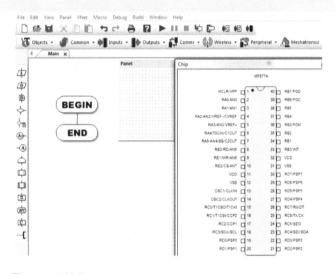

Figure 17.3. *An empty Flowcode project environment.*

Project 14: Step 2

▷ Click on the **Output** tab and select **LCD**.
▷ Right click on the **LCD** and select **Connections**.
▷ Double check the **LCD** is connected as shown in Fig. 17.4 and click **OK**.

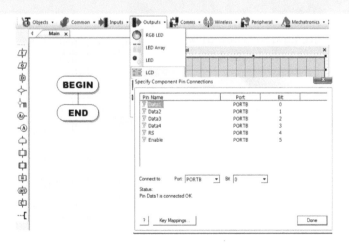

Figure 17.4. *Adding and connecting an LCD component..*

Project 14: Step 3

▷ Insert a **Component Macro** icon and double click on it.
▷ Select **LCDDisplay(0)** and **Start** in the **Component** and **Macro** fields.
▷ Click **OK**.

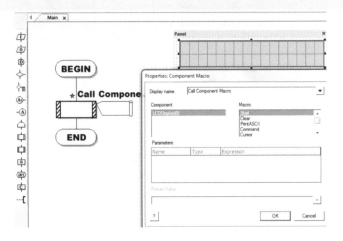

Figure 17.5. *Initializing the LCD component.*

Project 14: Step 4

▷ Insert a **Loop** icon.
▷ Click on the **Output** tab and select **ADC** to add an ADC device.
▷ Right click on the **ADC** device and select **Connections**.
▷ In the **Connect to** field select **ADC An0** and click **Done**.

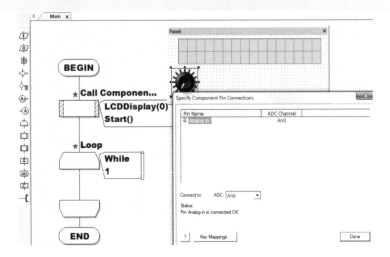

Figure 17.6. *Adding a loop and an ADC device.*

Project 14: Step 5

▷ Insert a **Component Macro** icon and double click on it.

▷ Select **ADC(0)** and **ReadAsInt** in the **Component** and **Macro** fields.

▷ Click on the **arrow** at the right end of the **Return value** field to create a new variable.

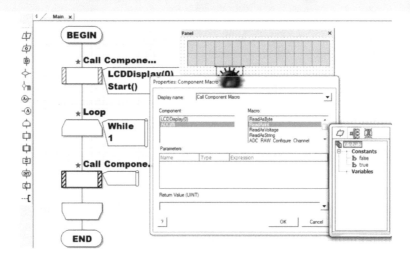

Figure 17.7. *Reading the ADC device on analogue channel zero.*

Project 14: Step 6

▷ Enter **RHsensorValue** in the **Name of new variable** field.

▷ Under **Variable type** select **Int**.

▷ Click **OK**.

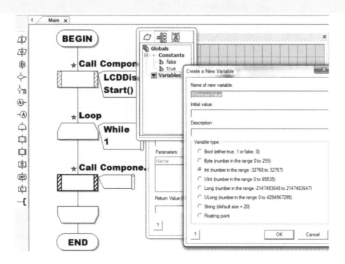

Figure 17.8. *Creating a variable to store the ADC device analogue input.*

Project 14: Step 7

▷ Enter **RHsensorValue** in the **Return value** field.
▷ Click **OK**.

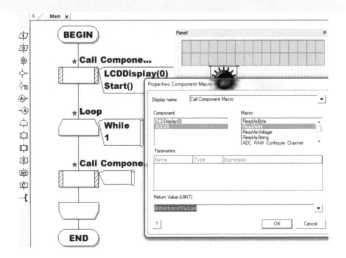

Figure 17.9. *Returning the ADC device analogue input to the Main program.*

Project 14: Step 8

▷ Insert a **Calculation** icon and double click on it.
▷ Double click on **Variables** to create a **Float** type variable.
▷ Enter **RH** in the **Name of new variable** field and click **OK**.

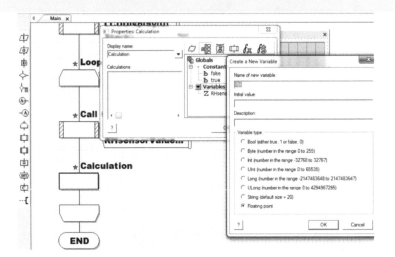

Figure 17.10. *Creating a new float type variable.*

Project 14: Step 9

▷ Double click on **Variables** again to create a **String** type variable.
▷ Enter **stringRH[5]** in the **Name of new variable** field.
▷ Click **OK**.

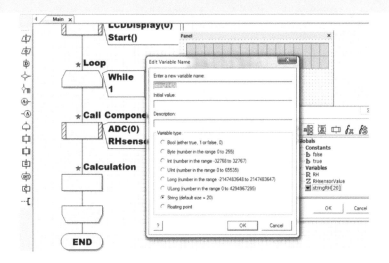

Figure 17.11. *Creating a string type variable.*

Project 14: Step 10

▷ Enter the following expressions in the **Calculations** field:
— **RH = fsub(int2float(RHsensorValue), 196)**.
— **RH = fdiv(RH, 6)**.
— **stringRH = FloatToString$(RH)**.
▷ Click **OK**.

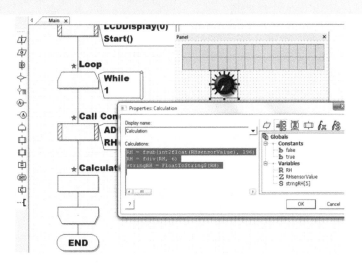

Figure 17.12. *Evaluating variables.*

Project 14: Step 11

▷ Insert a **Component Macro** icon and double click on it.
▷ Select **LCDDisplay(0)** and **Cursor** in the **Component** and **Macro** fields.
▷ Enter **4** and **0** in the **x** and **y** fields, click **OK**.

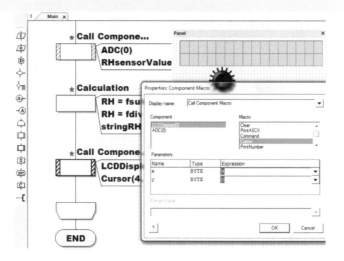

Figure 17.13. *Setting the LCD display cursor.*

Project 14: Step 12

▷ Insert a **Component Macro** icon and double click on it.
▷ Select **LCDDisplay(0)** and **PrintString** in the **Component** and **Macro** fields.
▷ Type **"Humidity"** in the **Expression** field and click **OK**.

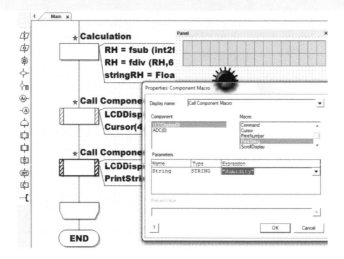

Figure 17.14. *Printing a string constant to the LCD.*

Project 14: Step 13

▷ Insert a *Component Macro* icon and double click on it.
▷ Select *LCDDisplay(0)* and *Cursor* in the *Component* and *Macro* fields.
▷ Enter *5* and *1* in the *x* and *y* fields, click *OK*.

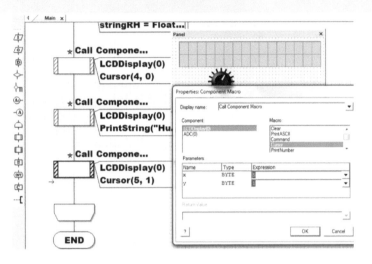

Figure 17.15. *Re-setting the LCD display cursor.*

Project 14: Step 14

▷ Insert a *Component Macro* icon and double click on it.
▷ Select *LCDDisplay(0)* and *PrintString* in the *Component* and *Macro* fields.
▷ Type *stringRH* in the *Expression* field and click *OK*.

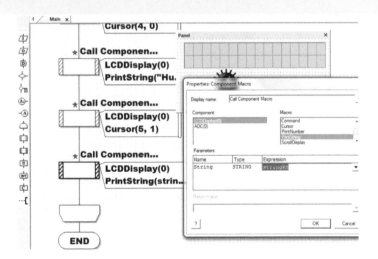

Figure 17.16. *Printing a string variable to the LCD.*

Project 14: Step 15

▷ Insert a **Decision** icon.
▷ Enter **RH > 75** in the **If** field.
▷ Click **OK**.

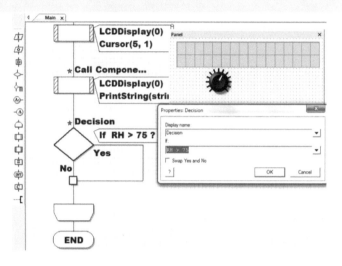

Figure 17.17. *Condition test.*

Project 14: Step 16

▷ Click on the **Output** tab and select **LED**.
▷ Right click on the **LED** and select **Connections**.
▷ Select **PORTD** and **Bit 2**, click **Done**.

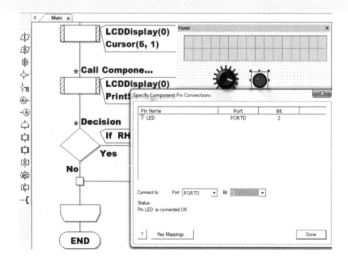

Figure 17.18. *Adding and connecting an LED to the output pin.*

Project 14: Step 17

▷ Insert a *Component Macro* icon and double click on it.
▷ Enter *Alarm_ On* in the *Display name* field.
▷ Select *LED(0)* and *LEDOn*, click *OK*.

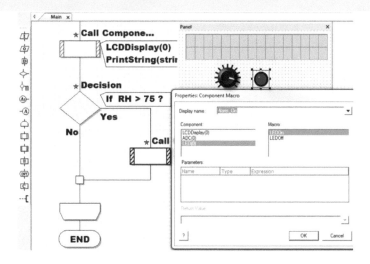

Figure 17.19. *Sending a high logic to the output pin.*

Project 14: Step 18

▷ Insert a *Component Macro* icon and double click on it.
▷ Enter *Alarm_ Off* in the *Display name* field.
▷ Select *LED(0)* and *LEDOff*, click *OK*.

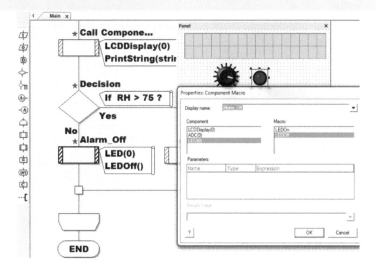

Figure 17.20. *Sending a low logic to the output pin.*

Project 14: Step 19

▷ Insert a **Delay** icon and double click on it.
▷ Set the delay time to **500 milliseconds**.
▷ Click **OK**.

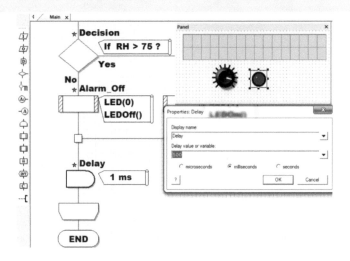

Figure 17.21. *Adding and configuring a delay.*

Project 14: Step 20

▷ Save the program and click on **Run** for simulation.

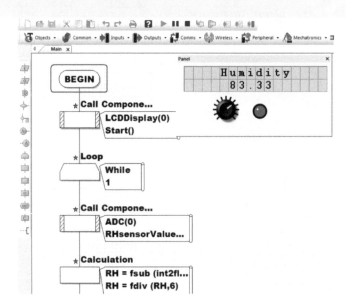

Figure 17.22. *Program is completed ready for simulation and downloading.*

17.5. Program Description

This program implements a humidity measuring and control system using the HIH-4030 humidity sensor. In the program, the humidity of the sensor's environment is read and displayed to an LCD. However, the system blows an alarm if the relative humidity of the environment goes above 75%. Details of the programme implementation steps are listed below.

Note: The **ADC device** referred to in the program represents the **HIH-4030** humidity sensor or any other analogue humidity sensor used to implement the project.

▷ **Step 1:**
— Launch Flowcode and start a new program.

▷ **Step 2:**
— Add an **LCD** component.
— Connect the **LCD** to **PORTB**.

▷ **Step 3:**
— Initialized the **LCD**.

▷ **Step 4:**
— Add a **Loop** to make the program runs repeatedly.
— Also add and an **ADC** device.
— Connect the **ADC** device to **An0** (analogue pin zero).

▷ **Step 5:**
— Read as **integer** the value at the ADC's device output.

▷ **Step 6:**
— Declare an integer type variable and name it **RHsensorValue**.

▷ **Step 7:**
— Return the content of the variable **RHsensorValue** to the **Main** program.

▷ **Step 8:**
— Declare a **float** type variable and name it **RH**.

▷ **Step 9:**
— Declare a **string** type variable and name it **stringRH**.

▷ **Step 10:**
— Evaluate variables **RH** and **stringRH** from the variable **RHsensorValue** using **Equation 17.1**.

▷ **Step 11:**
— Set the **LCD Cursor** to **column four** and **row zero**.

▷ **Step 12:**
— Print the string constant **Humidity** to the **LCD**.

▷ **Step 13:**
— Set the **LCD Cursor** to **column five** and **row zero**.

▷ **Step 14:**
— Print the string variable **stringRH** to the **LCD**.

▷ **Step 15:**
— Ensure **RH** (relative humidity) does not exceed **75%**.

▷ **Step 16:**
— Add an **LED** to represent the Piezo sounder for Flowcode simulation.

— ***Note:*** Flowcode does not have a Piezo sounder in its components library.

— Connect the ***LED*** to pin ***D2*** of the microcontroller.

▷ **Step 17:**

— Turn ***on*** the ***LED*** (blow alarm) if ***RH*** exceeds ***75%***.

▷ **Step 18:**

— Turn ***off*** the ***LED*** (turn off alarm) if ***RH*** is below ***75%***.

▷ **Step 19:**

— Update ***RH*** every ***500 milliseconds***.

▷ **Step 20:**

— Simulate the program by clicking on the ***Run*** button and download it to the micro-controller on the PhasePlus development board.

Chapter 18

Project 15: Accelerometer - Tilt Measurement

18.1. Objective

The purpose of this project is to demonstrate how to interface an accelerometer to a microcontroller. Accelerometers are used for applications such as vibration monitoring and control, vehicle collision sensing, shock detection and tilt measurement. There are varieties of accelerometers produced by different manufacturers. This project utilizes the ADLX 335 by ANALOG Devices.

Hardware

- ▷ ADLX 335 triple axis accelerometer
- ▷ Character-based LCD (16x2)
- ▷ Connection wires
- ▷ PhasePlus PIC16F877A development board
- ▷ Potentiometer (optional)
- ▷ 10K resistor (optional)

18.2. Accelerometers Overview

An accelerometer is a device which measures acceleration forces. In some applications, where the net acceleration or force on a system over time is gravity, an accelerometer can be used to measure the static angle of tilt or inclination. These forces could be static, like the constant force of gravity or they could be dynamic caused by moving or vibrating the accelerometer. Measuring the amount of static acceleration due to gravity, the angle the device is tilted at with respect to the Earth can be computed. Also, sensing the amount of dynamic acceleration, the device rate can be analysed. Commonly types of accelerometers are; capacitive, Piezo-resistive, Piezoelectric, hall effect, MEMs, etc. MEMS accelerometers usually come in the smallest surface mount package and can detect acceleration in up to 3 axes.

18.2.1. ADLX 335 Accelerometer

The ADXL335 accelerometer depicted in Fig. 18.1, is a small, thin, low power, complete 3-axes accelerometer with signal conditioned voltage outputs. The sensor measures acceleration with a minimum full-scale range of ±3 g. It can measure the static acceleration of gravity in tilt-sensing applications, as well as dynamic acceleration resulting from motion, shock, or vibration. The sensor works with between 1.8 to 3.6VDC, consuming only 320A. The device can be used in applications such as motion and tilt sensing systems, mobile devices, gaming systems, disk drive protection, image stabilization, sports and health devices.

Figure 18.1. *Sparkun breakout board for ADLX335 triple axis accelerometer.*

The following expression converts the sensor's output to angular position on the x-axis:

$$Tilt_{x-axis} = \frac{Sensor_{Reading} - 256}{0.76} \tag{18.1}$$

18.3. Circuit Schematic

The circuit schematic for this project is shown in Fig. 18.2. The x-axis output of the sensor connects to analogue pin An0 of the microcontroller and the power terminals connect to the 3.3V and GND of the voltage regulator IC. The two LEDs anodes connect to pins D2 and D5 of the microcontroller; while their cathodes connect to GND. The listing below indicates how the LCD connects to the microcontroller;

- ▷ Data lines (D1-D3) connect to PORTB pins RB0 - RB3.
- ▷ Enable, read/write and RS pins connect to B5, GND and B4 respectively.
- ▷ The LCD back light pins, A and K connect to VCC via a 220 resistor and GND.

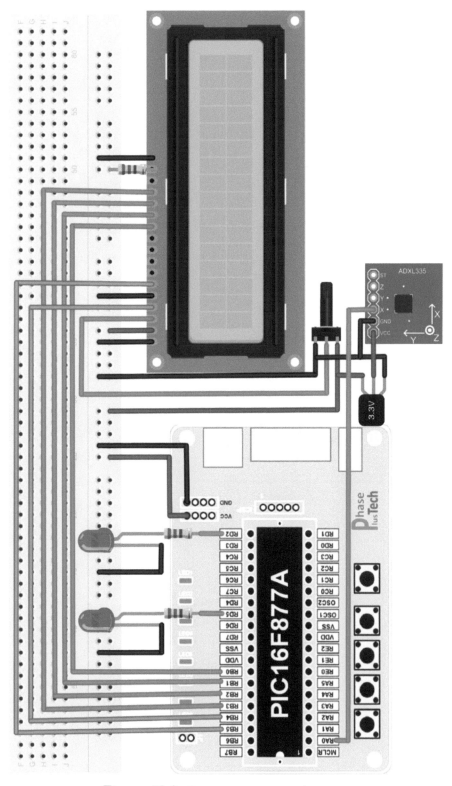

Figure 18.2. Project 15 circuit schematic.

18.4. Implementation Steps:

Project 15: Step 1

▷ Launch **Flowcode**.
▷ Select **Create a new Flowcode**, click **OK** and select **16F877A**.
▷ Click **OK**.

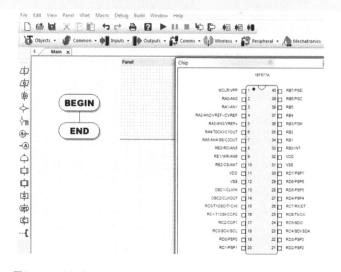

Figure 18.3. *An empty Flowcode project environment.*

Project 15: Step 2

▷ Click on the **Output** tab and select **LCD**.
▷ Right click on the **LCD** and select **Connections**.
▷ Double check the **LCD** is connected as shown in Fig. 18.4 and click **OK**.

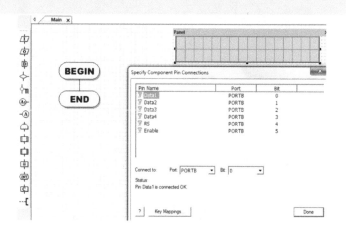

Figure 18.4. *Adding and connecting an LCD component..*

Project 15: Step 3

▷ Click on the **Input** and select **ADC**.
▷ Right click on the **ADC** and select **Connections**.
▷ Double check **An0** is selected in the **Connect to** ADC field and click **Done**.

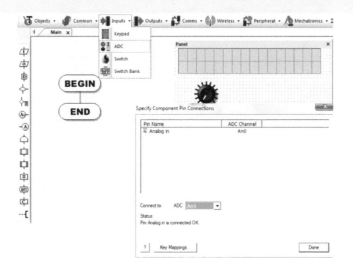

Figure 18.5. *An empty Flowcode project environment.*

Project 15: Step 4

▷ Click on the **Objects** tab and select **Text** to label the **ADC** component.
▷ Right click on the inserted **text-box** and select **Properties**.
▷ Enter **ADLX335 Accelerometer** in the **Caption** field, close the **Property** window.

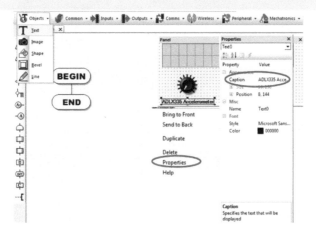

Figure 18.6. *labelling a Flowcode component.*

Project 15: Step 5

▷ Insert two *LEDs* and connect them to pins *D2* and *D5*.
▷ Label the two *LEDs* as *Horizontal Position* and *Vertical Position*.
▷ Position the two *LEDs* as shown in Fig. 18.7.

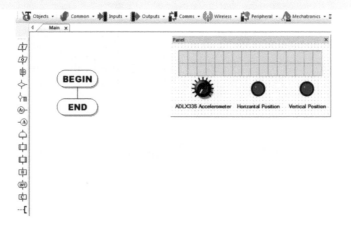

Figure 18.7. *Adding and labelling of more components.*

Project 15: Step 6

▷ Insert a *Component Macro* icon and double click on it.
▷ Select *LCDDisplay(0)* and *Start* in the *Component* and *Macro* fields.
▷ Click *OK*.

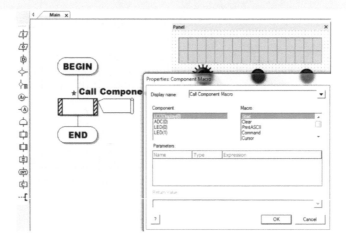

Figure 18.8. *Initializing the LCD component.*

Project 15: Step 7

▷ Insert a **Loop** icon.
▷ Then, insert a **Component Macro** icon and double click on it.
▷ Select **ADC(0)** and **ReadAsInt** in the **Component** and **Macro fields**.
▷ Click on the **arrow** at the right end of the **Return value** field to create a variable.

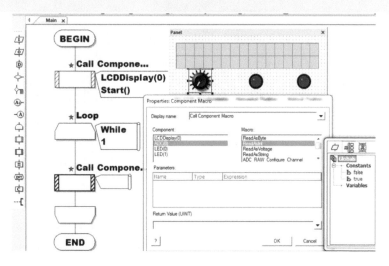

Figure 18.9. *Adding a loop and reading the ADC device output.*

Project 15: Step 8

▷ Double click on **Variables** to create an **unsigned integer** variable.
▷ Enter **x_axis_sensorValue** in the **Name of new variable** field.
▷ Click **OK**.

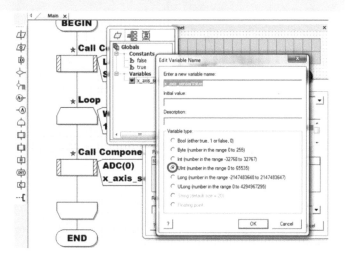

Figure 18.10. *Creating a variable.*

Project 15: Step 9

▷ Enter *x_axis_sensorValue* in the ***Return value*** field.
▷ Click ***OK***.

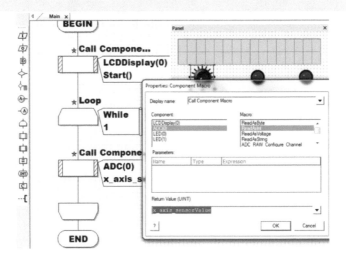

Figure 18.11. *Returning a variable to the Main program.*

Project 15: Step 10

▷ Insert a ***Calculation*** icon and double click on it.
▷ Double click on ***Variables*** to create a variable.
▷ Enter ***tilt_on_x_axis_f*** in the ***Name of new variable*** field and click ***OK***.

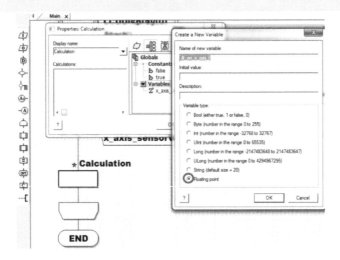

Figure 18.12. *Creating a new variable.*

Project 15: Step 11

▷ Double click on **Variables** again and create another variable.
▷ Enter **tilt_on_x_axis_string** in the **Name of new variable** field.
▷ Click **OK**.

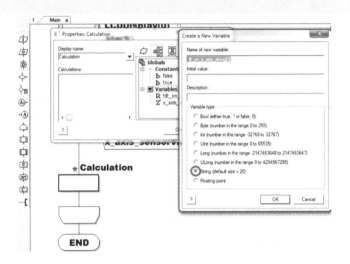

Figure 18.13. *Creating another variable.*

Project 15: Step 12

▷ In the **Calculations** field enter the following expressions:
  — *tilt_on_x_axis_f = fsub(int2float(x_axis_sensorValue), 256).*
  — *tilt_on_x_axis_f = fdiv(tilt_on_x_axis_f, 0.76).*
  — *tilt_on_x_axis_string = FloatToString\$(tilt_on_x_axis_string).*
▷ Click **OK**.

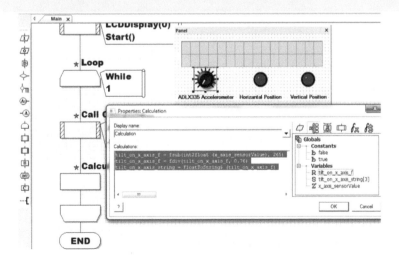

Figure 18.14. *Evaluating variables.*

Project 15: Step 13

▷ Insert a **Decision** icon an double click on it.
▷ Enter **tilt_ on_ x_ axis_ f** > 145 in the **If** field.
▷ Click **OK**.

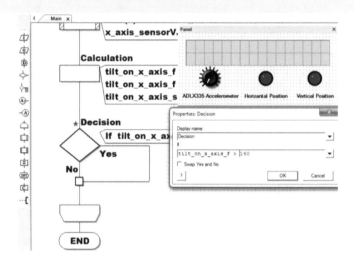

Figure 18.15. *Condition test.*

Project 15: Step 14

▷ Insert a user-defined **Macro Call** icon and double click on it.
▷ Under **Macro** field double click on **Create a New Macro**.
▷ Enter **Vertical** in the **Name of new macro** field and click **OK**.

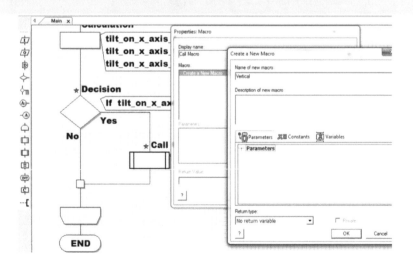

Figure 18.16. *Creating a user-defined macro.*

Project 15: Step 15

▷ Click on the **OK & Edit Macro** to edit the new macro.

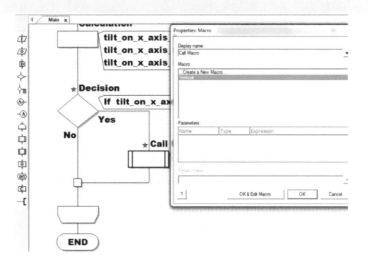

Figure 18.17. *Editing the user-defined macro.*

Project 15: Step 16

▷ Insert a **Component Macro** icon in the new **Macro** and double click on it.
▷ Select **LCDDisplay(0)** and **Cursor** in the **Component** and **Macro** fields.
▷ Enter **4** and **0** in the **x** and **y** fields, click **OK**.

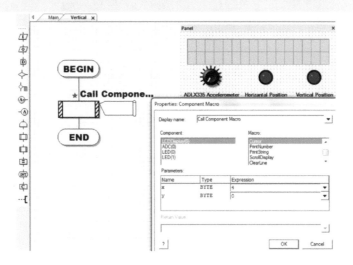

Figure 18.18. *Setting the LCD display cursor.*

Project 15: Step 17

▷ Insert another **Component Macro** icon and double click on it.
▷ Select **LCDDisplay(0)** and **PrintString** in the **Component** and **Macro** fields.
▷ Type **"Vertical"** in the **Expression** field and click **OK**.

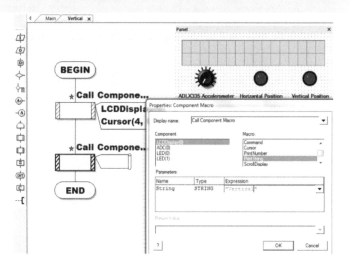

Figure 18.19. *Printing a string constant to the LCD.*

Project 15: Step 18

▷ Insert another **Component Macro** icon and double click on it.
▷ Select **LED(0)** and **LEDOn** in the **Component** and **Macro** fields, click **OK**.
▷ Switch to **Main** program by clicking on its tab.

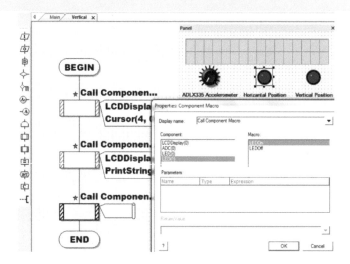

Figure 18.20. *Sending a high logic to D5 of the microcontroller.*

Project 15: Step 19

▷ Insert another user-defined **Macro Call** icon and double click on it.
▷ Under **Macro** field double click on **Create a New Macro**.
▷ Enter **Horizontal** in the **Name of new macro** field and click **OK**.

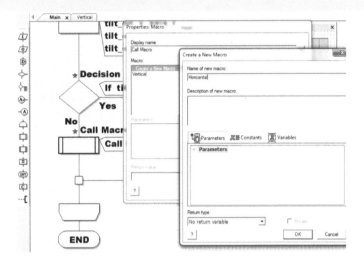

Figure 18.21. *Creating another user-defined macro.*

Project 15: Step 20

▷ Click on the **OK & Edit Macro** to edit the new macro.

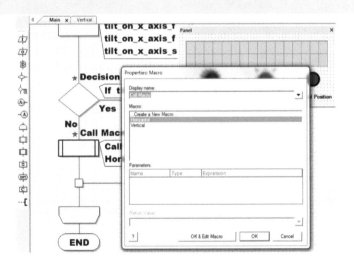

Figure 18.22. *Editing the user-defined macro.*

Project 15: Step 21

▷ Insert a **Component Macro** icon in the new **Macro** and double click on it.
▷ Select **LCDDisplay(0)** and **Cursor** in the **Component** and **Macro** fields.
▷ Enter **3** and **0** in the **x** and **y** fields, click **OK**.

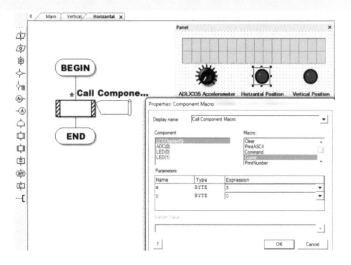

Figure 18.23. *Re-setting the LCD display cursor.*

Project 15: Step 22

▷ Insert another **Component Macro** icon and double click on it.
▷ Select **LCDDisplay(0)** and **PrintString** in the **Component** and **Macro** fields.
▷ Type **"Horizontal"** in the **Expression** field and click **OK**.

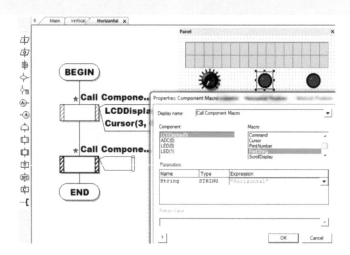

Figure 18.24. *Printing another string constant to the LCD.*

Project 15: Step 23

▷ Insert another *Component Macro* icon and double click on it.
▷ Select *LED(1)* and *LEDOn* in the *Component* and *Macro* fields, click *OK*.
▷ Switch to *Main* program by clicking on its tab.

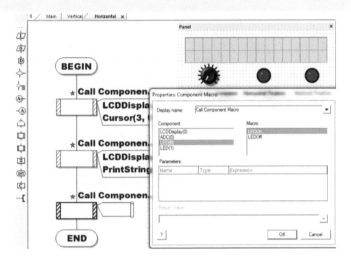

Figure 18.25. *Sending a high logic pin D2 of the microcontroller.*

Project 15: Step 24

▷ Insert a *Delay* icon and double click on it.
▷ Set the delay time to *1 second*.
▷ Click *OK*.

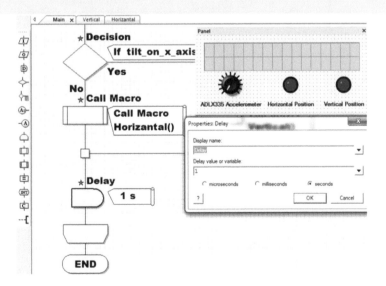

Figure 18.26. *Adding and configuring a delay.*

Project 15: Step 25

▷ Insert a *Component Macro* icon and double click on it.
▷ Select *LED(0)* and *LEDOff* in the *Component* and *Macro* fields.
▷ Click *OK*.

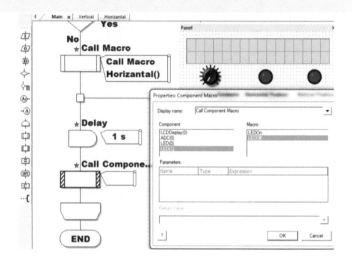

Figure 18.27. *Sending a low logic pin D5 of the microcontroller.*

Project 15: Step 26

▷ Insert a *Component Macro* icon and double click on it.
▷ Select *LED(1)* and *LEDOff* in the *Component* and *Macro* fields.
▷ Click *OK*.

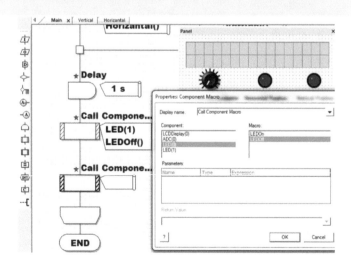

Figure 18.28. *Sending a low logic pin D2 of the microcontroller.*

Project 15: Step 27

▷ Insert another **Component Macro** icon and double click on it.
▷ Select **LCDDisplay(0)** and **Clear** in the **Component** and **Macro** fields.
▷ Click **OK**.

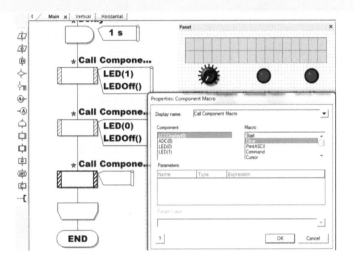

Figure 18.29. *Clearing the LCD screen.*

Project 15: Step 28

▷ Save the program and click on **Run** for simulation.

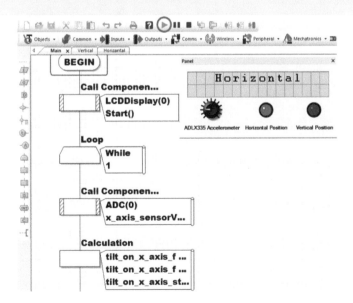

Figure 18.30. *Program is completed ready for simulation and downloading.*

18.5. Program Description

This program implements a single axis tilt measuring tool using an ADLX 335 triple axis accelerometer. The sensor senses and displays the orientation of the tool as either being vertical or horizontal. If the device is horizontal, the LED labelled horizontal turns on and the string "Vertical Position" is displayed on the LCD. Similarly, if the device is vertical, the LED labelled vertical turns on and the string "Vertical Position is displayed on the LCD.

Note: The **ADC device** referred to in the program represents the **ADLX 335 triple axis accelerometer** or any other analogue accelerometer used to implement the project.

▷ **Step 1:**
— Launch Flowcode and start a new program.

▷ **Step 2:**
— Add an **LCD** component.
— Connect the **LCD** to **PORTB**.

▷ **Step 3:**
— Add an **ADC** device to represent the accelerometer for **Flowcode** simulation.
  — **Note:** (Flowcode does have the ADLX 335 triple axis accelerometer in its components library).
— Connect the **ADC** device to pin **An0** (analogue channel zero) of the microcontroller.

▷ **Step 4:**
— Label the **ADC** device as **ADLX 335 Accelerometer** for better appearance.

▷ **Step 5:**
— Add two **LEDs** and connect them to pin **D2** and **D5** of the microcontroller.
— Label the **LEDs** as **Vertical** and **Horizontal** as indicated in Fig. 18.7.

▷ **Step 6:**
— Initialize the **LCD** component.

▷ **Step 7:**
— Add a **Loop** to make the program runs repeatedly.
— Read as **integer** the value at the **x-axis** terminal of the **ADC** device.

▷ **Step 8:**
— Declare an **unsigned integer** type variable and name it **x_ axis_ sensorValue**.

▷ **Step 9:**
— Return the content of the variable **x_ axis_ sensorValue** to the **Main** program.

▷ **Step 10:**
— Declare a **float** type variable and name it **tilt_ on_ x_ axis_f**.

▷ **Step 11:**
— Declare a **string** type variable and name it **tilt_ on_ x_ axis_ string**.

▷ **Step 12:**
— Evaluate the variables **tilt_ on_ x_ axis_f** and **tilt_ on_ x_ axis_ string** from **x_ axis_ sensorValue** using **Equation 18.1**.

▷ **Step 13:**
— Check if the device output (**tilt_ on_ x_ axis_f**) greater than **145**?
  — **Note:** In the program, the sensor has been calibrated to two states; outputting 90^0 when the device is horizontal and 180^0 when it is vertical.

▷ **Step 14:**
— Define a new *Macro* and name it *Vertical*.

▷ **Step 15:**
— Edit the new macro to display *Vertical* on the *LCD* and turn *on* the *LED* labelled *Vertical* when *step 13* evaluates *True*.

▷ **Step 16:**
— Set the *LCD Cursor* to *column four* and *row zero*.

▷ **Step 17:**
— Print the string constant *Vertical* to the *LCD*.

▷ **Step 18:**
— Turn *on* the *LED* attached to pin *D5* of the microcontroller.

▷ **Step 19:**
— Define another macro and name it *Horizontal*.

▷ **Step 20:**
— Edit the new macro to display *Horizontal* on the *LCD* and turn *on* the *LED* labelled *Horizontal* when *step 13* evaluates *False*.

▷ **Step 21:**
— Set the *LCD Cursor* to *column three* and *row zero*.

▷ **Step 22:**
— Print the string constant *Horizontal* to the *LCD*.

▷ **Step 23:**
— Turn *on* the *LED* attached to pin *D2* of the microcontroller.

▷ **Step 24:**
— Switch to the *Main* program.
— Update the device output (*tilt_ on_ x_ axis_f*) every *1 second*.

▷ **Step 25:**
— Turn *off* the *LED* attached to pin *D5* of the microcontroller.

▷ **Step 26:**
— Turn *off* the *LED* attached to pin *D2* of the microcontroller.

▷ **Step 27:**
— Refresh the *LCD* display to prepare it for the next display.

▷ **Step 28:**
— Simulate the program by clicking on the *Run* button and download it to the microcontroller on the PhasePlus development board.

Chapter 19

Project 16: Automatic Cooling System

19.1. Objective

This project is a follow up to project 13. It demonstrates how to build an automatic cooling system. The system can be incorporated into any independent system or process that requires temperature monitoring and control.

Hardware

▷ Brushless DC fan
▷ TMP102 digital temperature sensor
▷ 2N3904 NPN transistor
▷ 3.3V voltage regulator
▷ Character-based LCD (16x2)
▷ Connection wires
▷ PhasePlus PIC16F877A development board
▷ Potentiometer (optional)
▷ 1x10K resistor (optional)

19.2. Brushless DC fan Overview

A brushless DC fan motor depicted in Fig. 19.1 is made using a brushless DC (BLDC) motor. A BLDC motor is a synchronous electric motor powered by a direct current. As the name implies, the brushless DC motor does not operate using brushes; rather it operates with a controller via electronic commutation.

Figure 19.1. *A brushless DC fan.*

Brushless DC fans are in many cases the solution of choice for most systems or process which dissipates a lot of heat. These fans are quite reliable and easy to interface to microcontrollers. The basic DC brushless fan is a 2-wire device over which a DC voltage ranging from 5-48V is applied. The fans mainly operate at a nominal 5V, 12V, 24V, or 48V with the 5V fans being the most commonly used in mechatronics applications.

19.3. 2N3904 NPN transistor

The 2N3904 IC depicted in Fig. 19.2 is a common NPN bipolar junction transistor used for general purpose low-power amplifying or switching applications. It is a high gain low saturation transistor suitable for TV and home appliances equipment, an in small load switching.

Figure 19.2. *An NPN 2N3904 transistor.*

19.4. Voltage Regulator -LD1117V33

The LD1117V33 depicted in Fig. 19.3 is basic low drop voltage regulator and provides up to 800mA of output current. It is contained in the TO-220 package, perfect for low voltage 3.3V applications.

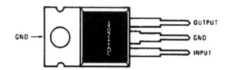

Figure 19.3. *A LD1117V33 voltage regulator.*

19.5. Circuit Schematic

The circuit schematic for this project is shown in Fig. 19.4. The power terminals of the motor connect +5V and GND of the development board. Signal terminal of the transistor connects to pin C2 of the microcontroller. The two serial communication terminals of the sensor SDA and SCL connect to pins C3 and C4 of the microcontroller. The sensor's power terminals connect to the output of the 3.3V regulator and GND. Voltage regulator's power terminals connect to the +5V and GND of the development board. While, the LED connects pin D2 of the microcontroller via 220 ohms current limiting resistor and GND. The listing below indicates how the LCD connects to the microcontroller;

▷ Data lines (D1-D3) connect to PORTB pins RB0 - RB3.
▷ Enable, read/write and RS pins connect to B5, GND and B4 respectively.
▷ The LCD back light pins, A and K connect to VCC via a 220 resistor and GND.

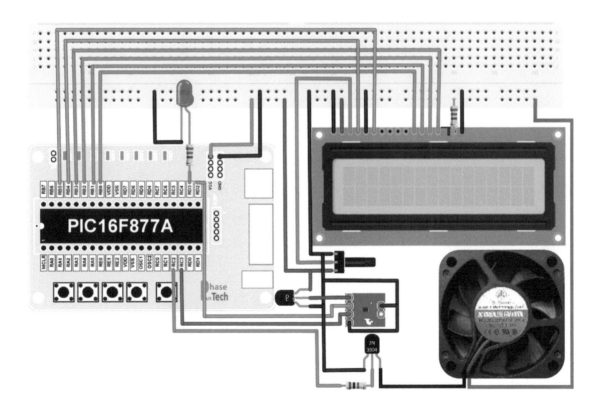

Figure 19.4. Project 16 circuit schematic.

19.6. Implementation Steps:

Project 13: Step 1

> ▷ Launch **Flowcode**.
> ▷ Select **Create a new Flowcode**, click **OK** and select **16F877A**.
> ▷ Click **OK**.

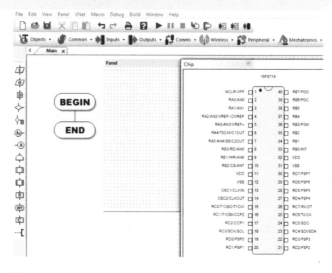

Figure 19.5. *An empty Flowcode project environment.*

Project 13: Step 2

> ▷ Click on the **Output** tab and select **LCD**.
> ▷ Right click on the **LCD** and select **Connections**.
> ▷ Double check the **LCD** is connected as shown in Fig. 16.4. and click **OK**.

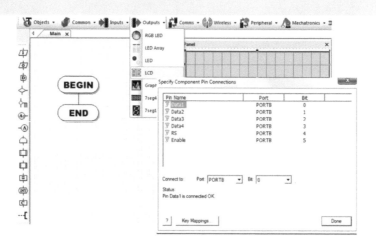

Figure 19.6. *Adding and initializing an LCD component..*

Project 13: Step 3

▷ Insert a **Component Macro** icon and double click on it.
▷ Select **LCDDisplay(0)** and **Start** in the **Component** and **Macro** fields.
▷ Click **OK**.

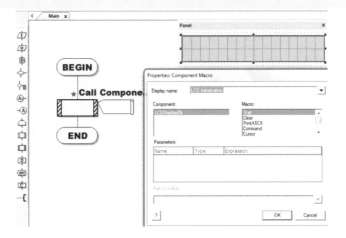

Figure 19.7. *Initializing the LCD display component.*

Project 13: Step 4

▷ Click on the **Comms** tab and select **I2C Master**.

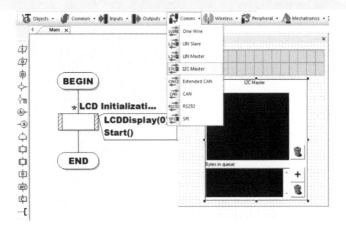

Figure 19.8. *Adding an I2C device.*

Project 13: Step 5

▷ Insert a **Component Macro** icon and double click on it.
▷ Select **I2C_ Master(0)** and **MI2C_ Init** in the **Component** and **Macro** fields.
▷ Click **OK**.

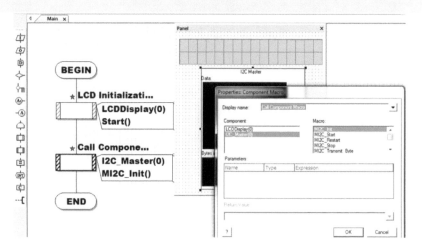

Figure 19.9. *Initializing the I2C device.*

Project 13: Step 6

▷ Insert a **Loop** icon.
▷ Also insert a **Component Macro** icon and double click on it.
▷ Select **I2C_ Master(0)** and **MI2C_ Start** in the **Component** and **Macro** fields.
▷ Click **OK**.

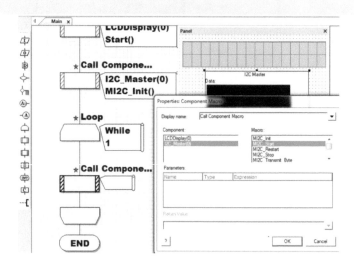

Figure 19.10. *Adding a loop and starting the I2C device.*

Project 13: Step 7

▷ Insert a **Component Macro** icon and double click on it.
▷ Select **I2C_ Master(0)** in the **Component** field.
▷ Also select **MI2C_ Transmit_ Byte** in the **Macro** field.
▷ Type **0×48** in the **Expression** field and click **OK**.

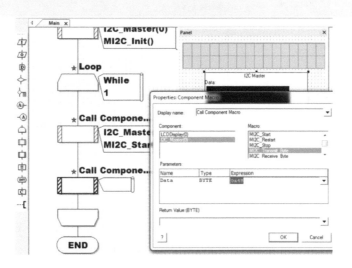

Figure 19.11. *Transmitting the I2C external device address.*

Project 13: Step 8

▷ Insert another **Component Macro** icon and double click on it.
▷ Select **I2C_ Master(0)** in the **Component** field.
▷ Also select **MI2C_ Transmit_ Byte** in the **Macro** field.
▷ Type **0×01** in the **Expression** field and click **OK**.

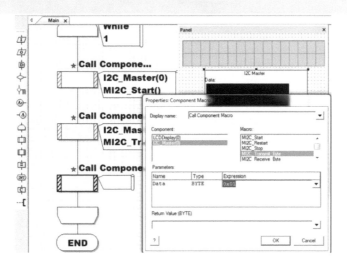

Figure 19.12. *Transmitting the I2C internal device address.*

Project 13: Step 9

▷ Insert another **Component Macro** icon and double click on it.

▷ Select **I2C_ Master(0)** and **MI2C_ Restart** in the **Component** and **Macro** fields.

▷ Click **OK**.

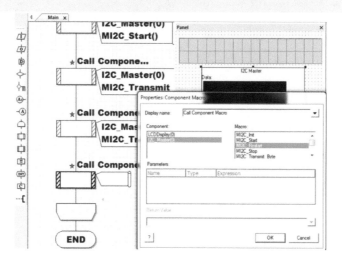

Figure 19.13. *Restarting the I2C device.*

Project 13: Step 10

▷ Insert another **Component Macro** icon and double click on it.

▷ Select **I2C_ Master(0)** in the **Component** field.

▷ Also select **MI2C_ Transmit_ Byte** in the **Macro** field.

▷ Type **0×91** in the **Expression** field and click **OK**.

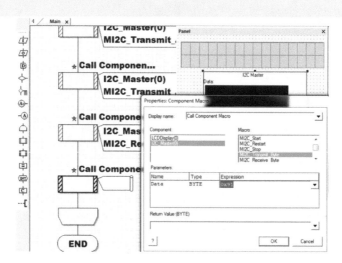

Figure 19.14. *Transmit the I2C external device address to receive the main significant byte of the data.*

Project 13: Step 11

▷ Insert another **Component Macro** icon and double click on it.
▷ Select **I2C_ Master(0)** in the **Component** field.
▷ Also select **MI2C_ Receive_ Byte** in the **Macro** field.
▷ Click on the arrow at the right end of the **Return value** field.

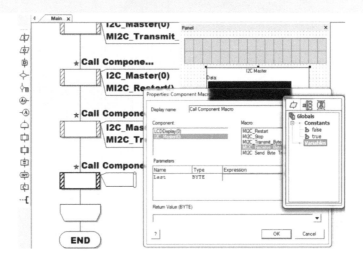

Figure 19.15. *Receiving the main significant byte of data from I2C device.*

Project 13: Step 12

▷ Double click on **Variables**.
▷ Enter **msb** in the **Name of new variable** field.
▷ Under **Variable type** select **Byte** and click **OK**.

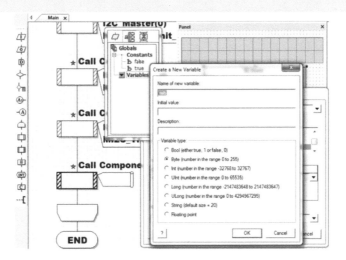

Figure 19.16. *Creating a variable to store the data received from I2C device.*

Project 13: Step 13

▷ In the **Expression** field enter0×91.
▷ Enter **msb** in the **Return value** field.
▷ Click **OK**.

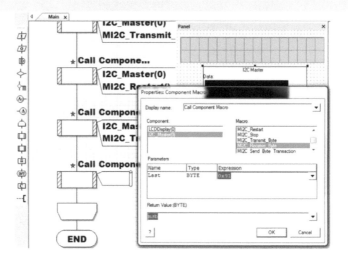

Figure 19.17. *Storing the data into the variable msb.*

Project 13: Step 14

▷ Insert a **Delay** icon and double click on it.
▷ Set the delay time to **5 milliseconds**.
▷ Click **OK**.

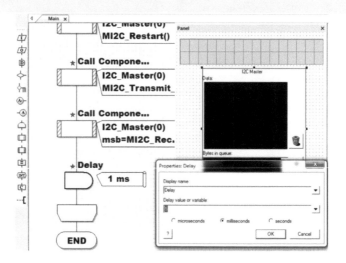

Figure 19.18. *Adding and initializing a delay.*

Project 13: Step 15

▷ Insert a **Component Macro** icon and double click on it.
▷ Select **I2C_ Master(0)** in the **Component** field.
▷ Also select **MI2C_ Transmit_ Byte** in the **Macro** field.
▷ Type **0×48** in the **Expression** field and click **OK**.

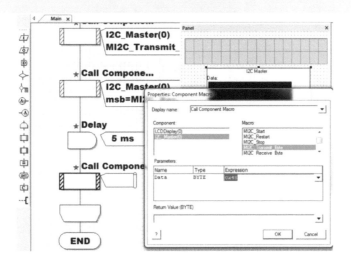

Figure 19.19. *Transmitting the I2C external device address.*

Project 13: Step 16

▷ Insert another **Component Macro** icon and double click on it.
▷ Select **I2C_ Master(0)** in the **Component** field.
▷ Also select **MI2C_ Transmit_ Byte** in the **Macro** field.
▷ Type **0×02** in the **Expression** field and click **OK**.

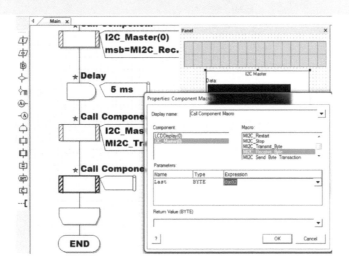

Figure 19.20. *Transmitting the I2C internal device address.*

Project 13: Step 17

▷ Insert a **Component Macro** icon and double click on it.
▷ Select **I2C_ Master(0)** and **MI2C_ Restart** in the **Component** and **Macro** fields.
▷ Click **OK**.

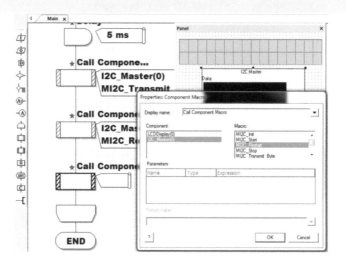

Figure 19.21. *Restarting the I2C device.*

Project 13: Step 18

▷ Insert another **Component Macro** icon and double click on it.
▷ Select **I2C_ Master(0)** in the **Component** field.
▷ Also select **MI2C_ Transmit_ Byte** in the **Macro** field.
▷ Type **0×91** in the **Expression** field and click **OK**.

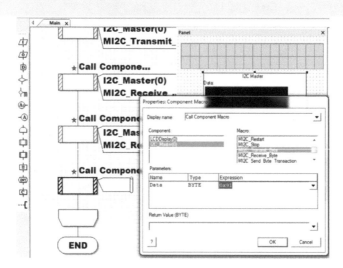

Figure 19.22. *Transmitting the I2C external device address to receive the least significant byte of the data.*

Project 13: Step 19

▷ Insert a **Component Macro** icon and double click on it.
▷ Select **I2C_Master(0)** and **MI2C_Receive_Byte** in the **Component** and **Macro** fields.
▷ Click on the **arrow** at the right end of the **Return value** field.

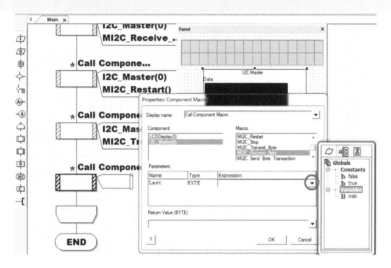

Figure 19.23. *Receiving the main significant byte of data from I2C device.*

Project 13: Step 20

▷ Double click on **Variables**.
▷ Enter **lsb** in the **Name of new variable** field.
▷ Under **Variable type** select **Byte** and click **OK**.

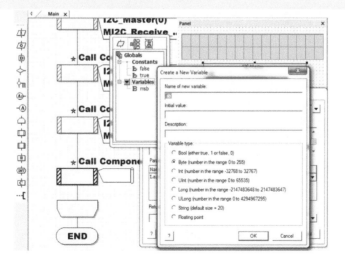

Figure 19.24. *Creating a variable to store the data received from I2C device.*

Project 13: Step 21

▷ Enter *0×91* in the ***Expression*** field.
▷ In the ***Return value*** field, enter ***lsb***.
▷ Click ***OK***.

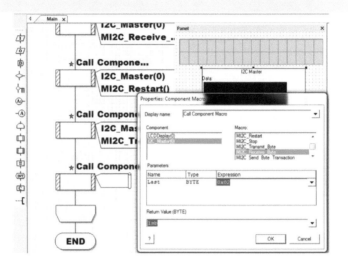

Figure 19.25. *Storing the data into the variable lsb.*

Project 13: Step 22

▷ Insert a ***Component Macro*** icon and double click on it.
▷ Select ***I2C_ Master(0)*** and ***MI2C_ Stop*** in the ***Component*** and ***Macro*** fields.
▷ Click ***OK***.

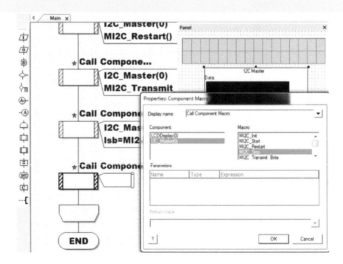

Figure 19.26. *Stopping the I2C device.*

Project 13: Step 23

▷ Insert a user-defined *Macro Call* icon and double click on it.
▷ Enter *computeTemp* in the *Name of new macro* field.
▷ Click *OK* and *OK & Edit Macro* button to edit the new macro.

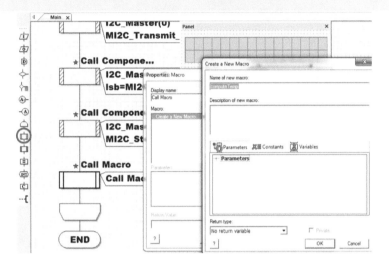

Figure 19.27. *Adding and editing a user-defined macro call icon.*

Project 13: Step 24

▷ Insert a *Calculation* icon and double click on it.
▷ Double click on *Variables* to create a new variable of *UInit* type.
▷ Enter *temp* in the *Name of new variable* field and click *OK*.

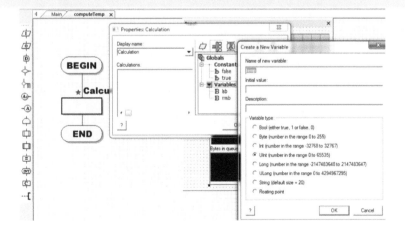

Figure 19.28. *Creating a new variable.*

Project 13: Step 25

▷ Create two other variables as follows:
  — Variable name **celsiusTemp**, type **Float**.
  — Variable name **stringTemp**, type **String**.

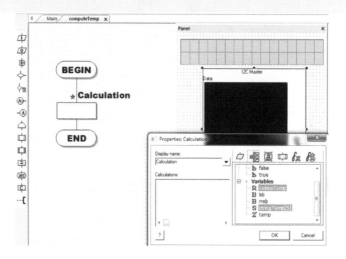

Figure 19.29. *Creating more variables.*

Project 13: Step 26

▷ Enter the following expressions into the **Calculations** field:
  — $temp = ((msb << 8) \: lsb) >> 4$
  — $celsiusTemp = int2float(temp)$.
  — $celsiusTemp = fmul(celsiusTemp, 0.0625)$.
  — $stringTemp = FloatToString\$(celsiusTemp)$.
  — Click **OK**.

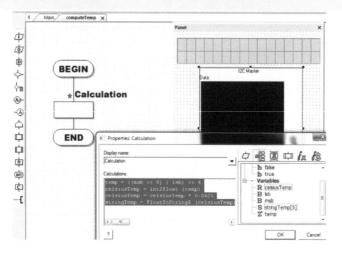

Figure 19.30. *Assigning values to variables.*

Project 13: Step 27

▷ Click on the *Macro* tab and select *New* to create a new macro.
▷ Enter *tempDisplay* in the *Name of new macro* field.
▷ Click *OK* to edit new macro.

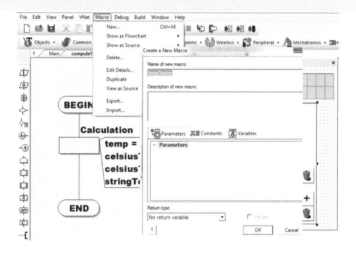

Figure 19.31. *Creating a user-defined macro.*

Project 13: Step 28

▷ Insert a *Component Macro* icon and double click on it.
▷ Select *LCDDisplay(0)* and *Cursor* in the *Component* and *Macro* fields.
▷ Enter *2* and *0* in the *x* and *y* fields, click *OK*.

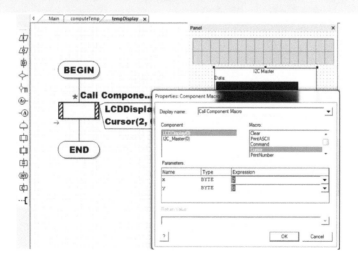

Figure 19.32. *Setting the LCD display cursor.*

Project 13: Step 29

▷ Insert another **Component Macro** icon and double click on it.
▷ Select **LCDDisplay(0)** and **PrintString** in the **Component** and **Macro** fields.
▷ Enter **"Temperature"** in the **Expression** field and click **OK**.

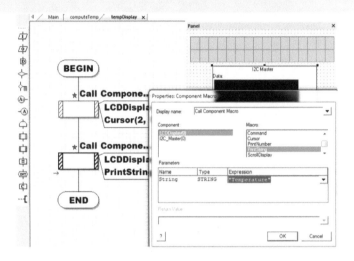

Figure 19.33. *Printing a string constant to the LCD.*

Project 13: Step 30

▷ Insert another **Component Macro** icon and double click on it.
▷ Select **LCDDisplay(0)** and **Cursor** in the **Component** and **Macro** fields.
▷ Enter *4* and *1* in the *x* and *y* fields, click **OK**.

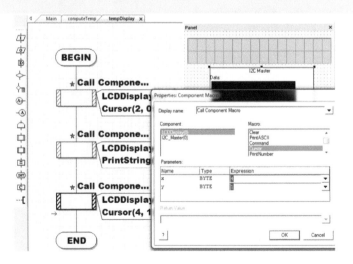

Figure 19.34. *Setting the LCD display cursor.*

Project 13: Step 31

▷ Insert another **Component Macro** icon and double click on it.
▷ Select **LCDDisplay(0)** and **PrintString** in the **Component** and **Macro** fields.
▷ Enter **"tempString"** in the **Expression** field and click **OK**.

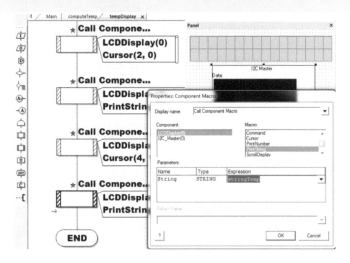

Figure 19.35. *Printing a string variable to the LCD.*

Project 13: Step 32

▷ Insert another **Component Macro** icon and double click on it.
▷ Select **LCDDisplay(0)** and **Cursor** in the **Component** and **Macro** fields.
▷ Enter **9** and **1** in the **x** and **y** fields, click **OK**.

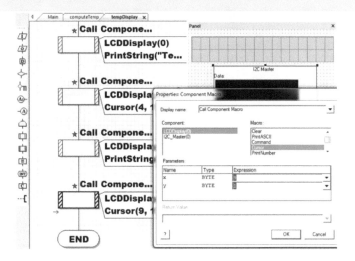

Figure 19.36. *Setting the LCD display cursor.*

Project 13: Step 33

▷ Insert another **Component Macro** icon and double click on it.
▷ Select **LCDDisplay(0)** and **PrintString** in the **Component** and **Macro** fields.
▷ Enter **"C"** in the **Expression** field and click **OK**.

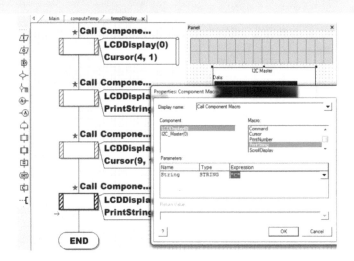

Figure 19.37. *Printing a string constant to the LCD.*

Project 13: Step 34

▷ Insert a **Decision** icon.
▷ Enter **temp > 40** in the **If** field.
▷ Click **OK**.

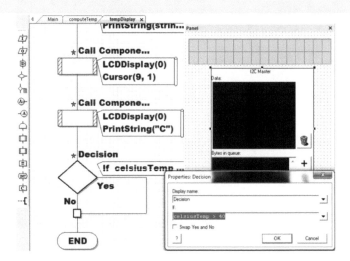

Figure 19.38. *Defining a condition to determine the flow direction.*

Project 13: Step 35

▷ Click on the **Output** tab and select **LED**.
▷ Right click on the **LED** and select **Connections**.
▷ Select **PORTD** and **Bits 3**, click **Done**.

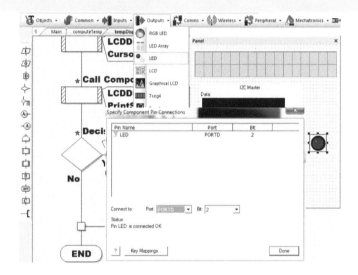

Figure 19.39. *Adding an LED component and connecting the LED to the output pin.*

Project 13: Step 36

▷ Insert a **Component Macro** icon and double click on it.
▷ Enter **LED_ON** in the **Display name** field.
▷ Select **LED(0)** and **LEDOn** in the **Component** and **Macro** fields, click **OK**.

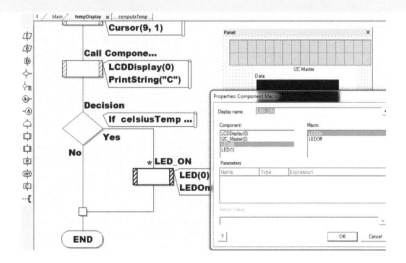

Figure 19.40. *Sending a high logic to the microcontroller output pin.*

Project 13: Step 37

▷ Insert another **LED** and label the two **LEDs** as shown in Fig. 19.41.
▷ Right click on the second **LED** and select **Connections**.
▷ Select **PORTC** and **Bits 2**, click **Done**.

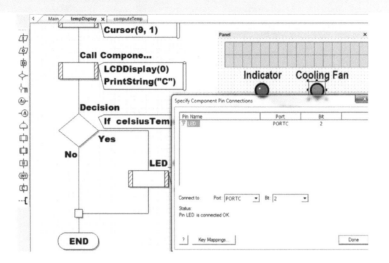

Figure 19.41. *Adding and configuring a delay.*

Project 13: Step 38

▷ Insert another **Component Macro** icon and double click on it.
▷ Enter **FAN_ON** in the **Display name** field.
▷ Select **LED(1)** and **LEDOn** in the **Component** and **Macro** fields, click **OK**.

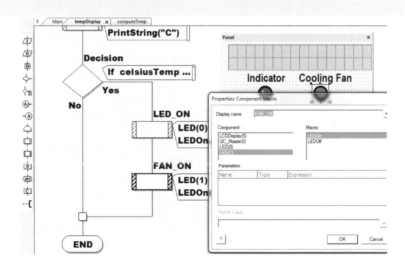

Figure 19.42. *Sending a low logic to the microcontroller output pin.*

Project 13: Step 39

▷ Insert a *Component Macro* icon and double click on it.
▷ Enter *LED_ OFF* in the *Display name* field.
▷ Select *LED(0)* and *LEDOff* in the *Component* and *Macro* fields, click *OK*.

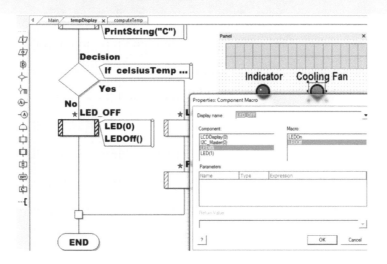

Figure 19.43. *Adding and configuring a delay.*

Project 13: Step 40

▷ Insert another *Component Macro* icon and double click on it.
▷ Enter *FAN_ OFF* in the *Display name* field.
▷ Select *LED(1)* and *LEDOff* in the *Component* and *Macro* fields, click *OK*.

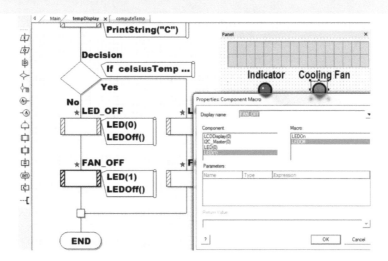

Figure 19.44. *Sending a low logic to the microcontroller output pin.*

Project 13: Step 41

▷ Insert a **Delay** icon and double click on it.
▷ Set the delay time to **200 milliseconds**.
▷ Click **OK**.

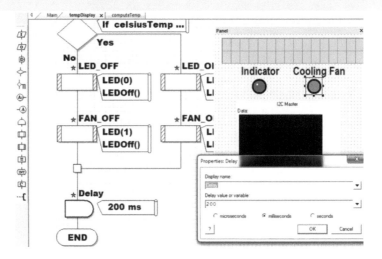

Figure 19.45. *Adding and configuring a delay.*

Project 13: Step 42

▷ Insert a user-defined **Macro Call** icon and double click on it.
▷ In the **Macro** filed select **tempDisplay** macro.
▷ Click **OK**.

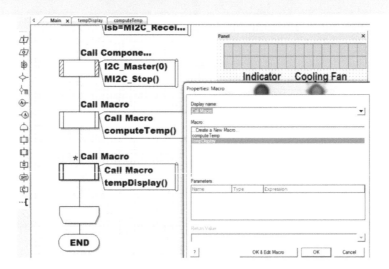

Figure 19.46. *Adding user-defined macro call icon.*

Project 13: Step 43

▷ Save the program and click on **Run** for simulation.

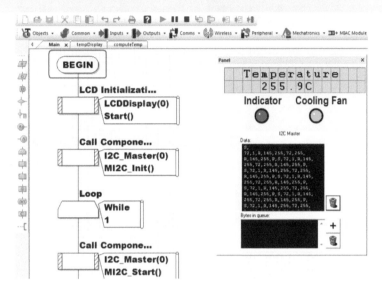

Figure 19.47. *Program is completed ready for simulation and downloading.*

19.7. Program Description

This program implements an automatic cooling system that can be integrated to other systems or processes. The system senses the ambient temperature and turns on the cooling fan and the high temperature indicator LED attached to it anytime the ambient temperature exceeds the defined threshold. Details of the programme implementation steps are listed below;

▷ **Step 1:**
 — Launch Flowcode and start a new program.
▷ **Step 2:**
 — Add an **LCD** component.
 — Connect the **LCD** to **PORTB**.
▷ **Step 3:**
 — Initialize the **LCD**.
▷ **Step 4:**
 — Add an **I2C** master device from **comms** tab.
▷ **Step 5:**
 — Initialize the **I2C** device.
▷ **Step 6:**
 — Start the **I2C** device.
  — This makes the device start listening to the I²C bus.

▷ **Step 7:**
— Transmit the external address of the *I2C* device.
    — This sets the address of the device to read data from.

▷ **Step 8:**
— Transmit the internal address of the *I2C* device.
    — This enables the device and set it to read mode.

▷ **Step 9:**
— Restart the *I2C master* device.

▷ **Step 10:**
— Transmit the external address of the *I2C* device to receive the **main significant byte** of the data.

▷ **Step 11:**
— Declare a variable to store the **main significant byte** of the data.

▷ **Step 12:**
— Name the variable *msb*.

▷ **Step 13:**
— Return the variable *msb* to the **Main** program.

▷ **Step 14:**
— Wait for **50 milliseconds** to finish receiving the data.

▷ **Step 15:**
— Transmit the external address of the *I2C* device again.
    — This sets the address of the device to read data from.

▷ **Step 16:**
— Transmit the internal address of the *I2C* device again.
    — This enables the device and set it to read mode.

▷ **Step 17:**
— Restart the *I2C master* device again.

▷ **Step 18:**
— Transmit the external address of the *I2C* device to receive the **least significant byte** of the data.

▷ **Step 19:**
— Declare a variable to store the **least significant byte** of the data.

▷ **Step 20:**
— Name the variable *lsb*.

▷ **Step 21:**
— Return the variable *lsb* to the **Main** program.

▷ **Step 22:**
— Stop the *I2C* device.

▷ **Step 23:**
— Define a macro to evaluate the sensor's ambient temperature based on **Equation 16.1**.
— Name the macro **computeTemp** and edit the macro.

▷ **Step 24:**
— Declare an **unsigned** integer variable and name it **temp**.

▷ **Step 25:**

— Declare *float* and *string* type variables.

— Name the *float* variable *celsiusTemp* and the *string* variable *stringTemp*.

▷ **Step 26:**

— Evaluate the three variables using the following relation;

— temp = ((msb << 8)lsb) >> 4.

— celsiusTemp = int2float(temp).

— celsiusTemp = fmul(celsiusTemp, 0. 0625).

— stringTemp = FloatToString$(celsiusTemp).

▷ **Step 27:**

— Define a macro.

— Name the macro *tempDisplay*.

▷ **Step 28:**

— Set the *LCD Cursor* to *column two* and *row zero*.

▷ **Step 29:**

— Print the string constant *"Temperature"* to the *LCD*.

▷ **Step 30:**

— Set the *LCD Cursor* to *column four* and *row one*.

▷ **Step 31:**

— Print the string variable *tempString* to the *LCD*.

— Note: The variable *tempString* is the sensor's ambient temperature.

▷ **Step 32:**

— Set the *LCD Cursor* to *column nine* and *row one*.

▷ **Step 33:**

— Print the string constant *"C"* to the *LCD*.

▷ **Step 34:**

— Monitor the ambient temperature.

— Ensure it does not exceeds 40^0C.

▷ **Step 35:**

— Add an *LED* component to indicate if the ambient temperature exceeds 40^0C.

— Connect the *LED* pin *D2* of the microcontroller.

▷ **Step 36:**

— Turn *on* the *LED* connected to pin *D2* of the microcontroller if the ambient temperature exceeds 40^0C.

▷ **Step 37:**

— Add another *LED* component to represent the *cooling fan* (Brushless DC fan).

— Connect the *LED* pin *C2* of the microcontroller.

▷ **Step 38:**

— For as long as the temperature is above 40^0, turn *on* the cooling fan attached to pin *C2* of the microcontroller to *cool* the system.

▷ **Step 39:**

— Turn *off* the indicator *LED* for as long the ambient temperature remain s below 40^0C.

▷ **Step 40:**

— Turn *off* the *cooling fan* also if the ambient temperature is below 40^0C.

▷ **Step 41:**

— Update the state of the ambient temperature every **200 milliseconds**.

▷ **Step 42:**

— Switch to the **Main** program and call the **tempDisplay** macro to handle the following tasks:

   — LCD display.

   — Commanding the indicator LED.

   — Commanding the cooling fan.

▷ **Step 43:**

— Simulate the program by clicking on the **Run** button and download it to the microcontroller on the PhasePlus development board.

Chapter 20

Project 17: Automatic Door System

20.1. Objective

The purpose of this project is to demonstrate how to build an automatic swinging door opening system. An automatic door is a type door which opens automatically if a someone approaches a building entrance allowing easy access to the building. These doors are becoming popular in most public buildings as they eliminate the need for hiring a doorman to usher in visitors.

Hardware

- ▷ Servo motor
- ▷ Sharp GP2Y0A02YK0F IR Proximity Sensor
- ▷ Character-based LCD (16x2)
- ▷ Connection wires
- ▷ PhasePlus PIC16F877A development board
- ▷ Potentiometer (optional)
- ▷ 10K resistor (optional)

20.2. Servo Motor Overview

Servo motors are motors which use error sensing negative feedback for effective position control based on a modulated signal. It could either be a DC or AC motor combined with a position sensing device, such as a digital decoder and could be of linear or rotary type. The motor incorporates a DC motor, a gear-train, limit stops beyond which the shaft cannot turn, a potentiometer for position feedback, and an integrated circuit for position control. The motor retains the shaft angular position so long as the modulated signal exists on the input terminal. The angular position of the shaft is changed by altering the modulated signal.

20.2.1. RC Servo Motor

There are different varieties and classes of servo motors. This project is based on the remote control (RC) servo motor, typically used on radio-controlled models to provide mechanism actuation. The three terminals of the motor are +5V, GND and control input signal. The input signal terminal takes in a pulse-width modulated (PWM) signal and commands the position of the motor shaft. RC servo motors are extremely useful in mechatronics applications. Despite their size compared to standard brushed or brushless motors, they are extremely powerful. For example, a standard servo motor such as HiTEC HC-422 shown in Fig. 20.1 is weighing 45.5g with a torque of 4.1kg-cm. It draws power proportional to the mechanical load.

Figure 20.1. *A bipolar stepper motor.*

20.2.2. Sharp GP2Y0A02YK0F IR Proximity Sensor

Sharp GP2Y0A02YK0F IR proximity sensor is a three terminal IR sensor module comprising a integrated combination of PSD (position sensitive detector), IRED (infrared emitting diode) and signal processing circuit. The sensor operates on the principles of triangulation where location of a point is determined by measuring angles to it from known points at either end of a fixed baseline. This device outputs a voltage which non-linearly corresponds to the detection distance. So this sensor can be used as a proximity sensor as well as distance measuring sensor. The three terminals of the sensor are output signal terminal, +5V and GND.

20.3. Circuit Schematic

Figure 20.2 depicts the circuit schematic for this project. The motor input signal terminal and the sensor's signal terminal connect to pin D1 and A0 of the microcontroller. While their power terminals connect to +5V and GND. The LED's anode connects to pins D4 of the microcontroller, and the cathode connects to GND. The listing below indicates how the LCD connects to the microcontroller;

 ▷ Data lines (D1-D3) connect to PORTB pins RB0 - RB3.
 ▷ Enable, read/write and RS pins connect to B5, GND and B4 respectively.
 ▷ The LCD back light pins, A and K connect to VCC via a 220 resistor and GND.

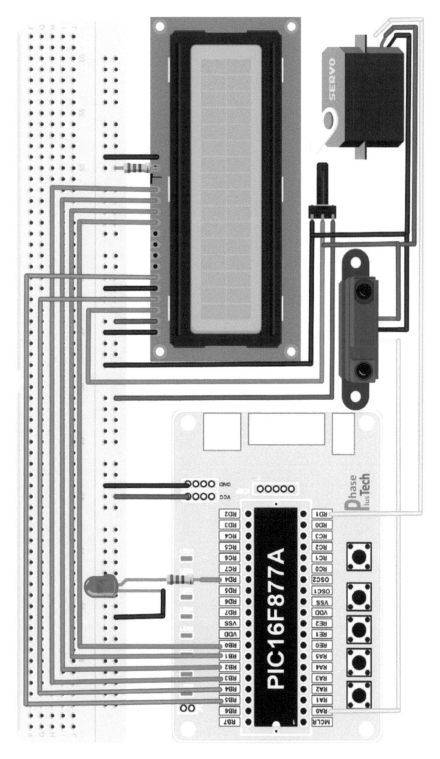

Figure 20.2. Project 17 circuit schematic.

20.4. Implementation Steps:

Project 17: Step 1

▷ Launch *Flowcode*.
▷ Select *Create a new Flowcode*, click *OK* and select *16F877A*.
▷ Click *OK*.

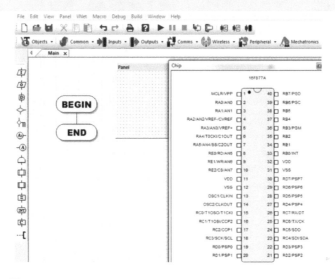

Figure 20.3. *An empty Flowcode project environment.*

Project 17: Step 2

▷ Click on the *Output* tab and select *LCD*.
▷ Right click on the *LCD* and select *Connections*.
▷ Double check the *LCD* is connected as shown in Fig. 20.4 and click *OK*.

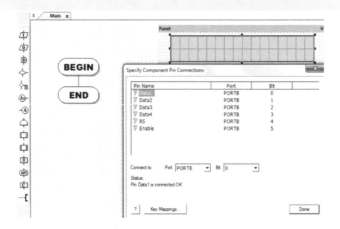

Figure 20.4. *Adding and connecting an LCD component.*

Project 17: Step 3

▷ Insert a **Component Macro** icon and double click on it.
▷ Select **LCDDisplay(0)** and **Start** in the **Component** and **Macro** fields.
▷ Click **OK**.

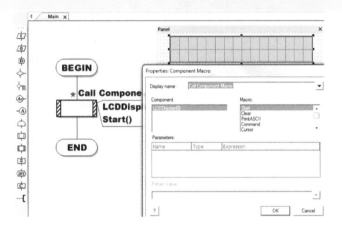

Figure 20.5. *Initializing the LCD component.*

Project 17: Step 4

▷ Click on the **mechatronics** tab and select **Servo** to add a servo motor.

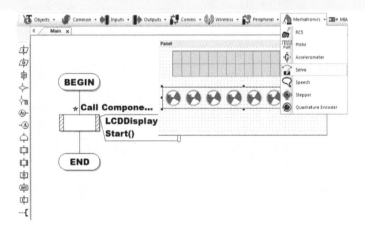

Figure 20.6. *Adding a servo motor.*

Project 17: Step 5

▷ Right click on the **Servos** and select **Ext Properties**.
▷ Select **1** in the **Number of channels** menu.
▷ Click **OK**.

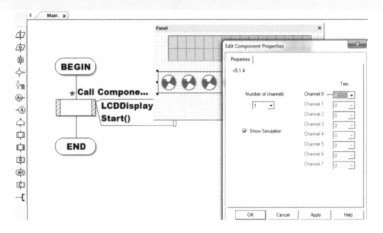

Figure 20.7. *Configuring the servo motor.*

Project 17: Step 6

▷ Right click on the **Servo** and select **Connections**.
▷ Connect the **Servo** to **PORTD Bit 1**.
▷ Click **OK**.

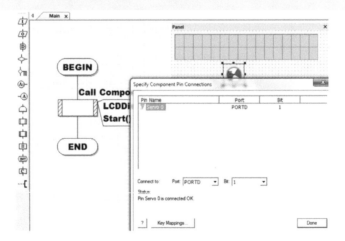

Figure 20.8. *Connecting the servo motor to the microcontroller output pin.*

Project 17: Step 7

▷ Insert a *Component Macro* icon and double click on it.
▷ Select *Servo(0)* and *EnableServo* in the *Component* and *Macro* fields.
▷ Type *0* in the *Expression* field and click *OK*.

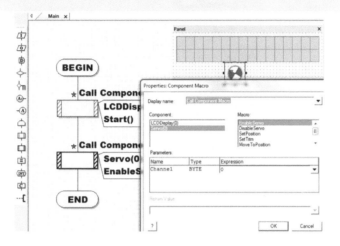

Figure 20.9. *Activating the servo motor.*

Project 17: Step 8

▷ Insert another *Component Macro* icon and double click on it.
▷ Select *Servo(0)* and *SetPosition* in the *Component* and *Macro* fields.
▷ Type *0* in the *Channel* and *Position* fields under the *Expression* field and click *OK*.

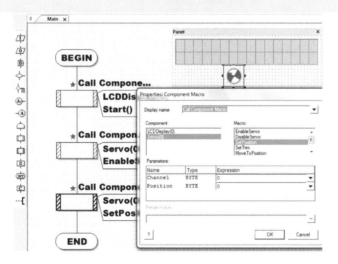

Figure 20.10. *Setting the servo motor position.*

Project 17: Step 9

▷ Insert a *Loop* icon.

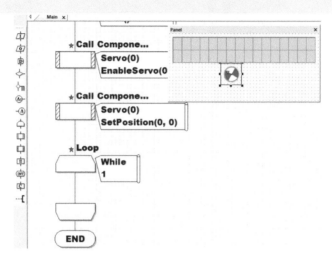

Figure 20.11. *Adding a continuous loop.*

Project 17: Step 10

▷ Insert a *Component Macro* icon and double click on it.
▷ Select *LCDDisplay(0)* and *Cursor* in the *Component* and *Macro* fields.
▷ In the *x* and *y* fields enter *2* and *0*, click *OK*.

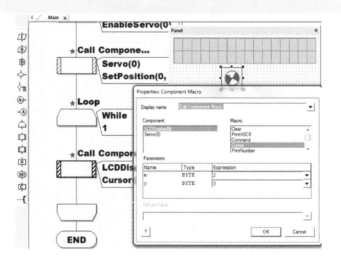

Figure 20.12. *LCD display cursor positioning.*

Project 17: Step 11

▷ Insert another **Component Macro** icon and double click on it.
▷ Select **LCDDisplay(0)** and **PrintString** in the **Component** and **Macro** fields.
▷ Type **"Door Closed"** in the **Expression** field and click **OK**.

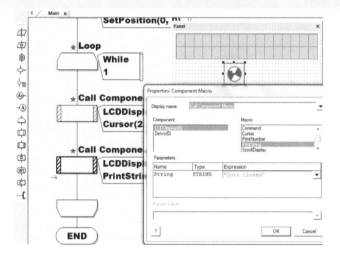

Figure 20.13. *Printing a string constant to the LCD.*

Project 17: Step 12

▷ Click on the **Input** tab and select **ADC**.
▷ Right click on the **ADC** and select **Connections**.
▷ Double check the **ADC** device is connected to pin **An0** and click **Done**.

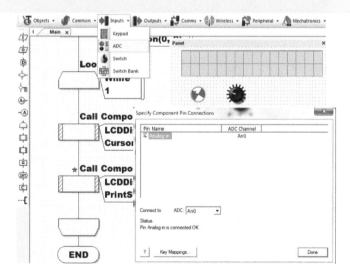

Figure 20.14. *Adding and connecting an ADC device to microcontroller's analogue input pin.*

Project 17: Step 13

▷ Insert a **Component Macro** icon and double click on it.
▷ Select **ADC(0)** and **ReadAsInt** in the **Component** and **Macro** fields.
▷ Click on the **arrow** at the right end of the **Return Value** field.

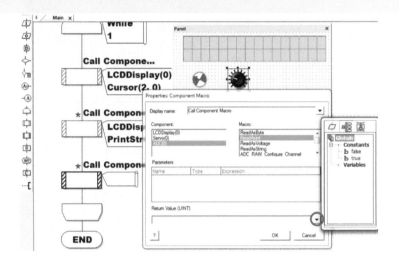

Figure 20.15. *Reading the ADC signal terminal .*

Project 17: Step 14

▷ Double click on **Variables** to create a new variable.
▷ Enter **irSensorValue** in the **Name of new variable** field.
▷ Select **UInt** under the **Variable type** and click **OK**.

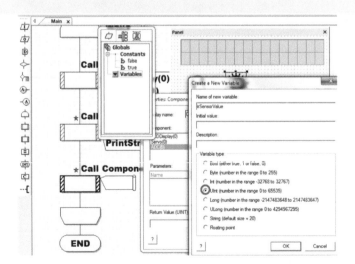

Figure 20.16. *Creating a variable.*

Project 17: Step 15

▷ Enter *irSensorValue* in the ***Return Value*** field and click ***OK***.

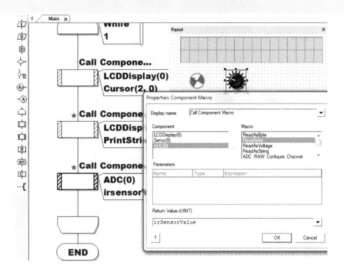

Figure 20.17. *Returning a variable to the Main program.*

Project 17: Step 16

▷ Insert a ***Decision*** icon and double click on it.
▷ Enter*irSensorValue > 200* in the ***If*** field.
▷ Click ***OK***.

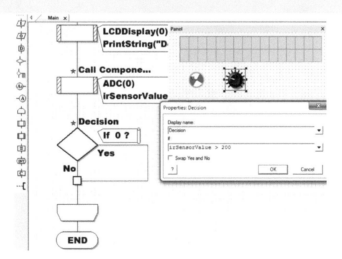

Figure 20.18. *Setting a condition to determine the program flow direction.*

Project 17: Step 17

▷ Insert a user-defined *Macro Call* icon and double click on it.
▷ Double click on *Create a New Macro* under *Macro* field.
▷ Enter *doorOpened* in the *Name of new macro* filed and click *OK*.

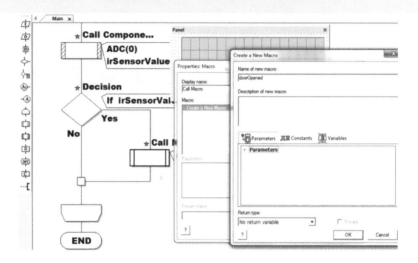

Figure 20.19. *Creating a user-defined macro.*

Project 17: Step 18

▷ Click *OK & Edit Macro* to edit the new macro..

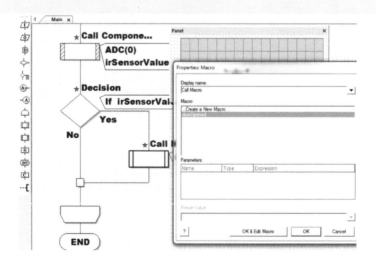

Figure 20.20. *Editing the the user-defined macro.*

Project 17: Step 19

▷ Insert a **Component Macro** icon and double click on it.
▷ Select **Servo(0)** and **SetPosition** in the **Component** and **Macro** fields.
▷ Type **0** and **130** in the **Channel** and **Position** fields under the **Expression** field and click **OK**.

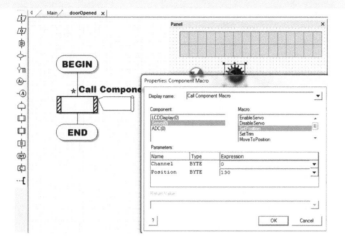

Figure 20.21. *Resetting the servo motor position.*

Project 17: Step 20

▷ Click on the **Output** tab and select **LED**.
▷ Right click on the **LED** and select **Connections**.
▷ Select **PORTD** and **Bits 4**, click **OK**.

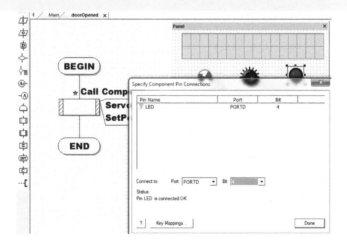

Figure 20.22. *Adding and connecting an LED component to the microcontroller output pin.*

Project 17: Step 21

▷ Insert a **Component Macro** icon and double click on it.
▷ Select **LED(0)** and **LEDOn** in the **Component** and **Macro** fields.
▷ Click **OK**.

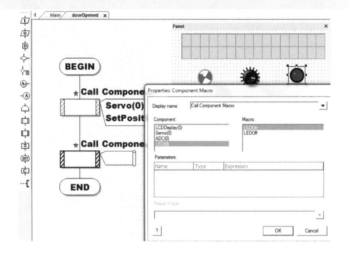

Figure 20.23. *Sending a high logic to the microcontroller output pin.*

Project 17: Step 22

▷ Insert another **Component Macro** icon and double click on it.
▷ Select **LCDDisplay(0)** and **Clear** in the **Component** and **Macro** fields.
▷ Click **OK**.

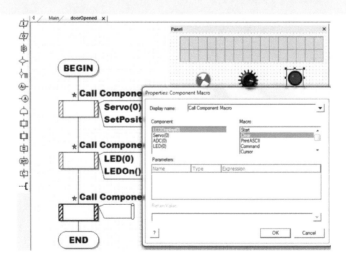

Figure 20.24. *Clearing the LCD display.*

Project 17: Step 23

▷ Insert a **Component Macro** icon and double click on it.
▷ Select **LCDDisplay(0)** and **Cursor** in the **Component** and **Macro** fields.
▷ In the **x** and **y** fields enter **2** and **0**, click **OK**.

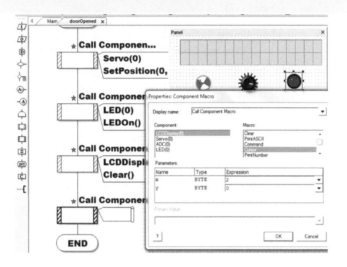

Figure 20.25. *LCD display cursor repositioning.*

Project 17: Step 24

▷ Insert another **Component Macro** icon and double click on it.
▷ Select **LCDDisplay(0)** and **PrintString** in the **Component** and **Macro** fields.
▷ Type **"Door Opened"** in the **Expression** field and click **OK**.

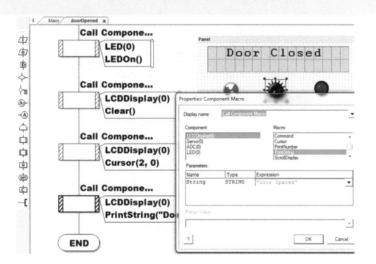

Figure 20.26. *Printing another string constant to the LCD.*

Project 17: Step 25

▷ Insert a **Delay** icon and double click on it.
▷ Set the delay time to **4 second**s.
▷ Click **OK**.

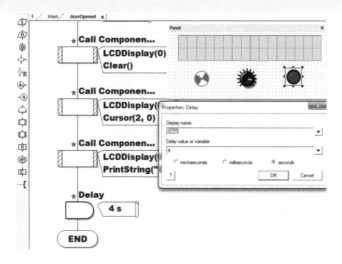

Figure 20.27. *Adding and configuring a delay.*

Project 17: Step 26

▷ Switch to the **Main** program by selecting its tab.
▷ Insert a **Component Macro** icon and double click on it.
▷ Select **Servo(0)** and **AutoMoveToPosition** in the **Component** and **Macro** fields.
▷ Type **0, 0** and **5** in the **Expression** field, click **OK**.

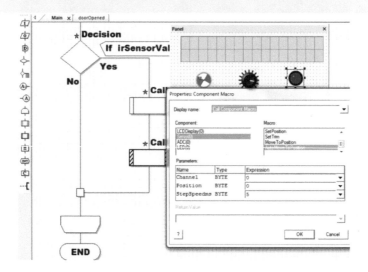

Figure 20.28. *Servo motor automatic positioning.*

Project 17: Step 27

▷ Insert a **Component Macro** icon and double click on it.
▷ Select **LED(0)** and **LEDOff** in the **Component** and **Macro** fields.
▷ Click **OK**.

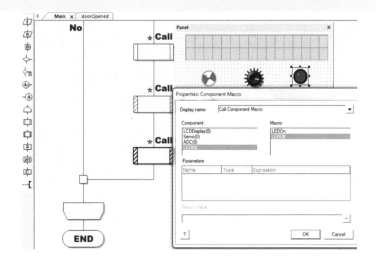

Figure 20.29. *Sending a low logic to the microcontroller output pin.*

Project 17: Step 28

▷ Declare a **Connection Point** just before the **ADC Read** macro.
▷ Also add a jump to **Connection Point** icon just below **LED Off** macro.

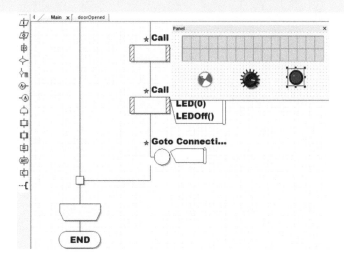

Figure 20.30. *Declaring connection points.*

Project 17: Step 29

▷ Insert a **Delay** icon and double click on it.
▷ Set the delay time to **200 millisecond**s.
▷ Click **OK**.

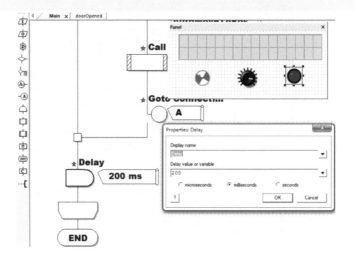

Figure 20.31. *Adding and configuring a delay.*

Project 17: Step 30

▷ Save the program and click on **Run** for simulation.

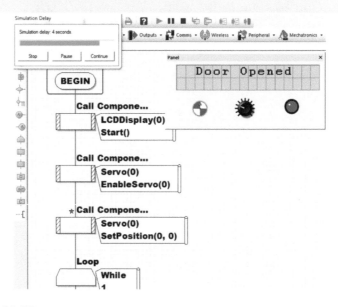

Figure 20.32. *Program is completed ready for simulation and downloading.*

20.5. Program Description

This program implements an automatic swinging door opening system that can be installed at any building entrance. By default; the door is always closed, the LED turned off and the LCD displaying *"Door Closed"*. However, if the system senses someone approaching the entrance, the door opens automatically, the LED turns on and the LCD displays *"Door Opened"*. After the person must have passed, the system reverts to its default operation mode. For safety, the door cannot close as long as someone is within the preset opening range.

Note: The ***ADC device*** referred to in the program represents the ***GP2Y0A02YK0F IR proximity*** sensor or any other IR sensor module used in implementing the project.

▷ **Step 1:**
— Launch *Flowcode* and start a new program.
▷ **Step 2:**
— Add an *LCD* component.
— Connect the *LCD* to *PORTB*.
▷ **Step 3:**
— Initialize the LCD component for display.
▷ **Step 4:**
— Add a servo motor component.
▷ **Step 5:**
— Selecting *one* servo on channel *zero*.
▷ **Step 6:**
— Connect the servo motor to pin *D1* of the microcontroller.
▷ **Step 7:**
— Servo need to be activated before use and deactivated when not in use.
— Therefore, enable the servo motor on channel *zero*.
▷ **Step 8:**
— Set the servo motor shaft to an initial position 0^0.
▷ **Step 9:**
— Add a *Loop* to make the program runs repeatedly.
▷ **Step 10:**
— Set the *LCD Cursor* to column *two* and row *zero*.
▷ **Step 11:**
— Anytime the door is closed indicate on the *LCD*.
— Print the string constant *"Door Closed"* to the LCD.
▷ **Step 12:**
— Add an *ADC* device to represent the *IR* sensor (for simulation).
— *Note:* (Flowcode does have an *IR proximity* sensor in its components library).
— *IR* sensors are analogue devices.
— Connect the *ADC* device to pin *A0* (analogue channel zero) of the microcontroller.
▷ **Step 13:**
— Read as an *integer* variable the value at the sensor signal terminal.
▷ **Step 14:**

— Declare a variable of *integer* type and name it *irSensorValue* to store the value read from sensor's signal terminal.

▷ **Step 15:**

— Return the variable *irSensorValue* to the *Main* program.

▷ **Step 16:**

— Check if the variable *irSensorValue* greater is than *200*.

— If someone is within the door-defined opening range, the value at the sensor signal terminal will be greater than 200 ADC value.

▷ **Step 17:**

— Define a macro to handle the opening and closing of the door.

— Name the *Macro* as *doorOpened*.

▷ **Step 18:**

— Edit the new macro to the following:

— command the door to open.

— command the *LCD* to display *Door opened*.

— command the *LED* attached to pin *D4* to turn *on*.

▷ **Step 19:**

— Set the servo motor to position 130^0 at once. (i.e., swing the door open)

▷ **Step 20:**

— Add an *LED* and connect the *LED* to pin *D4* to indicate when the door opens.

▷ **Step 21:**

— Turn *on* the *LED* attached to pin D4 anytime the is opened.

▷ **Step 22:**

— Delete the message *"Door Closed"* on the *LCD* and prepare it to display *"Door Opened"*.

▷ **Step 23:**

— Set the *LCD* display cursor again to *column two* and *row zero*.

▷ **Step 24:**

— Print *"Door Opened"* on the LCD.

▷ **Step 25:**

— Keep the door opened for *4 seconds*.

▷ **Step 26:**

— Gradually close the door when no one is within the door-defined opening range.

▷ **Step 27:**

— The door is now closed, so turn *off* the *LED*.

▷ **Step 28:**

— Check continuously for when the sensor's signal terminal will change from *High* to *Low*.

▷ **Step 29:**

— Check every *200 milliseconds* to keep track of *step 28*.

▷ **Step 30:**

— Simulate the program by clicking on the *Run* button and download it to the micro-controller on the PhasePlus development board.

Chapter 21

Project 18: Driving a Stepper Motor

21.1. Objective

The purpose of this project is to demonstrate how to interface stepper motors to a micro-controller. Stepper motors are employed in automation applications that require precision positioning of the motor shaft at a specific speed and specific direction. The two commonly used stepper motors in mechatronics systems are unipolar and bipolar, and this project is based on a bipolar stepper motor.

Note: Unlike the previous projects, this project and the subsequent projects details implementation steps would not be given. However, these can be downloaded from the book's website.

Hardware

- ▷ 1.8^0 Bipolar stepper motor
- ▷ Character-based LCD (16x2)
- ▷ Connection wires
- ▷ PhasePlus PIC16F877A development board
- ▷ Potentiometer (optional)
- ▷ 1x10K resistor (optional)

21.2. Stepper Motor Overview

A Stepper motor is a brushless DC motor which divides rotation of the motor shaft into smaller steps. Commutation in stepper motor is handled externally by the motor controller. This motor is perfect for automation which requires precision positioning of the motor shaft to a specific point, at a specific speed and in a specific direction. In some applications, stepper motors are preferable over servo motors; however, both motor types offer similar opportunities when it comes to precise position control.

Unlike servo motors and other brushed or brushless DC motors, stepper motors have the capability of holding their position when they are not moving and are typically fully powered all the time. Stepper motors are either bipolar or unipolar and are classified based on the minimum number of steps or degrees the motor can make. Commonly used stepper motors in mechatronics systems are the 200 steps, or 1.8° motors and can be controlled with a microcontroller and some few transistors. However, many drivers are available for stepper motors control. This project utilizes a driver called EasyDriver by Sparkfun Electronics.

21.2.1. Bipolar Stepper Motor

Figure 21.1 depicts schematic of a bipolar Stepper motor; this motor is similar to the unipolar stepper motor except the absence of centre tab in the coils. Because of this, a bipolar stepper motor requires a controller which is capable of reversing the current flow through the coils by alternating the polarity of the terminals.

Figure 21.1. *A bipolar stepper motor.*

The EasyDriver depicted in Fig. 21.2 is a simple to use bipolar stepper motor driver, compatible with any microcontroller that outputs a digital 0 to 5V pulse or 0 to 3.3V pulse. It requires a 7V to 30V supply to power the motor and can power any voltage of stepper motor. The EasyDriver has an on board voltage regulator for the digital interface that can be set to 5V or 3.3V. It works perfectly with any bipolar stepper motor.

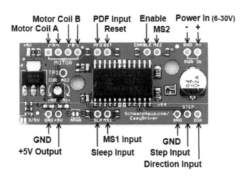

Figure 21.2. *Sparkun EasyDriver bipolar stepper motor controller.*

21.3. Circuit Schematic

Figures 21.3 and 21.4 depict the functional blocks diagram and circuit schematic for this project. There are five functional components in the system; the microcontroller, LCD, motor driver and the motor itself. The components connect to the microcontroller as follows: Four terminals of the motor connect to the motor driver board as indicated in the figure. The motor step and direction control terminals on the driver board connect to pin D0 and D1 of the microcontroller, while its power terminals connect to +5V and GND of the development board.

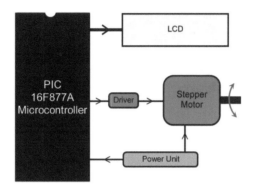

Figure 21.3. *Project 18 functional blocks diagram*

The listing below indicates how the LCD connects to the microcontroller;
  ▷ Data lines (D1-D3) connect to PORTB pins RB0 - RB3.
  ▷ Enable, read/write and RS pins connect to B5, GND and B4 respectively.
  ▷ The LCD back light pins, A and K connect to VCC via a 220 resistor and GND.

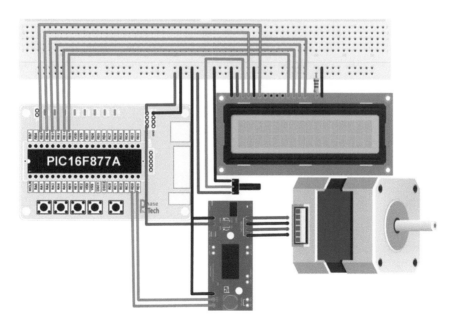

Figure 21.4. *Project 18 circuit schematic..*

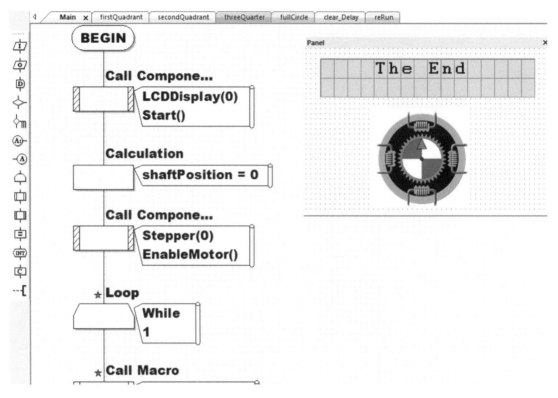

Figure 21.5. *Project 18 program and simulation layout.*

21.4. Program Description

This program implements a stepper motor shaft quadrant positioning. The program first drives the motor shaft through the first quadrant (90^0 clockwise) in 24 steps. The motor then stops for five seconds before proceeding to the next quadrant until a complete revolution of the shaft is achieved. At every stage, the shaft's current position (quadrant) is displayed on the LCD. Transition from one quadrant to the next is also indicated on the display and finally, at the end of the fourth quadrant, the message "The End" is displayed.

Chapter 22

Project 19: Generator/Main Grid Auto-Change-Over Switch

22.1. Objective

The purpose of this project is to demonstrate how to build an automatic electricity supply changeover from the main grid to the generator supply and back to the main grid when its supply is restored. This eliminates the inconvenience of having to physically change the electricity supply from the main grid to the generator and vice versa. For generating sets fitted with electrical starters, the system again solves the problem of manual starting of generators when the main grid supply ceased.

Hardware

- ▷ 25A Solid state relay
- ▷ Character-based LCD (16x2)
- ▷ Connection wires
- ▷ PhasePlus PIC16F877A development board
- ▷ 2 x Green LEDs
- ▷ 2 x red LEDs
- ▷ 4 x 220Ω resistor

22.2. Solid State Relay (SSR)

A solid state relay schematically shown in Fig. 22.1 is essentially an Integrated Circuit (IC) which acts like a mechanical relay (an electromechanical switch). It allows the control of high voltage AC loads from lower voltage DC control circuitry. Solid state relays have several advantages over mechanical relays. For instance, a solid state relay can be switched by a much lower voltage and at a much lower current than most mechanical relays. Also, because it does not have any moving contacts, solid state relays can be switched much faster and for much longer periods without wearing out. The electrical separation between the input control signal and the output load voltage is accomplished with the aid of an opto-coupler type light sensor.

Figure 22.1. *A bipolar stepper motor.*

22.3. Circuit Schematic

Figure 22.2 and 22.3 depict the functional blocks diagram and circuit schematic for this project. The system is composed of five major functional components; microcontroller, LCD, LEDs for status indication, solid state relay and signal sensing/conditioning circuit. These components connect to the microcontroller as follows: The signal terminals of the two signal sensing/conditioning devices connect to pins E0 and E1 and the relay positive input terminal connects to pin C0. The cathodes of the four indicator LEDs connect to pin C1, C2, C3 and D0. Ground terminals of all the components connect to the GND of the development board as indicated in Fig. 22.3

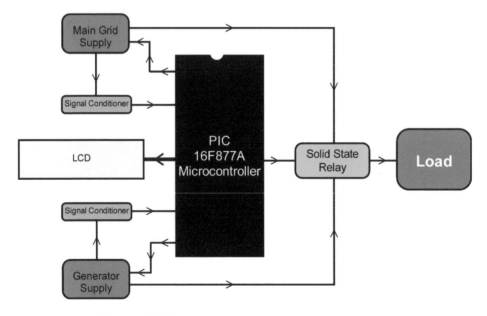

Figure 22.2. *Project 19 functional blocks diagram*

The listing below indicates how the LCD connects to the microcontroller;

▷ Data lines (D1-D3) connect to PORTB pins RB0 - RB3.

▷ Enable, read/write and RS pins connect to B5, GND and B4 respectively.

▷ The LCD back light pins, A and K connect to VCC via a 220 resistor and GND.

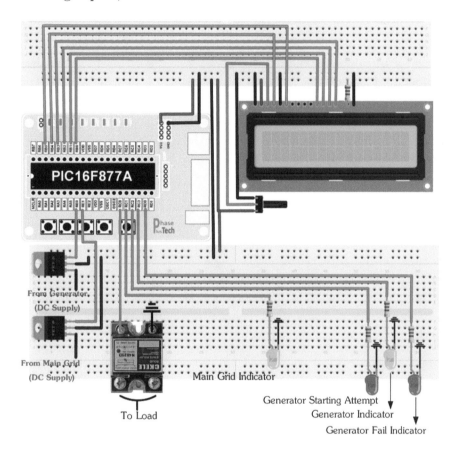

Figure 22.3. *Project 19 circuit schematic..*

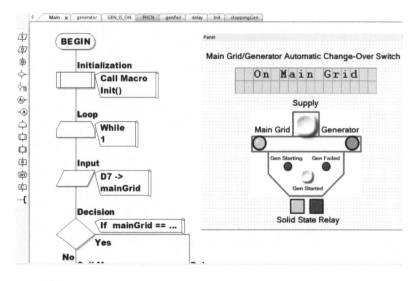

Figure 22.4. *Project 19 program and simulation layout.*

22.4. Program Description

This program implements an automatic main grid/generator electricity supply changeover switch. The system, by default is always connected to the main grid via a normally close solid state relay. When the absence of the main grid supply is sensed, the system generates a control signal that opens the relay contact. In the open state, the relay connects the generator supply to the load.

Provision is made for automatic generator starting for generators fitted with electrical starting system. The system makes three starting attempts, upon which if the generator fails to start after the three attempts, a failure is indicated on the LCD and the LED status display. The system then goes into waiting state until the generator is manually started or main grid supply is restored. Occurrence of either of the two connects the relay switch appropriately. System status is always indicated on the LCD and the indicator LEDs for ease of use.

Chapter 23

Project 20: Vehicle Reverse and Parking Guidance System

23.1. Objective

The purpose of this project is to demonstrate how to build an ultrasonic-based vehicle reverse and parking guidance system. The system is normally fitted on a vehicle's rear bumper to sense and alert the driver when the vehicle is close to an obstacle. The components used in this project have been discussed already in the previous projects. Therefore, for components background information reference should be made to the previous chapters.

Hardware

- ▷ 4 x Ultrasonic range finders
- ▷ 5A relay
- ▷ Connection wires
- ▷ PhasePlus PIC16F877A development board
- ▷ 10K resistor (optional)

23.2. Vehicle Reverse and Parking Guidance System (RPGS)

Vehicle Reverse and Parking Guidance System (RPGS) is an active sensor-based automatic car reversing and parking guidance system, usually fitted on a vehicle rear bumper to assist in proper and safe reversing or parking manoeuvres. The system is equipped with feedback signals to alert the driver of unseen obstacle while reversing or parking a vehicle.

Feedback to the driver is via audible beeps or tones. The frequency of the beeps indicates distance from an obstruction, with the beeps becoming faster the closer the vehicle moves to an object the free encyclopedia [12]. A continuous tone may be heard when the vehicle is extremely close, often warning a driver to stop immediately to avoid collision.

23.3. Circuit Schematic

The functional blocks diagram and circuit schematic for this project are shown in Fig. 23.1 and 23.2 respectively. Main functional components in the system are the microcontroller, four ultrasonic sensors, solid state relay, Piezo sounder and the conditioning circuitry.

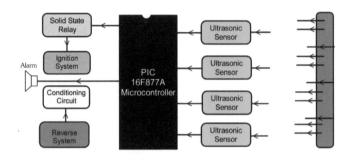

Figure 23.1. *Project 20: Program and simulation layout.*

The components connect to the microcontroller as follows: Analogue pins of the four ultrasonic sensors connect to analogues pins A0 to A3 of the microcontroller, and their power terminals connect to +5V and GND accordingly. The ignition system control relay connects to the microcontroller via a shielding transistor and the Piezo sounder connects to pin D2 and GND. While, the anodes of the two status LEDs connect to pins C6 and D3 via current limiting resistors, and the LEDs cathodes connect to GND. The reverse shift gear activation switch connects to pin D7 and GND.

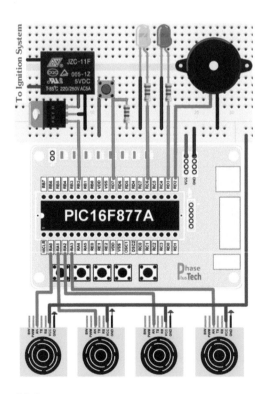

Figure 23.2. *Project 20: Program and simulation layout.*

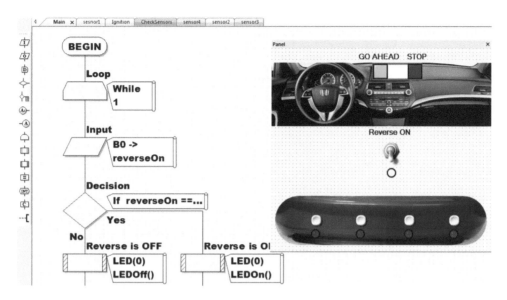

Figure 23.3. *Project 20: Program and simulation layout.*

23.4. Program Description

This program implements an automatic vehicle reverse and parking guidance system. In the program, distance thresholds were defined upon which the system raises alarm. The alarm is of low frequency at safer reverse distances and become high as the obstruction becomes closer. Persistence alarm signifies the vehicle should not move any further. If the driver ignores this alarm, the system automatically switches off the vehicle ignition system and prevents the vehicle from starting in as much the reverse gear is engaged or reengaged. The vehicle only starts in neutral or forward gear. When installed on a vehicle, the system becomes active anytime a reverse gear is engaged. In active state, each of the four sensors scans for obstructions within the defined range thresholds and reports to the microcontroller if any is detected.

Chapter 24

Project 21: Single Axis Solar Tracking System

24.1. Objective

The purpose of this project is to demonstrate how to build an automatic single axis solar tracking system for solar power plants. Solar panels are usually tilted at a fixed angle corresponding to the latitude of the location. However, incorporating a solar tracking system to a solar panel can increase the electricity yield of the plant by as much as 35% to 60%.

Hardware

▷ Stepper motor
▷ Stepper motor driver
▷ Character-based LCD (16x2)
▷ 2 x Photocells (LDR)
▷ 2 x 10K resistor
▷ Potentiometer (optional)
▷ 10K resistor (optional)
▷ PhasePlus PIC16F877A development board
▷ Connection wires

24.2. Solar Tracking System Overview

A solar tracker is a device which orients solar panel to the position of the sun where the solar radiation is highest at any given time. It positions the panel to face east when the sun rises and follows it as it travels west during the day. Solar trackers are either single axis or 2-axis. The single axis solar trackers adjust the panel's elevation only (i.e. east-west orientation), while the 2-axes tracker are capable of adjusting both elevation and azimuth orientations (i.e north-south and east-west orientations). Figure 24.1 depicts an illustration of the angle with which the sun's rays makes with the zenith (vertical direction) during different times of the day.

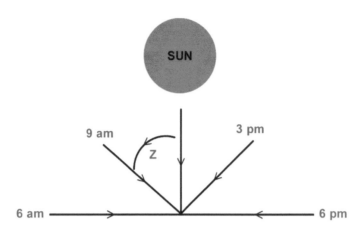

Figure 24.1. *The sun zenith angle.*

When the sun is directly overhead the zenith angle (Z) is zero, and the full intensity of sunlight is directed upon the Earth's surface. The zenith angle varies linearly with time from -90^0 at sunrise (6am) to $+90^0$ at sunset (6pm).

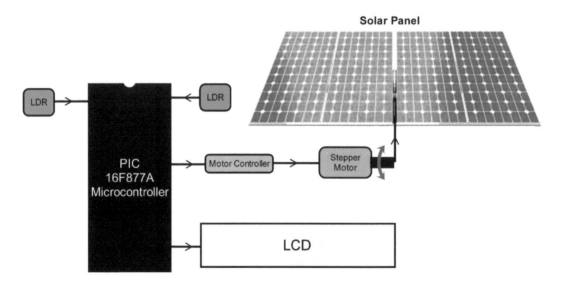

Figure 24.2. *Project 21: Functional blocks diagram*

24.3. Circuit Schematic

Figure 24.2 and 24.3 depict the functional blocks diagram and circuit schematic for this project. Microcontroller, LCD, motor driver and stepper motor are the main functional components in the system. These components connect to the microcontroller as follows: The two light sensors connect to the analogue pins A1 and A5, while the stepper motor connects to the microcontroller via its drive board.

The listing below indicates how the LCD connects to the microcontroller;
  ▷ Data lines (D1-D3) connect to PORTB pins RB0 - RB3.
  ▷ Enable, read/write and RS pins connect to B5, GND and B4 respectively.
  ▷ The LCD back light pins, A and K connect to VCC via a 220 resistor and GND.

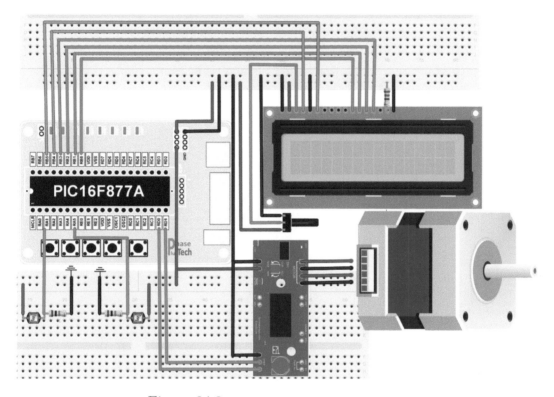

Figure 24.3. *Project 21: Circuit schematic..*

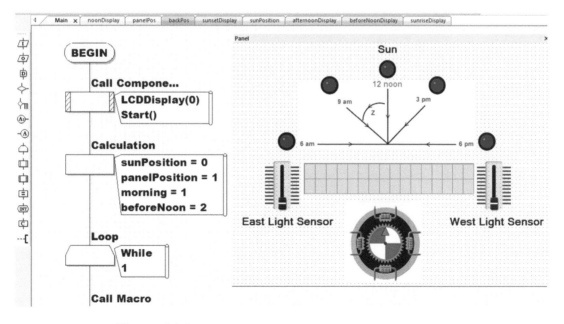

Figure 24.4. *Project 21: Program and simulation layout.*

24.4. Program Description

This program implements an automatic single axis solar tracking system. The two LDRs in the system are placed at an angle of 45^0 each to the vertical plane on the east and west ends of the solar panel. The function of the system is to position the solar panel in such that the two LDRs receive equal amount of sunlight. To achieve this, the system receives signals representing the light level detected by each LDR and then generates a control signal to the motor. The motor in turns positions the panel perpendicular to the incident sunlight. For instance, when sun rises into the sky the eastward LDR will receive more effective light as the sun is closer to being perpendicular to its surface while the westward LDR receive less. However, when the sun's zenith angle is zero, that is at 12 noon, the two LDR will receive the same amount of light.

Bibliography

[1] M. Acar and R. M. Parkin. Engineering education for mechatronics. *IEEE Transactions on Industrial Electronics*, 43(1):106 –113, march 1996.

[2] Automobile Industry Development Centre. Mechatronics: The new language of the automobile. `http://www.aidc.co.za/index.php?pid=336&ct=1&dc=6`, February 2006.

[3] Didactic South Africa FESTO. Mechatronics at colleges in south africa. http://www.festo-didactic.com/za-en, August 2011.

[4] M. Tomizuka F.Harshama and T. Fukuda. What is it, why, and how. *Mechatronics, IEEE/ASME Transactions on Mechatronics, on*, 1(1):1–4, march 1996. ISSN 1083-4435. doi: 10.1109/3516.491404.

[5] http://www.ehow.com/audio amplifiers. Audio amplifiers - how to information. http://www.ehow.com/audio-amplifiers, August 2012.

[6] K. Korb and A. Nicholson. *Mechatronics: Mechanical System Interfacing*. Prentice-Hall, Upper Saddle Rive, NJ, 2nd edition, 1996.

[7] L. S. Laura. Do you know what a pir sensor is? *Tech and gadgets*, 8:175–191, 2012.

[8] H. Bishop R. and Ramasubramanian M. K. A Simple Algorithm to Construct a Consistent Extension of a Partially Oriented Graph. Technical report, The University of Texas at Austin, 1992. Available as Technical Report R-185.

[9] Acroname Robotics. Open collector outputs. http://www.acroname.com/robotics, July 2006.

[10] D. Shetty and R. A. Kolk. *Mechatronic System Design*. PWS Publishing Company, Boston, MA, 2nd edition, 1997.

[11] D. Shetty and R. A. Kolk. *Mechatronics: Electrical Control Systems in Mechanical and Electrical Engineering*. Pearson Education Limited England, 4th edition, 2008.

[12] Wikipedia the free encyclopedia. Parking sensors. http://en.wikipedia.org/wiki/Parking-sensors, August 2012.

[13] New Zealand University of Canterbury Christchurch. Mechatronics engineering? `http://www.mechatronics.canterbury.ac.nz/what.shtml`, August 2012.

Index

CPSIA information can be obtained
at www.ICGtesting.com
Printed in the USA
LVHW070331160822
726058LV00002B/8